The Diversity Myth

"THE DIVERSITY MYTH charges that 'politicized' classes and student activities have led to an ironic intolerance on campus — intolerance of all things Western."

—*NEWSWEEK*

"The story of THE DIVERSITY MYTH is based at Stanford, but this book is larger than that. As a Harvard graduate, I recognize my own school in these pages, and quite likely you will too. By detailing the current corruption of our academic ideals with a larger audience, David Sacks and Peter Thiel have hastened the much-needed and long-awaited restoration of higher education."

— CHRISTOPHER COX
United States Congressman

"If you want to find out what went wrong at Stanford University, read THE DIVERSITY MYTH. There's hardly a better source than this book for learning why multiculturalism on campus cannot work."

—LINDA CHAVEZ
former Director, U. S. Commission on Civil Rights

"THE DIVERSITY MYTH is a carefully documented and sensitively recorded historical account of the whole tragic saga, together with keen analysis of how all this could have happened. Future historians will find this book indispensable."

— *NATIONAL REVIEW*

The Diversity Myth

Multiculturalism and Political Intolerance on Campus

DAVID O. SACKS
PETER A. THIEL

Foreword by Elizabeth Fox-Genovese

Oakland, California

Printed in the United States of America 1998 by

The Independent Institute
100 Swan Way
Oakland, CA 94621-1428
http://www.independent.org (Web site)
http://www.independent.org/catalog.html (on-line book catalog)
info@independent.org (for e-mail inquiries)

The Diversity Myth : "multiculturalism" and the politics of intolerance
at Stanford / David O. Sacks and Peter A. Thiel
Includes references and index.
Library of Congress Catalog Card Number 95-80321

ISBN 0-945999-76-3

The Independent Institute is a non-profit, scholarly research and educational organization which sponsors comprehensive studies on the political economy of critical social and economic problems.

The politicization of decision-making in society has largely confined public debate to the narrow reconsideration of existing policies. Given the prevailing influence of partisan interests, little social innovation has occurred. In order to understand both the nature of and possible solutions to major public issues, the Independent Institute's program adheres to the highest standards of independent inquiry and is pursued regardless of prevailing political or social biases and conventions. The resulting studies are widely distributed as books and other publications, and are publicly debated through numerous conference and media programs.

Through this uncommon independence, depth, and clarity, the Independent Institute pushes at the frontiers of our knowledge, redefines the debate over public issues, and fosters new and effective directions for government reform.

INDEPENDENT STUDIES IN POLITICAL ECONOMY

THE ACADEMY IN CRISIS
The Political Economy of Higher Education
Edited by John W. Sommer
Foreword by Nathan Glazer

AGRICULTURE AND THE STATE
Market Processes and Bureaucracy
E. C. Pasour, Jr.
Foreword by Bruce L. Gardner

ALIENATION AND THE SOVIET ECONOMY
The Collapse of the Socialist Era
Paul Craig Roberts
Foreword by Aaron Wildavsky

ANTITRUST AND MONOPOLY
Anatomy of a Policy Failure
D. T. Armentano
Foreword by Yale Brozen

ARMS, POLITICS AND THE ECONOMY
Historical and Contemporary Perspectives
Edited by Robert Higgs
Foreword by William A. Niskanen

BEYOND POLITICS
Markets, Welfare, and the Failure of Bureaucracy
William C. Mitchell and Randy T. Simmons
Foreword by Gordon Tullock

THE CAPITALIST REVOLUTION IN LATIN AMERICA
Paul Craig Roberts and Karen LaFollette Araujo
Foreword by Peter T. Bauer

FREEDOM, FEMINISM AND THE STATE
Edited by Wendy McElroy
Foreword by Lewis Perry

HAZARDOUS TO OUR HEALTH?
FDA Regulation of Health Care Products
Edited by Robert Higgs
Foreword by Joel J. Nobel

HOT TALK, COLD SCIENCE
Global Warming's Unfinished Debate
S. Fred Singer
Foreword by Frederick Seitz

MONEY AND THE NATION STATE
The Financial Revolution, Government and the World Monetary System
Edited by Kevin Dowd and Richard H. Timberlake,
Foreword by Merton H. Miller

OUT OF WORK
Unemployment and Government in Twentieth-Century America
Richard K. Vedder and Lowell E. Gallaway
Foreword by Martin Bronfenbrenner

PRIVATE RIGHTS & PUBLIC ILLUSIONS
Tibor R. Machan
Foreword by Nicholas Rescher

REGULATION AND THE REAGAN ERA
Politics, Bureaucracy and the Public Interest
Edited by Roger E. Meiners and Bruce Yandle
Foreword by Robert W. Crandall

TAXING ENERGY
Oil Severance Taxation and the Economy
Robert Deacon, Stephen DeCanio, H. E. Frech, III, and M. Bruce Johnson
Foreword by Joseph P. Kalt

TAXING CHOICE
The Predatory Politics of Fiscal Discrimination
Edited by William F. Shughart II
Foreword by Paul W. McCracken

THAT EVERY MAN BE ARMED
The Evolution of a Constitutional Right
Stephen P. Halbrook

For further information and a catalog of publications, please contact:
THE INDEPENDENT INSTITUTE
100 Swan Way, Oakland, CA 94621-1428
Telephone: 510-632-1366
Fax: 510-568-6040
E-mail: info@independent.org
Website: http://www.independent.org

For our parents,
who made a Stanford education possible.

Contents

Foreword

Ten years ago, Stanford University was enjoying its status as one of the most prestigious universities in the country, as much for the quality of the education it offered undergraduates as for its graduate schools and the research of its faculty, but most people would not have thought of the happenings at Stanford as material for the national media. Then, Stanford's "revision" of its Western Civilization requirement and, shortly thereafter, its administration's questionable financial practices captured national attention. The tendency to present Stanford as a unique case must have been reassuring for the leadership of other great universities, if only because it suggested that Stanford was anomalous rather than typical. In private, however, many university presidents, provosts, and deans must have been saying their novenas (if they remembered how to) for dodging the bullet that so easily might have hit them. For the real interest of Stanford's miseries lies precisely in their embodiment of trends that are sweeping through higher education in the United States.

David Sacks and Peter Thiel were attending Stanford during the great curriculum wars and the revelations about unseemly misuse of taxpayer dollars. Their engaging saga of Stanford's response to both compellingly draws readers into a surreal world of social engineering and institutional arrogance. Having lived through the campaign to reshape thought and behavior, these young authors are well positioned to chronicle the experience from the perspective of students who did not share the prevailing commitment to "multiculturalism" but were nonetheless caught in its throes. The chilling picture they paint is one of a pervasive arrogance that drove one of the country's most prestigious, elite universities to dismantle the educational system and quality that had built its reputation.

Let us note that there are principled reasons to support some aspects of what has, however vaguely and imprecisely, become known as multiculturalism; for many serious, honest people do, for a variety of reasons, support it. At first glance, there seem few reasonable grounds not to endorse a broadening and enrichment of undergraduate education, especially in a world in which women have become regular participants in the economy and politics, and in which the cultures of other civilizations enjoy increasing prominence in our national and international life. Presumably some professors among the vast majority of the Stanford faculty who endorsed the replacement of Western Civilization by Cultures, Ideas, and Values did so for the most honorable of reasons. But once all allowances have been made and all caveats filed, the authors' account commands serious attention, not least because it lays out the connections among superficially disparate tendencies.

In attacking multiculturalism, Mr. Sacks and Mr. Thiel readily acknowledge that neither they, nor apparently anyone else, know precisely what the term means. At Stanford, and other universities, where multiculturalism may have less to do with a coherent educational program or philosophy than with a series of interlocking attitudes and practices, what multiculturalism in the curriculum assuredly does *not* mean is a renewed emphasis upon the mastery of foreign languages or the close study of complex civilizations. All of the multicultural texts are read in English, and it appears that most of them were written since World War II. We are not, in other words, talking about close and respectful study of the *Koran* which has shaped the consciousness of millions of people throughout the world since the seventh century. We are not, to be blunt, talking about a substantive introduction to the values and identities of peoples who differ radically from today's youth. After all, distance in time offers one of the most promising avenues to an encounter with people whose values and assumptions have differed radically from our own. No. We are talking about various participants, many of them "revolutionaries," in today's increasingly homogenized global system. Thus the most popular multicultural texts are written by people who may differ from elite Stanford students by sex, "sexual preference," skin color, wealth, or place of birth and access to opportunity, but who share many, if not all, of the values of Stanford students and of a majority of the Stanford humanities faculty.

Even here, we might reasonably debate the value of including one or more such texts either to expand students' familiarity with the contemporary world or even out of respectful desire to "recognize" cultural variation among contemporary Americans. What is difficult to debate at all is the value—or, indeed, the intellectual and moral integrity—of requiring students to agree with or even applaud views and values that mock the values with which they have been reared. Yet Stanford built a radical sensibility into the very fabric of its residential and social life, censuring students for "incorrect" views and, at the extreme, excluding them from funding for speakers or even residence in the dorms. No less disturbing, the triumph of multiculturalism at Stanford coincided with a period of extraordinary and extravagant grade inflation that resulted in the vast majority of students ending up with only As or Bs on their record. It does not take much imagination to understand that this practice severely diminished the accomplishment of students who did take their work seriously. If the best way to get a good grade is to ignore the assigned readings, get a good night's sleep, and write "what the professor wants to hear," the value of reading the texts and thinking for yourself declines accordingly.

Mr. Sacks and Mr. Thiel provide abundant examples of the excesses they deplore, and even if Stanford provided more space for dissent than they suggest, they make a convincing case that the cause of responsible education and intellectual inquiry was being poorly served, if indeed it was being served at all. Obviously, some Stanford students, by whatever means, continued to acquire a quality education, for how else do we explain Mr. Sacks and Mr. Thiel? But the most chilling core of our authors' argument does not lie in the documentation of this or that excess or even this or that atrocity. It lies in their convincing argument that, at Stanford and beyond, the campaign to impose "multiculturalism" amounts to nothing less than a war on Western civilization and, beyond it, a war on the very idea of civilization.

In this respect, even those readers who do not agree with all of the authors' views, would do well to take *The Diversity Myth* as a timely and thoughtful warning about the real stakes in the culture wars on our campuses. Their frightening and thought-provoking account is appearing at a moment of mounting public consciousness of the ways in which our educational system is failing our young people. We all know that we are doing something wrong. Some turn to national standards, others to a voucher system for school choice, others to merit increases for teachers, others to multicultural curricula, others simply to more funding. Most colleges, especially the handful of truly elite private universities (the Stanfords of this world) seem to avoid, as if magically, the most debilitating problems that plague our schools. Their immunity, however, has nothing to do with magic. It derives directly from their position as gatekeepers of our most prestigious and remunerative careers. In this light, it does not matter that much what curriculum Stanford offers its students. No matter what Stanford does with or to them, most will go on to the law, business, medical, or graduate school of their choice—or at least their second choice.

Seen in another light, however, what Stanford does matters tremendously to all of us, which may be why its doings merit national media attention. For if Stanford declares war on Western civilization or on the very idea of civilization, it will have to answer for its role in shaping a national leadership that treats with contempt the values of Western civilization—from individual freedom to respectful manners to the open debate of contested issues. It will, in short, contribute to the formation of a leadership that does not stand for anything beyond personal self-interest and that, in not honoring its forebears, will have lost all reason to believe in itself. This book, above all, makes clear that the educational collapse of our most exclusive universities must be of deep concern to us all.

—Elizabeth Fox-Genovese
Elénore Raoul Professor of Humanities
Emory University

Preface to the Second Edition

The "diversity myth" is the myth that universities are doing a good job promoting diversity. In reality, America's leading schools have been stifling diversity, and the situation has improved only modestly since the original release of this book in hardcover two years ago. We believe universities could be doing a much better job promoting diversity, and we wrote this book both to articulate the problem and to provide a blueprint for improvement. The largely favorable response to the first edition suggests that many people across the political spectrum share our concerns and that change may be in the winds. We are gratified, therefore, that the Independent Institute has reissued this book in a more accessible paperback form, and we hope the new edition will spark a broad-based discussion about what terms like "multiculturalism" and "diversity" really mean.

Just in the last two years, the diversity debate seems to have taken on a new urgency. On college campuses and beyond, new controversies abound. Many of these developments are adumbrated in this book. For example:

- Georgetown University recently dropped its "great authors" requirement. English majors there will no longer have to know anything about Shakespeare, Chaucer, or Milton in order to graduate. English departments at more than a dozen other schools have followed suit.[1] This development has inspired controversy, but it also has vindicated this book. In Chapter 1, we predict that the dismissal of the classics will become the norm as what passes for "multiculturalism" spreads.

- An indication of what might replace the classics is the so-called "-ISM Project," a controversial new course on "diversity" being taught on twelve college campuses. "The purpose of the project is to create yet another way for students to articulate their feelings about diversity to other students," an organizer explained. Yet the course defines the study of "diversity" only to mean the study of racism, sexism, ageism, and capitalism (apparently a form of discrimination). And the class is one-sided. Capitalism, for instance, was described as "the root of all evil in our society."[2] Again, this new development has vindicated our book. In Chapter 3, we show that new curricular offerings are not always as diverse as they might at first appear.
- Recently-revised national history standards continue to draw fire. The new standards de-emphasize Western ideas, including the view that the American republic evolved as the extension of Western civilization in the New World. As a result, no mention is made of the *Federalist Papers*. Instead, the new standards promote the notion that "three worlds" (African, Native American, and European) engaged in a "great convergence" to form a "composite American society created out of such human diversity."[3] Anticipating this debate, our book discusses the merits of the West vis-à-vis the rest of the world (see Chapters 1 and 8).
- With the recent passage of Proposition 209, Californians voted to reject racial preferences in a broad range of state functions, including admission and hiring at public universities.[4] Similarly, the U.S. Court of Appeals for the 5th Circuit, considering affirmative action at the University of Texas, has ruled that racial preferences can never be justified as a means of achieving "diversity."[5] Foreshadowing this debate, Chapters 2 and 3 discuss attempts to achieve faculty diversity through racial preferences.
- The University of California at Berkeley has a controversial new branch of ethnic studies: "whiteness studies." The program analyzes what it calls the "white racial identity" and "white privilege." At a recent conference, Harvard professor Noel Ignatiev suggested that whites were responsible for many of the world's social problems. His paper advocated that citizens follow police around with video cameras in hopes of filming another Rodney King incident, and thus provoking outrage against whites.[6] We predicted such an increase in race consciousness, and this book analyzes views on "whiteness" in some detail (see Chapters 2 and 5).
- Elementary schools have begun to follow the lead of curricular

activists at the university level. In 1996, the Oakland school board unanimously recognized "Ebonics" as a legitimate dialect of the English language that should be taught in schools. "Ebonics" is rap-music slang, characterized by its use of the verb "to be"—as in, "He be going to the store"—and multiple negatives, such as "Didn't nobody see nothing."[7] As discussed in Chapter 3, universities have been teaching Ebonics for many years, and at Stanford University the course even fulfills a graduation requirement.

- At James K. Polk Elementary School in Alexandria, Virginia, fifth-graders tore up the words to "The Twelve Days of Christmas" last December and instead sang about "the 12 days of the holidays." While Christianity was out, however, "Kwanzaa" was in. Organizers explained the move as an attempt to promote "diversity."[8] We anticipated this trend, and Chapter 4 describes the animosity of many educators towards religion, especially Christianity.
- Outside education, the diversity debate continues to arise in new settings. For instance, there is the world of "multicultural therapy." The American Psychological Association and the American Psychiatric Association have published treatment guidelines for racial and ethnic groups. And a popular textbook for psychotherapists asks: "As a member of the White group, what responsibility do you hold for the racist, oppressive, and discriminatory manner by which you personally and professionally deal with minorities?" At San Francisco General Hospital, one of the new "educational objectives" for the staff is to "break down denial of one's own participation in racism." Staff members who claim not to be racist are said to be in "denial" and are assigned to re-education.[9] These indoctrination campaigns began on university campuses, and we predicted they would spread elsewhere. Chapter 6 describes the phenomenon.
- At the national level, diversity and multiculturalism continue to be popular themes for politicians seeking office. At the 1996 Republican Convention, vice presidential nominee Jack Kemp said that his goal was to "transform the party" into one attractive to "diversity" and "multiculturalism."[10] At the same time, his party in the U.S. House of Representatives voted to declare English the official language of the United States. Backers of the bill portrayed it as "a defense of American society against the assault of multiculturalism."[11] This national political conflict over multiculturalism (including Bill and Hillary Clinton's views on the subject) is analyzed in Chapter 8.

The original publication of this book, therefore, was well-timed to shed light on these ongoing debates. Indeed, many of our predictions have already been realized. And the rapid rate at which diversity issues continue to arise in new contexts suggests that this book is more timely than ever.

Of course, at the time we began writing *The Diversity Myth*, these thoughts were not foremost in our minds. Our primary goal was simply to present an accurate account of what "diversity" politics and its alter-ego "multiculturalism" have meant at a major university, the place these doctrines originated and have been most fully developed and implemented. Such an account would help to resolve the larger diversity debate taking place across America—a debate unfortunately engulfed in confusing rhetoric. We wanted to illuminate that debate with hard facts. For example, "multiculturalism," as practiced on today's college campuses, is hardly the source of cosmopolitanism and openness that the term connotes. In practice, it has nothing to do with the study of other cultures, and it actually has resulted in budget cuts for departments teaching foreign languages. Requirements that graduating students be proficient in a foreign language have also been gutted in recent years.[12] The main purpose of multiculturalism, it seems, is to propagate intellectual conformity in the name of "diversity."

Indeed, it may come as a surprise that universities have limited diversity in a number of significant ways. At the same time, they have been very successful in promoting the myth that diversity is alive and well. But consider the reality:

Economic diversity. The enormous cost of multicultural programs, personnel, services, and departments—what Stanford's president has collectively called a "mini-welfare state"—has stifled economic diversity. The price of an elite undergraduate education now exceeds $100,000 for four years, and steep tuition hikes continue to squeeze middle- and low-income families who do not qualify for financial aid. The result has lent credence to the view that elite universities are playgrounds for the rich.

Political diversity. Multicultural hiring policies, despite their stated goal of diversifying the faculty, have led to ideological conformity in many departments. At Stanford, more than eighty percent of the faculty are members of the same political party. (That party happens to be the Democratic Party, but the problem would be just as acute if eighty percent of the faculty were members of the GOP.) This figure actually understates the lack of political diversity because the few Republican professors tend to be moderates or centrists, while many Democratic professors are far-left.

Racial diversity. Segregation still exists on our college campuses. In the name of multiculturalism, universities like Cornell, University of California at Berkeley, and Stanford segregate African-Americans, Latino-Americans, Asian-Americans, and Native Americans into "race dormitories."[13] The net result of this ghettoizing is to remove a large number of minority students from the rest of the campus and to limit diversity of interaction. Not surprisingly, there are fewer interracial friendships. Stanford even conducts separate graduation ceremonies for different minority groups, further dividing the campus along racial lines.

Intellectual Diversity. The most important kind of diversity on a college campus is intellectual diversity, and this is the kind which has suffered most. Speech restrictions, political grading, ostracism of nonconformists, unqualified denunciations of the West, and a curricular obsession with oppression theory and victimology (all discussed at length herein) make clear that toleration of dissenting viewpoints is not a multicultural virtue. Because some students may be recalcitrant about losing their free-speech rights, Stanford also has hired a "Multicultural Educator" to "inculcate ideas" in those eighteen- and nineteen-year-olds who "resist educational efforts" and "avoid personal commitment" to the new regime. Ironically, as if to confirm our point, Stanford's leaders responded to the first edition of this book with a new public-relations strategy to trumpet their school's supposed diversity in which they warned independent-minded faculty to shut up because "an institution must speak with one voice, not many."[14] To university administrators, apparently, diversity means a chorus of voices all saying the same thing.

Since myths tend to evaporate if people think about them, the new restrictions essentially are designed to stop people from thinking—or at least from expressing their suspicions. Thus, if "multiculturalism" is universities' euphemism for the myth of diversity, "political correctness" may be defined as the sad reality. We called our book *The Diversity Myth* to summarize the uniformity that has occurred: campuses are full of people who look different but think alike. This is not real diversity, but pseudo-diversity. Real diversity requires a diversity of ideas, not simply a bunch of like-minded activists who resemble the bar scene from *Star Wars*.

As we have made these points in various contexts over the last two years—in newspapers, in magazines, at speeches, or on television and radio programs—we have been a bit surprised by the response. Not unexpectedly, traditional critics of the university have been supportive, and we received words of praise from the writers and editors of such magazines as

Insight, *The Washington Times*, the *Weekly Standard*, and the *American Spectator*. *National Review* wrote that "future historians of the period will find this book indispensable."[15] And *Crisis* further observed that, of the books on multicultural higher education, this one "may well be the best."[16] What also delighted us, however, was the encouragement from nontraditional quarters—liberal supporters who defended us in print, such as feminist scholar Elizabeth Fox-Genovese, former Democratic Governor Richard Lamm, and Philip Merrill, publisher of *The Washingtonian*. A number of Stanford students—of all political stripes—approached us and said they wished they had written this book.

This response has been rewarding, but much more importantly it has suggested to us that there is a common mischaracterization of the diversity debate. Usually it is framed as a debate between conservatives and liberals—or, more precisely, between angry conservative white men and everybody else. Little could be further from the truth. The prevailing orthodoxy on campus demands conformity from conservatives and liberals, blacks and whites, men and women alike; dissenters have been targeted at all ends of the spectrum. Thus, in *The Diversity Myth* we describe liberal Mexican-American students who were "encircled" and threatened for not uniting with the radicals; a liberal male student hounded out of an all-female feminist studies class; and black students who were "blacklisted" and persecuted for befriending white students. The problem on America's campuses has more to do with intolerance than with ideology.

Fortunately, as more people turn their attention to the problem, the myth of diversity is starting to unravel. As the reaction to the first edition demonstrated, fewer and fewer people are buying the politically-correct line that political correctness does not exist. For one thing, there are too many anecdotes, too much evidence that the problem has grown out of control—and new horror stories seem to arrive daily. But more important than the sheer number of examples and anecdotes is the fact that these anecdotes have resonated powerfully with people across the political spectrum. The reason is simple: almost everybody has experienced something similar. The reader's personal experience with political correctness may not have been quite as catastrophic, but it was unpleasant nonetheless. That is why there is such a broad coalition emerging against multiculturalism—all the way from traditional conservatives to 1960s-style liberals who believe in the virtue of free speech to Marxists who teach Shakespeare.

The first step in thinking about "diversity," both on and off college campuses, must involve an understanding of what is actually happening. It is for this reason that the two of us wrote this book. We need to have the courage to confront "multiculturalism" and "diversity" honestly. And once the rhetoric has been stripped away, our readers can decide for themselves whether they would prefer genuine diversity on our campuses and beyond, or merely the myth of it.

—David Sacks
—Peter Thiel

Notes

1. Carol Innerst, "'Teach-in' goes all-out in hailing Shakespeare," *The Washington Times*, May 1, 1996.

2. Carol Innerst, "Project on '-isms' is causing schisms on 12 campuses," *The Washington Times*, May 22, 1996.

3. "Ripe for the dustbin of history," *The Washington Times*, May 18, 1996.

4. Peter Baker, "Clinton Vows to Fight for Affirmative Action," *The Washington Post*, July 18, 1997.

5. George F. Will, "Subverting Diversity," *The Washington Post*, March 28, 1996.

6. Quentin Hardy, "School of Thought: The Unbearable Whiteness of Being," *The Wall Street Journal*, April 24, 1997.

7. "Ebonics proponent quits school post," *The Washington Times*, August 7, 1997.

8. Rex Bowman, "First Noel comes last in schools; Holidays marked without religion," *The Washington Times*, December 20, 1996.

9. Sally Satel, "Psychiatric Apartheid," *The Wall Street Journal*, May 8, 1996.

10. William Claiborne, "Kemp Invokes Spirit of Lincoln and Dr. King," *The Washington Post*, August 16, 1996.

11. John E. Yang, "House Votes English as Official U.S. Language for First Time," *The Washington Post*, August 2, 1996.

12. A study of the 50 most elite colleges and universities showed that foreign language requirements have declined by a third since the 1960s. *See* "Lowering Higher Education," *The Washington Times*, March 19, 1996.

13. *See*, for example, "Drastic Housing Change Planned At Cornell," *New York Times News Service*, October 9, 1997.

14. Ironically, Stanford's public relations strategy itself caused so much bad publicity that it had to be dropped. *See* Bill Workman, "Stanford Drops Promotional Word List," *The San Francisco Chronicle*, December 2, 1995.

15. Robert Greer Cohn, "Books in Brief," *National Review*, April 22, 1996.

16. A. J. Bacevich, "Diversity Blues," *Crisis*, April 1996.

Acknowledgments

The arduous research and labor necessary to document and then write this story began several years ago, and many people have been helpful and kind to us along the way. We will always be deeply indebted to these good samaritans for investing their confidence in two young authors.

Our odyssey began with the compilation of the numerous examples in this book, collected with the assistance of several generations of Stanford students, beginning with John Abbott, Greg Kennedy, and Kevin Warsh and continuing with Adam Ross, Michael Petras, Bob Schmidt, and Eric Jackson. Mention also should be made of the writers and editors of *The Stanford Daily*, *The Stanford Review*, and *Stanford University News Service* — without these primary sources of information, our job would have been made immeasurably more difficult.

At the writing and editing stage of this book, Neil Morganbesser, Brad Benbrook, Nathan Linn, John Harkins, Mary Gacek, and Keith and Mary Ann Eiler offered constructive comments to early drafts. Useful suggestions and guidance also came from Jennifer Caterini, Jerry Martin, John Miller, Raphael Sagalyn, Williamson Evers, John Reynen, Rich Lowry, Adam Meyerson, Mary Parker Lewis, Diana and Harold Furchtgott-Roth, Tom Duesterberg, Antony Korenstein, Mark Moller, Vincent Sollito, and Peter Uhlmann. Dr. Angelo Codevilla, a gentleman and a scholar, offered numerous suggestions and constant encouragement from beginning to end.

A special thanks goes to Keith Rabois and the other victims of multiculturalism interviewed for this book, who selflessly shared their special insights. Many others in the Stanford community also helped us but cannot be named for fear of repercussions.

Finally, at the publishing stage, we are particularly grateful to Independent Institute president David Theroux, and research director Robert Higgs who, in seeing the value of this book, sponsored its publication and provided invaluable assistance throughout. We are also grateful for the further assistance of Theresa Navarro and the rest of the professionals at the Institute, not only for setting words to paper but also for offering ideas, advice, and true dedication to this project. For those interested in exploring the further contours of the problem of higher education, we strongly recommend the Independent Institute's book, *The Academy in Crisis: The Political Economy of Higher Education*, edited by John W. Sommer (*see* page vi).

Introduction

Christopher Columbus, the First Multiculturalist

In 1492, Christopher Columbus set sail from the Western havens of medieval Spain. Fraught with myriad unforeseen consequences, his lonely voyage to the ends of the known world would prove to be the most fateful exploration in an age of discovery. The legacy of Columbus's first contacts between Western civilization and non-Western cultures would haunt the New World for centuries to come.

To the end of his life, Columbus remained uncertain of exactly what he had found. The Admiral's reaction to his initial encounters, recorded in his extensive journals, clearly was one of delight. He marvelled at the apparent harmony and peacefulness of the Taino natives, whose simple existence seemed to hearken back to an innocence that had been lost amidst the growing complexity of European life. At times, Columbus even believed that he had reached Eden, a sacred land whose inhabitants dwelt in a state of preternatural grace. Columbus's early adulation of New World primitivism would be reflected in one of Montaigne's essays, favorably contrasting the "perfection" of noble savages with the fallen West:

> I would tell Plato that those people have no trade of any kind, no acquaintance with writing, no knowledge of numbers, no terms for governor or political superior, no practice of subordination or of riches or poverty, no contracts, no inheritances, no divided estates, no occupation but leisure, no concern for kinship—except such as is common to them all—no clothing, no agriculture, no metals, no use of wine or corn.[1]

Of course, Montaigne had no intention of trading his privileged place in the French court for a teepee in the American outback. For him, ennobling the savage merely represented a useful ploy to attack aspects of the West he found ideologically distasteful. But for Columbus, who began to confront first-hand some of the stark realities lurking beyond the familiar confines of the West, such optimistic pieties would not last. As he came into contact with another non-Western culture, that of the warlike Caribs, his delight turned to horror: The Caribs were systematically hunting, capturing, imprisoning, gelding, and eating the Tainos. This Eden also contained its serpent.

Unfettered by any sort of a prime directive against cultural intervention, Columbus responded to the Tainos' plea for help in the only moral way possible. He intervened and took sides, favoring the Taino culture over the Carib culture—and the rest is history. Stripped of his initial illusions, Columbus would return to Europe at the end of his quest with a more balanced impression of the world outside the West. The explorer who first depicted the "noble savage" also had discovered the Carib tribe, whose name later would provide the basis for the word "cannibal." For Columbus at least, the once–lusterous appeal of multiculturalism had dulled.

***

Five hundred years later, modern-day explorers still seek alien cultures, hoping therein to find models of enlightened justice, collective well-being, or personal liberation. Of course, nobody today believes, as did Columbus, that such a hidden country—an El Dorado or Shangri–la—will be found in some forgotten physical corner of the planet. And so, the voyage has taken an intellectual turn: By travelling to the ends of the humanities, some hope to recreate a lost utopia that can serve as a conceptual alternative to the modern West, as a vehicle *á la* Montaigne for denouncing unpalatable aspects of our society.

The most aggressive manifestation of this quest is the multicultural movement. This movement had its genesis at elite universities in the 1980s, but today it is national in scope. No longer just concerned with learning about new ideas, multiculturalism is, as the word suggests, a cultural phenomenon, with rules of etiquette, codes of conduct, and precisely assigned roles for each of the participants. Dozens of articles a day are written on the subject, and even the country's elected leaders have gotten in on the act. The Clinton administration, beginning with its inauguration and its filling of government positions, has been particularly diligent in stressing multicultural themes at every turn.[2] The arbiters of taste in the media agree, praising Bill Clinton for "modeling the behavior other executives need and setting a good example."[3] Corporate America, too, has followed suit: 40 percent of all businesses now require "diversity training" in issues of race, gender, and sexual preference.[4] Such blue-chip companies as Xerox, IBM, and Coca-Cola pay professional educators as much as $10,000 a day for specialized multicultural workshops.[5]

In all of these contexts, multiculturalism is presented as a way to rediscover lost cultures (or at least lost cultural identities) and bring them back to life, as part of a richer, more diverse America. The resulting societal transformation, argue multiculturalists, will be needed to accommodate the diversity that has become part of contemporary America and should take place on every level: local and national, private and public, and in the hearts and minds of individuals everywhere. "To achieve a rich culture," multicultural educators proclaim, "we must weave a social fabric in which each diverse human gift will find a fitting place."[6]

It is not difficult to see why the promise of radical change should hold great appeal to many Americans. At the close of the 20th century, the country faces some great challenges—racial animosities are on the rise, gender relations are increasingly troubled, and the public's fear of social disintegration is growing. Across the political spectrum, there is little faith that the approaches of the last several decades are sufficient to fix America's problems. Many feel that some new course is needed, and multiculturalism seems to offer a fresh approach that transcends the conventions of everyday politics. Multiculturalism promises to abate the many tensions between America's disparate factions—white and black, rich and poor, religious and secular, heterosexual and homosexual, male and female. Moreover, multiculturalism promises to achieve these results by utilizing America's historical source of pride and energy—its diversity. The promise of multiculturalism is that a potential liability will once again become an asset, that a cause of faction will become a tool for harmony and strength.

Admittedly, multiculturalism's commercial packaging is attractive. But is the new consciousness about race, gender, and sexual preference really the antidote to America's problems or a cause of them? An answer requires that we know more about this powerful new presence emerging on the American scene. How does it operate where it really holds sway? What are the values and habits of its leaders? And what animates its followers? To answer these fundamental questions, we must examine the phenomenon's roots.

If one had to identify a single location where multiculturalism began, the best candidate would be Stanford University, located near Palo Alto, California. Privileged by ideal climate, sumptuous facilities, and lots of money (by the end of the 1980s, its endowment was well over $2 billion, and its annual budget approached $300 million), Stanford is one of America's leading institutions, sustained by hundreds of millions of dollars in taxpayer grants each year. In 1985, *U.S. News and World Report*, in its annual survey of colleges and universities, ranked Stanford first in the nation; the competition for admission reflected this status, as over 17,500 applicants vied for 1,500 places in the entering class.

But beginning about 1986, capping long–term trends, the most powerful administrators and faculty, along with many student leaders, moved aggressively to turn Stanford into the nation's first multicultural academy. In his welcoming remarks to Stanford's entering class of 1993 (given in September 1989), university president Donald Kennedy went so far as to declare that Stanford's multicultural venture was "a bold experiment that *must* succeed."[7] Conducted on the 25,000 human beings who made up the Stanford community, this "bold experiment" transformed the campus—revamping the curriculum, reshaping student "awareness," and implementing new codes of conduct. The experiment certainly was more all-encompassing than anything Kennedy had done to a lab animal in his former incarnation as a biology professor. Once successfully constructed at Stanford, this new multicultural community would serve as a prototype for the nation. "If we cannot succeed here," Kennedy declared, "we cannot succeed anywhere."[8]

But President Kennedy never got the chance to report on the progress of the multicultural experiment at the graduation ceremonies for the class of 1993. In August 1992, Stanford's Board of Trustees forced his resignation. The immediate cause centered on a financial scandal in which the university had misappropriated millions of dollars in federal research monies. The real reasons for this crisis of confidence, however, went far deeper: Trustees, congressional representatives, alumni, and the general public had begun to perceive that the great multicultural experiment had brought the very opposite of higher learning. It had brought speech restrictions, a new kind of intolerance known as "political correctness," a hysterically anti-Western curriculum, the increasing politicization of student life, and campus polarization along racial and ethnic lines. Like Columbus's multicultural journey, which turned from delight to disillusionment, the Stanford community had gradually soured on multiculturalism. Before doing so, however, multiculturalism had changed the outlook of a generation of American leaders, and because it is still deeply entrenched, it continues to graduate new disciples into society who will seek to implement multicultural policies.

As a leading university and breeding ground for new ideas, Stanford is a bellwether for the nation. Where Stanford stood with respect to multiculturalism eight years ago, America stands today. By the same token, Stanford's present represents one of America's possible futures—a probable outcome if the nation continues on its current path down the multicultural road. The multicultural trajectory at Stanford—from its inception to its growth to its gradual implosion—stands as a stark warning, of both the temptations and perils that lie in the multicultural future. Indeed, with a student body that is among the brightest in the country, a tranquil suburban location, and vast financial resources, the Stanford community should have been able to make the multicultural future work—if this future could work anywhere. But rather than producing utopia, multiculturalism caused Stanford to resemble less a great university than a Third World country, with corrupt ideologues and unhappy underlings. Stanford's failed experiment should give pause to a nation being pushed towards multiculturalism.

Notes

1. Michel de Montaigne, "Of the Cannibals," *The Complete Essays* (New York: Penguin, 1987).
2. Eloise Salholz, "Something for Everybody: Clinton's Cabinet is an exercise in diversity," *Newsweek*, January 4, 1993. Matthew Cooper, "Clinton's focus on diversity: Is the administration more concerned with statistics than success?" *U.S. News and World Report*, March 20, 1995.
3. *See* Patricia Galagan, "Navigating the Differences," *Training and Development*, April 1993.
4. Max Boot, "Oppression Studies Go Corporate," *The Wall Street Journal*, August 24, 1994.
5. *Ibid.*
6. Galagan, *supra* note 3.
7. "DK welcomes freshmen to 'real world': 'Pluralism experiment must succeed,'" *Campus Report*, September 27, 1989.
8. Jeff Brock, "Kennedy, panelists explore models of multiculturalism," *The Stanford Daily*, April 20, 1990.

Part I:

The New Academy

1

The West Rejected

First, Stanford capitulated to separatist know-nothings and abandoned its "Western Civilization" course because of its bias toward white males (you know: narrow-minded ethnics like Socrates, Jesus, and Jefferson).[1]

— Columnist Charles Krauthammer

In the beginning, before the creation of the multicultural world, Stanford was divided by demonstrations and protests. The most important of these rallies took place on January 15, 1987, when a throng of 500 indignant students and faculty gathered near the University's centrally located White Plaza to hear the Reverend Jesse Jackson.[2]

This assembly was not concerned about founding a new "multicultural" state. In fact, the term "multiculturalism" had not yet entered common usage in early 1987, and most of the demonstrators probably had never heard of the word. Rather, the purpose of the rally was to show support for the "rainbow agenda," for minority set-asides in admissions and teaching, and for other causes popular with university activists. In short, it began as the sort of protest commonplace on today's college campuses. But on that day, events would be set in motion that would push Stanford towards becoming the nation's first multicultural academy.

As the crowd stomped across the manicured lawns to present a list of demands to a meeting of the Faculty Senate, it translated its grievances into a chant: "Hey hey, ho ho, Western Culture's got to go! Hey hey, ho ho, Western Culture's got to go!"[3] This collective outpouring of anger, both spontaneous and intense, was reminiscent of protests in Teheran or Tripoli; however, the implausible source of these sentiments was not a mob of Islamic fundamentalists, but some of America's best and brightest students at a bucolic college campus, near sunny Palo Alto, California, an affluent suburban community.

Even at the time, campus observers were struck by the strange spectacle of some of America's elite students and faculty engaged in an unqualified denunciation of the West—the very civilization, after all, that had established universities like Stanford in the first place. Even Jesse Jackson, the leader of the march, was taken aback by the fury he had unleashed. Reverend Jackson actually tried to quiet the mob, but his admonitions were ignored.[4] The angry chant could not be stopped—and would go on to become the unofficial motto of a revolution with implications far beyond Stanford—because it succinctly articulated exactly what important people in higher education had been saying for some time. Similar demonstrations followed in the tempestuous months ahead, and the slogan became synonymous with the university's growing identity crisis, as many of Stanford's leaders came to insist that the academy's mission needed a thorough overhaul.

The nominal target of these demonstrations and protests was Stanford's core curriculum, a required course called "Western Culture" in which freshmen surveyed the history and classics of the West. This course gave many students—especially engineering and science majors—their primary exposure to the humanities. But the real target was much broader. The "Hey hey, ho ho" chant resonated powerfully because the "Western culture" that "had to go" was a double entendre: It referred not just to a single class at Stanford, but to the West itself—to its history and achievements, to its institutions of free-market capitalism and constitutional democracy, to Christianity and Judaism, to the complex of values and judgments that help shape who we are.[5]

These complaints about the West—present and past—would be repeated over the next several years in many different contexts at Stanford. Increasingly, they would also be heard beyond: at the universities for which Stanford is a model; in watered–down form in elementary and high school classes; and in the popular media and arts where graduates of schools like Stanford have influence. Quite arbitrarily, it seemed at the time, the university's required reading list, or canon, had symbolically come to represent deep grievances about an assortment of broader cultural issues. Somehow, the "Farm," as undergraduates affectionately call Leland Stanford's old plot, had been chosen as the pastoral site of an intellectual and cultural rebellion. Although nobody knew it then, this landmark skirmish—the Bull Run, so to speak, of America's ongoing "culture war"—would prove to be the labor pains of a nationwide multicultural movement.

As was well-reported at the time, this inchoate movement centered its complaints around the fact that most of the books studied in the Western Culture program had been written by "dead white males."[6] This charge was new and extraordinary because it attacked not the quality or historical significance of the great books, but rather the authors themselves—for being of the wrong race, gender, or class. To the protestors, the reading list was perceived as a cross-cultural celebration, and their groups had not been invited to the party. Their exclusion had to end, and so Bill King, president of the Black Student Union (BSU), told *Time Magazine*, "We want the idea of a canon eliminated."[7]

The protestors succeeded in exacting this demand, and in January 1988 Stanford's administration replaced the Western Culture program with a new requirement called "Cultures, Ideas, and Values" (CIV). As its name hinted, the new course was based on relativist notions of cultural parity, with a mandated emphasis on race, gender, and class.[8] To ensure this emphasis, the CIV Committee, which was charged with overseeing the transition from Western Culture to CIV, immediately began recruiting minority faculty for the new course. One committee member, comparative literature professor Marjorie Perloff, resigned after finding that "the main role of the committee was to discuss issues of personnel rather than course content. It seemed to be taken as a given that literature dealing with minority issues must be taught by minority professors. This is a very problematic ghettoizing of knowledge."[9]

According to the new thinking, upper-class white males may have been born with silver spoons in their mouths, but the minorities they oppressed were born with teaching credentials. This thinking would have profound implications for the entire university. As the late philosopher Sidney Hook aptly observed, if only minority professors were qualified to teach books authored by minorities, similar reasoning would dictate that only women could teach gynecology, only fat people obesity, only hungry people the physiology of starvation—or, for that matter, only Nazis could teach about the Third Reich.[10] Whereas the Western Culture canon had been based upon a belief in universalism—the belief that the insights contained within the West's great works were potentially available to everybody—the new curriculum embraced particularism: What one may know is determined by the circumstances of one's birth.

This was the crux of the whole debate. The Western Culture protestors were attacking not just "dead white males," but the idea of universalism itself. The idea they rejected was this: There exist truths that transcend the accidents of one's birth, and these objective truths are in principle available to everyone—whether young or old, rich or poor, male or female, white or black; individuals (and humanity as a whole) are not trapped within a closed cultural space that predetermines what they may know.

Within this framework, the university served as a refuge, somewhat outside the confines of a given culture, where individuals could disregard parochial blinkers of ethnicity, age, gender, class, or race and search for these transcendent truths. In rejecting the West, the protestors repudiated this entire framework.[11] In doing so, their fateful protest of January 1987 would pave the way for a very different kind of academy.

The New Classics

Founded upon the twin plinths of cultural relativism and cultural determinism, CIV sought to refit the reading list to a world devoid of universal truths. Having embraced race, gender, and class as proxies for some kind of special knowledge, or *gnosis*, the educators who taught CIV divided the reading list among cultural and racial constituencies, much the same way a city council might gerrymander districts.[12] The "Common Elements" among the CIV tracks, according to the 1992–93 program syllabus, were not perennial questions like "What is justice?" or "What constitutes a good life?" but:

- Works by women, minorities and persons of color
- Works introducing issues of race, gender and class
- Works of non-European provenance[13]

As Provost James Rosse wrote in a revealing letter, the new freshman requirement would "include the study of great works as well as works reflecting the role and contributions of minorities and women."[14] Provost Rosse unwittingly admitted the truth: The latter group of works often could be distinguished from the former. Included works did not necessarily have to be "great" if they fulfilled the function of "reflecting the role and contributions of minorities and women." As we shall see, many CIV books would meet one criterion or the other, but few would meet both.

During 1988–89, a compromise transition year, all the CIV tracks read the Bible, Plato, Augustine, Machiavelli, Rousseau, and Marx. Thereafter, quite a bit more was left to the discretion of professors, as the "Common Readings" (a term preferred to "canon") consisted of:

- Hebrew Bible and Christian Bible
- A Classical Greek philosopher
- An Early Christian thinker
- A Renaissance dramatist
- An Enlightenment thinker
- Marx[15]

In short, Plato was replaced with the more general category of "classical Greek philosophers," Augustine with "early Christian thinkers," Machiavelli with "Renaissance dramatists," and Rousseau with "Enlightenment thinkers." With the important exception of Marx (who is never deconstructed), the altered list implied that individual writers are the delegates of certain constituencies—ancient Greeks, early Christians, etc.—from which they derived their right to serve on the reading list. In a reverse of direction from the old course, authors were chosen precisely because they typified some cultural group, rather than because their writings are immortal and have transcended such particulars.

Few questioned how studying cultural differences could possibly be of value if ethnic experiences were incomprehensibly foreign to others. On the contrary, history professor Paul Robinson remarked, "We are eager to replace a canonized and seemingly unalterable 'core list' with a process aimed to create 'a common intellectual experience.'"[16] Professor Robinson was referring to CIV's founding legislation, which mandates that the class "provide students with the common intellectual experience of broadening their understanding of ideas and values."[17] The goal of the freshman requirement had shifted subtly from providing students with a common *background*, defined objectively in the form of a great works reading list, to providing a common *experience*, subjectively defined by those doing the reading. What each author actually wrote (and whether any of it is true) was much less important than the effect on students. Hence, in 1992 the Philosophy track added Chief Seattle to the Course Reader.[18] Because American Indian culture is as alien to most freshmen as ancient Greek culture, Chief Seattle presumably had instructional, or "broadening," value roughly equivalent to that of Plato or Aristotle. In this way, although the different tracks shared few authors in common, they were still able to provide 1,500 freshmen with a "common intellectual experience"—not by transmitting common knowledge, but by transmitting a common sensation of "broadening understanding." The course instructors, however, never explained in what direction students' minds should be broadened, or why any particular direction was preferable to another.

In practice, of course, a number of faculty members found it far from easy to create a new canon *ex nihilo*. Some professors chose to keep most of the old books, but changed the course focus. The Philosophy track, for instance, continued to require both Plato and Aristotle, but wedged readings about Australian aborigines between the two.[19] Among aboriginal "philosophical" insights are the concept of "dream-time"—a circular and antirational way of viewing cause and effect—and the belief that women become pregnant by crossing spiritually enchanted patches of ground. The class paid little attention to whether the aboriginal claims are actually true. Rather, discussions contrasted the readings with the "logocentric" approach of Western philosophers like Aristotle or Descartes. The upshot was that logic and illogic were put on the same plane and that truth and consistency were considered just two values among many. The course instructors ignored the fact that the *raison d'etre* of philosophy is the discovery of transcultural truth, and that *ipso facto* the discipline is predominantly a Western pursuit. The anti-Western focus required glossing over another embarrassing detail: The aboriginal readings were actually written by Western anthropologists because the aborigines lacked a written language—not to mention anthropology itself.

For instructors in other tracks, the CIV program provided the desired vehicle for a comprehensive revolution. Perhaps most extreme is "Europe and the Americas," a CIV track developed by anthropology professor Renato Rosaldo, one of the foremost advocates of curricular change. The new track focuses on issues of race, class, and gender—to the exclusion of almost everything else.[20] Marx's historic treatise on class warfare, the *Communist Manifesto*, is still required, and from there the 17- and 18-year-old freshmen's educational experience deteriorates rather rapidly. They study Guatemalan revolutionary Rigoberta Menchu, whose book *I...Rigoberta Menchu* relates "the effects on her of feminist and socialist ideologies." The story tracks Menchu's journey from poverty and despair to the center of the Central American revolutionary movement. Next, Zora Neale Hurston's book *Their Eyes Were Watching God* presents a semiautobiographical critique of male domination in American society. The hero of *With His Pistol in His Hand*, by America Parades, is a Mexican who shoots a local sheriff in Texas and runs away from the law, as he realizes that "there is one law for Anglo-Texans, another for Texas-Mexicans." "Impotence and despair reign" in Juan Rulfo's *The Burning Plain*, as Mexican Indians struggle to eke out a living in the howling desert. Sandra Cisneros's *House on Mango Street* emphasizes the stultification and drudgery of the life of a little girl in a downtown slum.[21] The last week of Fall quarter, lectures are devoted to the topic of "Forging Revolutionary Selves."

In the Spring quarter, students are required to complete a project or lengthy paper as a significant portion (one-third) of the final grade. The Spring 1992 course syllabus explained that "projects in the past have included:"

- A skit on the debates around culture curricula
- A photoessay on San Francisco, organized around a theme
- A report on a field work project on a migrant workers camp
- A violin duet designed to create an intercultural esthetic
- An Aztec newspaper from the year 1524
- A board game called "First Contact"
- A video on the course
- A dance articulating themes of identity
- A history of women's athletics in the US[22]

According to one student in the class, that year's projects even included a documentary on a Grateful Dead rock concert. Of course, what migrant workers, violin and dance performances, women's athletics, or Jerry Garcia have to do with great literature, Europe, the Americas, or any serious study of non-Western culture is a complete mystery.

CIV's amorphous mission—to "broaden" the experience of students—should not, however, be confused with "anything goes." Rather, the new canon is vague precisely so that teachers can canonize their personal beliefs. Professor Rosaldo's fundamental assumptions regarding the unique evils of the West, which formed the basis of his complaints against the Western Culture program, have become enshrined in the "Europe and the Americas" reading list, as even the handful of more traditional Western works are "deconstructed" to show hidden "Eurocentric" biases. Augustine's *Confessions*, rather than a discourse on religious faith, becomes a study in "the body and the deep interior self," followed by a discussion of "multicultural selves in Navajo country" (a topic no Navajo likely discussed outside contemporary American universities).[23] The *Book of Genesis* accompanies a lecture on "labor, gender, and self in the Philippine uplands," and Plato's *Republic* helps illustrate "anti assimilationist movements."[24] In the Winter quarter, the course compares the U.S. Bill of Rights with Lee Iacocca's "Car Buyer Bill of Rights."[25] In pairing the sublime with the trivial, the exercise intends to prove the assumption upon which it is based—that a founding document of our country is not incommensurably superior to any other document written by Western males.

Courses like "Europe and the Americas" promote a certain type of diversity, to be sure. Marx's demands for a class-based revolution contrast with Menchu's utopian feminism which in turn differs from other writers' stress on the deprivations of American Indians, inner-city slums, and everyday life. But the new CIV tracks do not accomplish the one educationally justifiable thing they promised to, namely, an examination of non-Western cultures, like Confucian China or medieval Islam. This, it must be remembered, had been a major rationale for the change from Western Culture to CIV. Instead, Professor Rosaldo and his colleagues remained solidly focused on the West in an effort to expose racism, sexism, and classism. In its practical application, then, CIV actually narrowed diversity significantly. For instead of surveying the ideas of a range of thinkers over the last 25 centuries (who cannot collectively be placed in any ideological categories), many of the new tracks focus largely on issues relevant to late-20th-century political activists like Professor Rosaldo.

A Tempest Over *The Tempest*

An honest study of other cultures might entail a drastic reassessment of the role and nature of the West, but hardly in the direction Stanford's activists probably imagine. While many cultures have practiced slavery, only in the West did the doctrine of individual rights develop, that shattered the cultural basis for slavery. More generally, the various forms of oppression with which activists charge the West—racism, sexism, elitism—pale in comparison to those found in non-liberal societies such as the ethnocentrism of China, the subordination of women in Islamic states, and the oppression of the untouchables in India. The belief in the dignity and freedom of the individual was not affirmed by societies that bound women's feet, sold their own people into slavery, routinely performed clitorectomies, or enforced rigid caste systems.

If there is a consistent intellectual mistake made by the West's critics, it appears to be this: Because the West has recognized its episodes of historical injustice, it is judged more harshly than cultures that present a rosier, but less accurate, accounting of themselves. In the process, the West appears uniquely baneful, when the reverse is the case: Without Western classical liberal ideas and rhetoric (regarding the unquestionable evils of racism, sexism, etc.) the CIV debate could never have gotten off the ground. Instead of recognizing their debt to the West, the CIV advocates carried their critique too far, mistaking the ability to diagnose a disease for the disease itself.

This complex and paradoxical relationship between the West and its denouncers is well illustrated by another example drawn from the new curriculum. "Europe and the Americas" required two readings that exemplify both the new way in which classics are taught and the true nature of works added for the sake of "diversity." The classic is *The Tempest;* the new work, read alongside it, is a revised version of Shakespeare's play, called *A Tempest*, written in 1969 by Aime Cesaire. Cesaire, a black French intellectual, devoted his spare time to radical politics, as a representative in the French Assembly and as mayor of Fort-de-France (two positions not usually occupied by the disempowered).

Shakespeare's play is the story of the magician Prospero, a former Duke of Milan stranded on an island after his brother, Antonio, usurped his dukedom with the connivance of Alonso, King of Naples. Rather than seeking revenge when a storm delivers Alonso and Antonio to the island, Prospero accepts Alonso's atonement. The theme of repentance and forgiveness is central to the play, symbolized in the final marriage of Prospero's daughter, Miranda, to Alonso's son, Ferdinand. Prospero is aided by Ariel, an airy spirit who helps thwart the rebellion of Prospero's servant, Caliban, a savage and deformed monster who had once attempted to rape Miranda.

Prospero's mastery of Caliban—who would be harmful to others were he free—is a subtheme of the play. At the end, Prospero disavows sorcery, and since the play is the last of Shakespeare's greats, the act is widely interpreted as symbolic of the Bard's sentimental decision to put aside the writing arts.

Hardly the multifaceted original, *A Tempest* is a transparent morality play about colonial imperialism. Cesaire's characters are "as in Shakespeare" with two alterations—Ariel is "a mulatto slave," Caliban "a black slave"—and an addition—Eshu, "a black devil-god." Prospero is depicted as a megalomaniac ("I am Power," he rants) as well as a heartless master, sniping at Ariel, "As for your freedom, you'll have it when I'm good and ready," and remarking of the restless Caliban, "He's getting a little too emancipated." For good measure Prospero is also an environmental nemesis who pollutes the isle; "Prospero is Anti-Nature!" exclaims Caliban. To complete the black-and-white scenario, Caliban is transformed into a revolutionary hero, who demands to be called "X" (for Prospero has stripped him of his "identity") and whose *leitmotif* is "Uhuru!" (a Swahili yell announcing his entrance on stage). Caliban chastises the more reserved slave, Ariel, for his "Uncle Tom patience" and for "sucking up to [Prospero]" before embarking on his rebellion. Whereas Prospero represents Shakespeare in the Bard's play, Caliban is Cesaire's voice in the new construction, which ends in a final indignant tirade indicative of Aime Cesaire's own revolutionary politics:

> Understand what I say, Prospero:
> For years I bowed my head,
> for years I took it, all of it—
> your insults, your ingratitude...
> and worst of all, more degrading than all the rest,
> your condescension,
> But now, it's over!
> Over, do you hear?
> Of course, at the moment
> You're still stronger than I am.
> But I don't give a damn for your power
> or for your dogs or your police or your inventions!
> And do you know why?
> It's because I know I'll get you!...
>
> And you lied to me so much,
> about the world, about yourself,
> that you ended up by imposing on me
> an image of myself:

underdeveloped, in your words, incompetent,
that's how you made me see myself!
And I loath that image... and it's false!...

And I know that one day my bare fist, just that, will be enough to crush your world. The old world is falling apart!

And by the way... you have a chance to get it over with: you can fuck off.
You can go back to Europe. But in a pig's eye you will!
I'm sure you won't leave. You make me laugh with your "mission"!
Your "vocation"!
Your vocation is to give me shit.
And that's why you'll stay... just like those guys who founded the colonies
and who now can't live anywhere else.
You're just an old colonial addict, that's what you are![26]

Cesaire's tempestuous diatribe has many targets, not the least of which is Shakespeare himself. According to Cesaire (and CIV more generally), Shakespeare portrayed the relations between Europe and the New World from a distorted "white, male, European" perspective that did not sufficiently consider the deprivations of New World peoples—hence Shakespeare's mistaken portrayal of Caliban as a "monster" and of Prospero as a benevolent protagonist. With a *gnosis* that Shakespeare lacked, Cesaire is able to correct the distortion and offer a true account of the relation between "colonizer" and "colonized." In Cesaire's inverted drama, Caliban becomes the revolutionary hero, while Prospero is the vile oppressor. In the process of this refutation, Cesaire simultaneously seeks to diminish Shakespeare's status as a great writer: *The Tempest* is reduced from a universal text, addressing questions that are of relevance in all places and times, to a case study of 16th-century British provincialism. Aime Cesaire is killing two birds with one book—Western ethnocentrism and transcultural universalism.

Whatever one may think of the literary merits of Cesaire's work or the revolutionary politics advocated therein, as a Shakespearean critic he leaves something to be desired. The crux of his problem is the same as that of Stanford's CIV advocates: Committed as they are to a framework of historicist relativism, they cannot even imagine that Shakespeare might be dealing with issues that transcend the boundaries of Elizabethan England. And so they read *The Tempest* as a (biased) reflection on the narrow political questions of that distant era. But this interpretation is almost certainly not the way Shakespeare conceived of his endeavor, and any serious criticism of Shakespeare's work should begin with a more careful study of the universal book Shakespeare thought he had written.

In particular, even though *The Tempest* draws upon reports of the New World discovered by European explorers, it is meant to be more than a meditation upon the enlightenment of not-so noble savages. Even if one concedes (to Cesaire and the CIV instructors) that questions concerning the liberation of Caliban are of central importance, then one should begin by looking at the problems with such a liberation, as described by Shakespeare. Consider the words of Caliban (in Shakespeare's original) as he chants his desire to be free:

> No more dams I'll make for fish,
> Nor fetch in firing
> At requiring,
> Nor scrape trenchering, nor wash dish.
> 'Ban, 'Ban, Ca-Caliban
> Has a new master, get a new man.
> Freedom, high-day! high-day, freedom! freedom,
> high-day, freedom!

The words summarize the problem with any "liberation," naively conceived: How can one be certain that liberation from one particular form of oppression (like collecting wood and washing dishes) will not give way to another, more grotesque and hideous than the first? Caliban's words hint at the relation: He can become "a new man" only by finding "a new master." In the play, this new master turns out to be Stephano, a drunken butler. Caliban's adulation of this fraudulent savior merely renders his resulting position all the more slavish:

> I'll swear upon that bottle [of wine] to be thy true subject,
> for the liquor is not earthly....
> Hast thou not dropp'd from heaven?...
> I'll show thee every fertile inch o' th' island;
> And I will kiss thy foot. I prithee be my god.

Only Trinculo, the Shakespearean fool, sees through Caliban's delusion:

> A most ridiculous monster, to make a wonder of a poor drunkard!

Objectively, Caliban is worse off than before—the degree of subservience is greater, and Stephano is far less worthy than Prospero. But subjectively,

Caliban feels like he has achieved a great liberation—for the time being he is rid of Prospero, and that is all about which he cares to reflect. Indeed, as the action unfolds, Caliban even becomes willing to risk his life, gladly following Stephano into battle against Prospero. Only at the very end, when the revolt has failed utterly, does Caliban obtain a measure of insight into the ridiculous nature of his actions:

> I'll be wise hereafter,
> And seek for grace. What a thrice-double ass
> Was I to take this drunkard for a god,
> And worship this dull fool!

There is no guarantee that Caliban has learned his lesson and will not follow a different "dull fool" should another come along. But for the moment at least, Caliban has recognized that there is no easy formula or chant that will ensure the liberation of the oppressed peoples of the world.

Far from being uniquely primitive, Caliban's last words may represent a degree of enlightenment many critics of the West have yet to reach. Indeed, if one reads Cesaire's text in light of Shakespeare (rather than vice versa), one is left with the impression that Cesaire's interpretation of Shakespeare involves a mistake anticipated and refuted, some 350 years in advance, by Shakespeare himself. If Shakespeare did not enable Caliban's revolt to succeed and a happy ending to follow, then perhaps it was because the Bard believed that revolutionary politics would ultimately prove rather unconvincing. Such an ending might be fitting for a fairy tale or a myth, but it would serve only to fool the credulous.

Instead of being exhausted or rendered irrelevant by the passage of time, *The Tempest* actually suggests a timely critique of the Stanford crowd that declared, "Hey hey, ho ho, Western Culture's got to go!" Like Caliban with his chant about "freedom," Stanford's rebels succeeded only in creating another pantheon, filled with a host of new demigods—with names like Rigoberta Menchu and Aime Cesaire—to replace the old. In pursuit of "liberation," they simply enthroned a new mythology (albeit one of demystification)—but, like Stephano, one much less worthy of adulation. There exists a crucial difference between Caliban's primitivism and Stanford's neoprimitivism, however: Caliban's actions, in a sense, are relatively innocent. Being a savage monster, he really does not know better; he does not have great books (such as *The Tempest*) available for his edification and would, in any case, be incapable of reading any such books. The same cannot be said for Stanford's humanities faculty.

Rhetoric and Reality

The fallowing of Shakespeare and the cultivation of political chaff were not the result of a mysterious process. This harvest was reaped from seed sown years before, during the long and truculent drive to eliminate the Western Culture program. From the outset, the drive to overhaul the canon and to staff the new classes was politically motivated. The "Hey hey, ho ho" chant was only the best publicized example. Even before that January 1987 march, at a forum in May 1986, history professor Kennell Jackson described the Western Culture protestors as "a kind of underground movement" that was "just beginning to explode."[27] Noting that the forum had the characteristics of a "revival meeting," lecturer Jonathan Reider exulted that "two of my students are up there yelling and screaming."[28]

"There have been faculty concerned about this issue from the beginning," noted anthropology professor James Gibbs, a former dean of undergraduate education. "The process of marshaling support for curricular change is both intellectual and political—and properly so."[29] In the fall of 1987, another series of political protests targeted the Committee on Undergraduate Studies (CUS), a group of key faculty charged with drafting possible legislation for a new freshman requirement. At one such rally, freshman Naomi Martin declared that "we are here to send a message to the CUS that racism in our education will not be tolerated."[30] Chanting "Down with racism, down with Western Culture, up with diversity," students disrupted the meeting.[31] Bill King, president of the Black Student Union, described the purpose of the protest: "[The CUS] was getting a bit timid and we wanted them to be well aware of the dedication to changing the Western Culture program."[32]

Vice Provost William Chace was one of the few to express alarm at the politicization of the university: "It's a version of academic populism, and populism is always dangerous for a university."[33] But Mr. King had correctly gauged the faculty's bearing as "timid," though perhaps not in the sense he had intended.[34] The more common reaction to the protestors was one of appeasement, as characterized by CUS chairman Craig Heller, who heralded the same rally as "an enthusiastic expression of interest."[35] The faculty's plaudits belied the fact that the sort of "enthusiasm" expressed by student activists discouraged careful deliberation over the merits and faults of the existing Western Culture program. One professor went so far as to compare the atmosphere on campus to that of Vichy France.[36] At the very least, the charges of racism, sexism, and ethnocentrism—often explicit, always implicit, and constantly repeated in protests, classroom discussions, dormitory programs, and the *Stanford Daily*—discouraged supporters of the existing program from voicing their views.[37]

By the end of the fall of 1987, the CUS had considered four sets of proposals, each more radical than the one that had come before.[38] The final proposal mandated the study of one "non-Western" culture and eviscerated the core reading list of great Western works.[39] History professor Paul Seaver euphemistically explained that because of the uproar that had followed the first draft, additional drafts were written that yielded a more "positive" response.[40] He was hopeful that the final draft would pass, because he "didn't get the sense of hostility" that had greeted the CUS's earlier work.[41] Professor Seaver's optimism was premature: A last-minute protest by the BSU almost derailed the CUS report,[42] until the CUS also agreed to hire additional minority and female professors to teach the new classes.[43]

By the time Vice Provost Chace launched a last-ditch effort in early 1988 to keep part of the core reading list, he was too late to turn the tide of the debate.[44] Denouncing the Chace proposal, feminist studies professor Diane Middlebrook wrote that "a vote in favor of retaining a core list is a vote against the spirit of criticism in which the whole review of Western Culture was undertaken."[45] There could be no better summary of the "whole review of Western Culture" that had taken place: Driven by protest, its "spirit" was entirely reluctant to accept even a partial list of the West's great books. By the time the matter came to a vote in Stanford's Faculty Senate in March 1988, Chace's compromise was compromised further: Western Culture would be replaced with a new requirement called "Cultures, Ideas, and Values," but the new CIV classes would retain six token books from the original core during a "transition year."[46]

As the Faculty Senate deliberated, protesters waited outside, ready to disrupt should Stanford's faculty vote the "wrong" way.[47] Based on his experiences over the previous year, Professor Seaver voiced apprehension: "If the Senate shoots [the proposal] down, it would be terribly disillusioning. As a University, we would be in trouble."[48] Presumably, the "disillusionment" would be on the part of those activists who had fought for so long and so hard, and the "trouble" would arise because no one knew who they might go after next. The Western Culture debate involved a vital issue, Mr. King had ominously warned, and would "set the tone for the next couple of years in terms of minority relations to the University."[49] But the agitators had little cause for concern. The Faculty Senate approved the so-called "CIV compromise" by an overwhelming margin of 39 to 4.[50] Most members of the Faculty Senate did not want to be labelled "racist" or "sexist." Stanford had received some bad press because of the protests,[51] and the administration desired a speedy end to the debate and the public relations problem it posed.

The administration's expedient response to the crisis recalled the late 1960s, when Stanford's faculty caved in to radicals demanding the elimination of the then-required "Western Civilization" course, a precursor of and the model for the Western Culture program established in 1980. As in the 1960s, Stanford's capitulation to protestors would only spark new rebellions, encourage more far-reaching demands, and pave the way for even more abject institutional acquiescence. Both the process and the substance of these demands would significantly alter the nature and climate of the university. The most noticeable of these changes was the disappearing distinction between a political attack and an intellectual attack. To the emerging vanguard of activists, the two were the same. They saw curricular debates as simply another setting in which groups struggled for political advantage. In the years to come, academic reform would be driven less by compelling arguments than by coercive protests.

Even at the time, the expediency of the Stanford administration only created a new public relations crisis because its shameful capitulation was easily recognized for what it was. As the heat from the media spotlight grew more intense, the administration tried to cover its tracks. The administration was not eager for alumni and parents, whose contributions finance the university, to identify the political motivations behind the change from Western Culture to CIV. As the national media spotlighted the curricular battle, Official Stanford launched an aggressive public relations campaign aimed at convincing parents and alumni that the changes were benign, modest, and academically motivated. A signed two-page letter in the fall of 1988 from Dean Junkerman and Thomas Wasow, Dean of Undergraduate Studies, exemplified this effort. "Dear Stanford Parent," they began the letter:

> We hope that a concise insiders' summary of what happened will serve to allay any misapprehension you may feel from accounts you may have read of what is, in fact, a fairly *modest* (although imaginative) curricular reform....The discussion was carried on at an impressively high intellectual level, clearly putting questions of pedagogical principle above any political considerations.[52] (emphasis added)

Meanwhile, activists on campus received precisely the opposite message. In a "Statement by the Dean of Undergraduate Studies," circulated only on campus in the spring of 1988 (just shortly before the letter to parents), Thomas Wasow wrote:

> As has been widely reported in the press, Stanford's Faculty Senate voted on March 31, 1988 to make *substantial* changes in its Western Culture Program; those changes will take effect in the autumn of 1989.[53] (emphasis added)

Now, "modest" and "substantial" are relative terms, and it is certainly possible that the same curricular change could be viewed as modest by one observer and substantial by another. But in this case, the same observer described the same change in diametrically opposed ways! Dean Wasow could have believed only one of the statements he wrote. The statement circulated on campus was more likely to be the accurate one, because campus activists (unlike parents scattered across the country) were in a better position to ascertain its veracity. If they believed the changes were merely incremental, protests would have quickly resumed. Needless to say, they did not.

Dean Wasow's double-talk echoed the equivocation of Stanford's president. Throughout the year of protest and intimidation, Donald Kennedy maintained a strange silence. Earlier, in May 1986, he had voiced his support for change: "I think it should be changed," he said on campus radio, "and changed in significant ways."[54] He appreciated the "powerful critique" of the Western Culture program, based on "a really impressively sustained effort on the part of a number of students, faculty, and others—over a period I measure at not less than two and a half years, and maybe longer than that—to express serious dissatisfaction, to present alternatives, and to be heard on the matter."[55] President Kennedy did not distinguish between a political attack and an intellectual critique; for him, as for many others, that difference seemed to have collapsed. But by early 1988, he declared that it was not his place to dictate the content of the curriculum, and that such decisions should be left to the faculty. He had "reached no a priori conclusion about what the outcome should be," and would await the votes of others.[56] While washing his hands of the impending decision, President Kennedy said little about the misuse of political force at these academic discussions. Having failed to make the distinction between politics and academics earlier, he was in no position to do so then. Once the change was enacted, however, the president again vigorously defended the new program before the public: "The decision-makers really operated in a very free and a very rational and very constructive environment."[57]

On campus, the administration endorsed the efforts of the protestors, if not explicitly, then by tacit approval of inappropriate conduct. Off campus, in order to facilitate fundraising efforts among parents and alumni who supported the popular Western Culture survey, it carefully maintained the image of diligent educational patricians. In the wake of the Western Culture debate, Official Stanford sent Professor Rosaldo to alumni meetings across the country, directing the same eloquence which had galvanized student protestors at reassuring disgruntled donors. Even Vice Provost Chace, stalwart of the core list and critic of academic populism, closed ranks with the new regime, defending substance and process in *The Washington Post*: "There is a widespread conviction here that a very good course, now modified in reasonable ways, will continue to be taught effectively."[58] In its own diplomatic fashion, the administration was as politically minded as the young protestors. The rejection of academic standards in favor of political goals—raising money, garnering favorable publicity—went to the highest levels of the administration. The resulting loss of intellectual integrity was university wide. The fall of Stanford had begun.

Despite the obvious parallels between the Stanford of the late 1960s and the Stanford of the late 1980s, the debate over the canon pointed to one key difference—a distinction more telling than any of the similarities: Whereas the Western Civilization program of the 1960s was replaced with nothing at all, the Western Culture program of the 1980s was replaced with Cultures, Ideas, and Values. Whereas the protestors of the 1960s failed to replace the Western tradition with anything of their own, the protestors of the 1980s and 1990s would invent a new system to put in its place. Activists insisted that "new perspectives" were needed. In accordance with these new perspectives, the conception of the academy was revamped. No longer merely an impartial refuge for those pursuing enlightenment, the university would now actively seek to promote particular ideas and values in an effort to transform society. The word for these new perspectives—and for the brave new world towards which Stanford's social engineers hope to lead America—is "multiculturalism."

Notes

1. Charles Krauthammer, "The Tribalization of America," *The Washington Post*, August 6, 1990.

2. Bob Beyers, "Faculty Senate Unanimously Approves New Western Culture Course Emphasizing Contribution Of Women And Minorities," *Stanford University News Service*, January 16, 1988. Richard Bernstein, "Stanford Set to Alter Freshman Program In a Dispute on Bias," *The New York Times*, January 19, 1988.

3. Bernstein, *supra* note 2.

4. Stanford's protestors were more radical even than Jesse Jackson. Although press accounts mistakenly attributed the "Hey hey, ho ho" slogan to him, Reverend Jackson actually tried to quiet the mob, reasoning "The issue is not that we don't want Western culture. We're from the West," but other cultures also should be studied. *See* Bob Beyers, "Machiavelli Loses Ground at Stanford; Bible Holds Its Own," *The Chronicle of Higher Education*, June 19, 1991.

5. The indictment of Stanford's core curriculum, issued by student leaders such as Amanda Kemp, chair of the Black Student Union (BSU), was really an indictment of Western civilization itself: "[It is] racist, and numbs us...we don't really count." Under this extended meaning, the protestors were chanting not just to overhaul a year-long survey of our shared heritage, but to redefine the very nature of that heritage—it was "racist." Even the notion of a shared experience was disputed because Western culture "didn't really count" everybody. The message sent by Western culture (both the course and the civilization), Kemp declared, was "nigger go home." *See* Bob Beyers, "Western culture changes proposed: Faculty, students debate evolution toward more coverage of women, minorities," *Stanford Observer*, November 1987. *See also* Bernstein, *supra* note 2.

6. Bill King, president of the Black Student Union, denounced the existing program as "a disservice to the Stanford community" because it "fails to acknowledge the contributions and impact of women and peoples of color on American and European culture." And anthropology professor Renato Rosaldo said the requirement was "set up with a list of sacred books, eternal monuments," with few, if any, women or minority authors. *See* Eileen Walsh and Bob Beyers, "For Observer Only. Add to Western Culture Story By Eileen," *Stanford University News Service*, undated. The press release was an addendum to: Eileen Walsh, "Stanford Undergraduate Dean Recommends Revision Of Western Culture Program," *Stanford University News Service*, June 13, 1986. For a similar account of the forum, *see also* Leslie Kaufman, "Tempers flare at forum," *The Stanford Daily*, May 21, 1986.

7. Ezra Bowen, "The Canons Under Fire; Stanford cuts its book list," *Time*, April 11, 1988.

8. CIV's founding legislation mandated: "Stanford minority faculty and faculty with expertise in the study of cultures outside the European cluster of cultures shall be actively recruited to teach in program tracks." Upon first glance, the hiring clause seemed sensible. Since CIV was to expand the range of topics in the freshman requirement to include the study of non-Western cultures, it seemed appropriate to hire teachers with "expertise in the study of cultures outside the European cluster of cultures." Similarly, since the range of topics was expanded to include the study of issues pertaining to race, class, and gender, it would seem sensible also to add teachers familiar with those issues. But the hiring clause did not stipulate hiring "faculty with expertise in the study of race, gender, or class." In a sleight of hand, it stipulated, rather, hiring "minority faculty." *See* text of the final legislation for the Area One Requirement: Culture, Ideas, and Values (CIV), *Campus Report*, April 6, 1988. The legislation was adopted by the Faculty Senate on March 31, 1988.

9. Norm Book, "CIV Committee Lacks Balance," *The Stanford Review*, February 1989.

10. Sidney Hook, "Civilization and Its Malcontents," *The National Review*, October 13, 1989.

11. In accepting cultural relativism and determinism, the protestors denied the existence of universal truths. This belief dates as far back as the monotheism of Mount Sinai and is embedded in the Judeo-Christian core of Western civilization. Since universalism is central to the West, the Western Culture protestors were also rejecting the West itself. *See* Dennis Prager, "The Evils of Multiculturalism: A Jewish perspective," *Policy Counsel*, Spring 1993. Prager argues: "Multiculturalism is simply the latest attempt to undermine the concept from Mount Sinai that there is one God, and there is one moral law for all humanity. It is an attempt to undermine ethical monotheism, which is the basis for our society."

12. The text of the final legislation for the Area One Requirement required the new CIV classes "to give substantial attention to the issues of *race*, *gender*, and *class* during each academic quarter, with at least one of these issues to be addressed explicitly in at least one major reading each quarter" (emphasis in original). Text of the final legislation for the Area One Requirement, *supra* note 8.

13. Syllabi of CIV tracks, listing "Common Readings" and "Common Elements," are printed and released each year by the Program in Cultures, Ideas, and Values.

14. Bob Beyers, "Reports of the Death of Western culture greatly exaggerated, say Kennedy, Rosse," *Campus Report*, February 17, 1988.

15. This remained the "core" list through the 1992–93 school year,

when Freud was restored. *See* Syllabi, *supra* note 13.

16. Bob Beyers, "Four of Stanford's Best Known Scholars to Join Colleagues Teaching in New Cultures, Ideas, and Values Program," *Stanford University News Service*, March 13, 1989.

17. Text of the final legislation for the Area One Requirement, *supra* note 8.

18. Syllabi, *supra* note 13.

19. *Ibid.* David Sacks also took the Philosophy CIV track in 1990–91 and observed this first-hand.

20. The course's 1988 outline described the goals of the new track: "First quarter: The Spanish debate over indigenous rights raises issues around race as well as religion; readings on European enlightenment include Wollstonecraft on question of gender, and Flora Tristan on question of class. Race, gender and class are all thematized in Chungara de Barrios' autobiography and Anzaldua's poetic essays. Second quarter: Race is a central focus of materials on the Haitian revolution, and materials from the twentieth century negritude movement which developed in the post-emancipation context of modern 'scientific' racism. Gender is a central issue in Jamaica Kincaid's novel 'Annie John,' a mother-daughter story. Roumain's 'Masters of the Dew' plays out a class drama around the conflict between traditionalist peasant culture and modern proletarian consciousness. Third quarter: Marx and Weber are essential sources on class; Franz Fanon on race; gender, ethnicity and class are central themes in Rulfo, Menchu, Chavez and Anzaldua." *See* "Stanford Slights The Great Books For Not-So-Greats," *The Wall Street Journal*, December 22, 1988.

21. Mike Iwan and Norm Book, "CIV involves destruction and deconstruction of the West," *The Stanford Review*, November 1988. *See also* "The Stanford Mind," *The Wall Street Journal*, December 22, 1988.

22. "Europe and the Americas," Course Syllabus, Spring 1992. The syllabus was distributed on the first day of class by Professor Mary Pratt.

23. "Stanford Slights The Great Books For Not-So-Greats," *supra* note 20. "The Stanford Mind," *supra* note 21. Iwan and Book, *supra* note 21.

24. "Stanford Slights The Great Books For Not-So-Greats," *supra* note 20. "The Stanford Mind," *supra* note 21. Iwan and Book, *supra* note 21.

25. "Stanford Slights The Great Books For Not-So-Greats," *supra* note 20. "The Stanford Mind," *supra* note 21. Iwan and Book, *supra* note 21.

26. Aime Cesaire, *A Tempest*, trans. Richard Miller (New York: Ubu Repertory Theater Publications, 1985).

27. Walsh and Beyers, *supra* note 6.

28. *Ibid.*

29. *Ibid.*

30. Erin Martin, "Protesters rally during meeting," *The Stanford Daily*, November 5, 1987.

31. *Ibid.*

32. *Ibid.*

33. Bernstein, *supra* note 2.

34. Dean of undergraduate studies Carolyn Lougee, for instance, earlier had argued that the time had come "to ask whether...the Western Civ course that has served American Universities so well for so long is adequate to the new political exigencies, the new social realities, and the new scholarly understandings." Of course, the "new political exigencies" she referred to were the protests themselves. Walsh, *supra* note 6.

35. Martin, *supra* note 30.

36. As reported by Secretary of Education William Bennett on the *MacNeil/Lehrer NewsHour*, April 19, 1988. For a transcript, see *Campus Report*, April 27, 1988. For understandable reasons, the professor wished to remain anonymous.

37. The CUS pandered to the protestors outside its window and joined the attack on the core's putative bigotry in its report: "[The Western Culture classes] have also been open to the charge of being socially irresponsible, however unintentionally and inadvertently, for they seem to perpetuate racist and sexist stereotypes that are wounding to some and dangerous to all in a world of such evident diversity." Many supporters of the Western Culture course feared that they too would be labelled "racist," "sexist," or "socially irresponsible" if they spoke up. *See* Bob Beyers, "Stanford Task Force Unanimously Recommends New Freshman Requirement in Culture, Ideas, and Values (CIV), Starting in 1989," *Stanford University News Service*, October 12, 1987.

38. Russell Korobkin, "Approval likely for panel report," *The Stanford Daily*, October 9, 1987.

39. "Report of CUS on Area 1 Legislation Proposed by the Provostial Task Force," as reprinted in "CUS endorses changes in Area One tracks: 'criticisms valid,'" *Campus Report*, January 20, 1988.

40. Korobkin, *supra* note 38.

41. *Ibid.*

42. Haru Connolly, "BSU rejects Area 1 report," *The Stanford Daily*, October 15, 1987. For other BSU demands, *see also* Bob Beyers, "Students criticize 'back room dealing' on course proposal," *Campus Report*, April 6, 1988. For instance, BSU leader Amanda Kemp demanded that Provost James Rosse "commit himself to having students as voting members in the Faculty Senate."

43. Erin Martin, "W. Culture plan set for easy passage," *The Stanford Daily*, November 5, 1987.

44. Diane Bisgeier, "New proposal alters today's Area 1 debate," *The Stanford Daily*, January 21, 1988.

45. Brooke Harrington and Elizabeth Howton, "Chace plan loses a supporter," *The Stanford Daily*, January 25, 1988.

46. Beyers, *supra* note 14.

47. Chris Shuttlesworth, "Students plan 'silent vigil' at Fac Senate," *The Stanford Daily*, January 20, 1988. The demonstrators referred to their protest as an "educational activity." Students formed a line through which faculty members had to cross in order to enter the meeting.

48. Haru Connolly, "W. Culture plan set for approval," *The Stanford Daily*, December 7, 1987.

49. Patsy Mickens, "Agenda optimistic about Western Culture changes," *The Stanford Daily*, October 2, 1987.

50. Romesh Ratnesar, "Reform nothing new to undergraduate education," *The Stanford Daily*, November 1, 1993.

51. *See*, for instance, David Gates and Tony Clifton, "Say Goodnight, Socrates: Stanford University and the decline of the West," *Newsweek*, February 1, 1988.

52. Charles Junkerman and Thomas Wasow, "Process and Product: The Inside Story on the Western Culture Debate," *The Farm Report*, Fall 1988.

53. Tom Wasow, "Statement by the Dean of Undergraduate Studies,"*Stanford University News Service*, Spring 1988.

54. Bob Michitarian, "Kennedy: change Western Culture; Careful thought is needed, he says," *The Stanford Daily*, May 20, 1986.

55. Mickens, *supra* note 49.

56. "Kennedy lauds debate as 'significant intellectual inquiry,'" *Campus Report*, January 27, 1988.

57. *MacNeil/Lehrer NewsHour*, *supra* note 36.

58. William Chace, "There Was No Battle to Lose at Stanford," *The Washington Post*, May 9, 1988.

2

Multiculturalism: A New Word for a New World

I do not know what a clear meaning of multiculturalism is. Maybe you have one, you have a clear definition. I have yet to encounter one.[1]

—Stanford President Gerhard Casper,
who succeeded Donald Kennedy in 1992

Multiculturalism" filled the vacuum created by the elimination of the West. By the fall of 1989, it seemed as though almost everybody at Stanford enthusiastically supported "multiculturalism," or at least was invoking this word in every imaginable context: A Multicultural Educator advised Stanford's residential staff on implementing multicultural programming in the dormitories, specially selected Multicultural Editors helped the *Stanford Daily* provide more multicultural perspectives, and ethnic theme dorms and focus houses placed multiculturalism at the center of student life. As the *Stanford Daily* observed, "multiculturalism is evident in various classes, dorm events, ethnic community centers, and other aspects of daily campus life—from top-level curriculum decisions all the way down to what you'll be eating for dinner tonight."[2] These efforts culminated with the establishment of the Office for Multicultural Development (OMD) in 1990, whose prominent location on the same floor as the Office of the University President underlined its importance to campus life.[3] Sharon Parker, the new director of the OMD, reported directly to President Kennedy, a status otherwise enjoyed only by vice presidents and deans.[4]

The curricular activists, while successful, had nevertheless invited the fear of divisiveness: If every culture possessed its own unchallengeable values and standards, some began to wonder, what common ground could possibly be left? In a remarkable sleight of hand, the OMD sought to turn this liability into an asset: The celebration of differences itself would become the new unifying theme, around which the new university would be structured. Proclaiming itself "the lead office for change and the advancement of multiculturalism throughout the University community,"[5] the OMD described its overall mission in terms bordering on the messianic:

> The Office for Multicultural Development is predicated upon the knowledge that our society is composed of interdependent, multi-racial/multi-ethnic peoples and that our future requires new thinking and new structures which incorporate diversity as a means to harmony, unity and equity. Moreover, diversity is fundamental to the pursuit of excellence and knowledge. In understanding and accepting this reality, Stanford University begins a transformation to ensure that multiculturalism is infused into (not appended to) all aspects of teaching, research, planning, policies, practices, achievement, and institutional life. It is the mission of the Office for Multicultural Development to develop the multicultural model of the future and guide Stanford University through the transformation.[6]

"Multiculturalism" is the word describing this synthesis of unity and diversity. Rather than creating divisiveness, the "multicultural model of the future" instead would forge diversity into "harmony, unity and equity." The educational process, once "infused" and enhanced with multiculturalism, would take on a highly moral mission: not only to heal racial division in our society, but, since multiculturalism would include all groups, perhaps to end factiousness altogether.

In his welcoming speech to Stanford's Class of 1993, President Donald Kennedy expanded on this idea. He declared that the university was working "to create a new kind of community: one that realistically embraces the diversity that is part of contemporary America—a model of stimulating, constructive pluralism and of the examined life."[7] And then came the punchline:

> It is a bold experiment that *must* succeed if we are not to fail an important test of institutional leadership....The tasks we perform here are exactly the ones we will need

> to accomplish in building communities elsewhere later on.[8] (emphasis in original)

Just as the OMD would guide the university through a millenarian "transformation," Stanford's mission would be rededicated to leading America towards its own utopian goal. Stanford's redefined mission, its "bold experiment," would be to train students to build new multicultural communities elsewhere upon graduation—or, in other words, to promulgate multiculturalism.

Multiculturalism as Diversity

Like the *glasnost* and *perestroika* of the former Soviet Union, the "new thinking" and "new structures" of multiculturalism would seek to effect a comprehensive transformation of the university. But despite the central importance of "multiculturalism" to the new Stanford, the term itself proved remarkably slippery. Consider the OMD's definition of the implementation of multiculturalism as "ensuring University-wide influence of [the] multicultural agenda" through:

> a. Creation of a working model of multiculturalism;
> b. Development and coordination of new financial resources to support initiatives and projects which are important to institutionalizing multiculturalism at Stanford;
> c. Appropriate placement of the Office [for Multicultural Development] in the University structure; and
> d. Office [for Multicultural Development] functions as University-wide clearinghouse for activities and information on multiculturalism; and
> e. Development of cross-University networks including the Cabinet, Operations Council, Faculty Senate, Staff Affairs Office, Vice-Presidential Representatives, and Human Relations managers, and the Board of Trustees to increase their exposure to diverse aspects of University offices and operations, and to expand upon linkages with University offices and the local geographic community.[9]

The most striking feature of all of these "definitions" of multiculturalism is that they are not really definitions at all. They are little more than tautologies: The implementation of "multiculturalism" is defined to mean "the multicultural agenda," which in turn is defined as "a working model of multiculturalism," as "institutionalizing multiculturalism at Stanford," or as "activities and information on multiculturalism." Descriptions in terms of "diversity" or "unity, harmony, and equity" do not have very much content either and do not provide a definition of what multiculturalism, the new guiding philosophy of Stanford University, actually is. What kinds of diversity count, and how is it to be measured? What can "unity" possibly mean in the context of "multi-racial/multi-ethnic" diversity? Will "harmony" exist because everybody will be in agreement (certainly unusual for a university)? And what of "equity"—does it refer to equality of opportunity, or an equality of results, or something altogether different? What *exactly* is multiculturalism?

Answers to these questions require more than tautologies, but Stanford's leaders provide little else. They might say that we should study other cultures, but they rarely specify which cultures should be studied. Nor do they answer a more fundamental question: Since the word "culture" is used to refer to everything from "the drug culture" to "pop culture," what precisely counts as a culture?

There are, to be certain, some commonsense answers to these kinds of questions. If not just Europe and North America, then we should be studying the cultures of Latin America, Africa, the Middle East, India, China, and Japan. More specifically, to obtain a better understanding of other cultures, students should learn languages other than English. Knowledge of other languages, after all, is essential to any in-depth understanding of a different culture, since many of the words, phrases, and books that fully describe a culture's understanding of itself are not entirely translatable.

Remarkably, however, Stanford's multicultural leaders have made clear that these commonsense answers are not the ones they have in mind. As understood at Stanford, multiculturalism has next to nothing to do with a thorough study of other cultures. Confucius and Solzhenitzyn are nowhere on the list of multicultural priorities. Chinese, Japanese, Slavic, Indian, Arabic, African, or Latin American cultures have nothing to do with the OMD's vision of an "interdependent, multi-racial/multi-ethnic" future, and neither do the non-Western world religions, such as Islam, Buddhism, or Hinduism. Nor are student and faculty activists ever found marching in favor of new language requirements. On the contrary, the study of other languages simply is unrelated to the multicultural "transformation." During the 1980s, while the overall number of professors in Stanford's School of Humanities and Sciences was increasing, Stanford sharply decreased the staffing of its language departments and closed a number of its overseas campuses.[10] The OMD, which has insisted that any financial cuts in university spending should not affect the multicultural experiment (because "change was beginning to take hold" and "more people were opening their minds to a new way of thinking") remained altogether silent as these language programs were gutted.[11]

Yet, despite the lack of a clear definition, campus activists have advanced a vast array of causes in the name of "multiculturalism." These include AIDS awareness weeks, a "1960s" theme dormitory, speech restrictions, and a new course requirement in feminist studies. During the month of November 1991 alone, the OMD cosponsored a campus talk by Rigoberta Menchu (yes, the same Marxist revolutionary we met in "Europe and the Americas") entitled "500 Years of Oppression;"[12] helped draft a controversial new policy on sexual harassment, which concluded that "psychological coercion" (a euphemism for verbal seduction) might be equivalent to rape;[13] established the Faculty Incentive Fund, as "an incentive to departments to make faculty appointments of members of targeted racial/ethnic groups by providing special, additional funds for such an appointment;"[14] orchestrated a boycott on grapes in solidarity with a local farmers' union, which was enforced with the help of Casa Zapata, one of the multicultural theme dormitories;[15] and banned the use of cardboard axes at Stanford football's annual "Big Game" with the University of California at Berkeley, because the symbol might be offensive to Native Americans and therefore incompatible with multiculturalism.[16] In just one month, multiculturalism was invoked to give a platform to a Guatemalan revolutionary, to redefine rape, to provide financial incentives for affirmative action, to ban grapes, and to determine proper etiquette at football games.

One begins to understand the reluctance of Stanford's leaders to define "multiculturalism." A precise definition would have to possess sufficient content to explain why football game spectators cannot wave cardboard axes and why rape may include seduction; it would have to reveal why grapes are *non grata* at Stanford, and why Rigoberta Menchu was invited to give a campus talk and not Alexander Solzhenitzyn (on, say, "74 Years of Oppression"). Such a precise definition would, no doubt, be far more controversial than vague generalities about "harmony, unity, and equity" or "ways for our racial minorities and majority to acknowledge and build mutual respect for their similarities as well as their differences."[17] For if multiculturalism involves nothing more than these vague generalities, no sensible person would have any reason to oppose it. On the other hand, if multiculturalism involves more than vague generalities—and the actions of the OMD suggest that it does—then there may be far less consensus on the specifics of multiculturalism. The biggest obstacle to achieving a consensus in favor of the "multicultural agenda" may in fact be a detailed exposition of what "multiculturalism" really means.

"Multiculturalism" is an elastic term, used in several different senses. When confronted with outsiders or critics, multiculturalists make reference to broad and convenient generalities, which suggest that nothing very dramatic or controversial is going on and that no well-meaning person should have any reason to be alarmed or critical. At the same time, however, there exists another aspect of "multiculturalism," far more precise and understood by all of Stanford's multiculturalists, which explains why Menchu receives an invitation to campus, grapes are boycotted, and cardboard axes are banned. A comprehensive understanding of this unspoken definition is essential to an understanding of multiculturalism and to the new Stanford that was to be founded on this idea.

Multiculturalism as Relativism

If pushed to provide more details on what "multiculturalism" means, the average Stanford student would define the term in roughly the following way: Multiculturalism represents a bold and hopeful attempt at dealing with the changing nature of American society. Whereas the America of the 19th and early 20th centuries was overwhelmingly white, European, and Judeo-Christian, the America of the future will become increasingly multiracial, multiethnic, multilingual, and multireligious. It will confront problems that did not exist in the earlier, more homogeneous society, as people with different backgrounds will have to learn new ways of getting along with one another. In the earlier America, each new wave of immigrants entered into society by integrating its identity in the "melting pot." And, while such attempts were only partially successful in the past (as many distinct American subcultures have retained key aspects of their identity), such attempts will prove utterly inadequate in the future. It will not be possible to impose a "monocultural"[18] standard on all people in the United States, as there will be too many individuals for whom such a standard would be unacceptable. More generally, in the global and interdependent world of the future, it will be necessary for people to have a better understanding of a wide variety of different cultures, upon which a unitary (Western) standard cannot be imposed. Harmonious relations will depend upon knowing about other cultures and evaluating them on their own terms.[19]

This characterization of multiculturalism is highly attractive because its conclusions appear to follow from objective demographic facts. It seems incontrovertible that America's ethnic make-up is currently changing, and will continue to change dramatically in the 21st century. Nevertheless, none of these demographic "facts" translates easily into multicultural policies. Student leader Stacey Leyton inadvertently revealed some of the weaknesses of the demographic paradigm when she used the new thinking to justify a ruling of Stanford's Student Senate. The Student Senate, as on many occasions, was busy appointing student senators to a university committee—this one being the important University Committee on Minority Issues (UCMI). This time, however, the Senate decided to forgo its usual constitutional process of selecting representatives from among its ranks in order to let campus minority organizations choose the delegates instead. Ms. Leyton explained:

> We in the ASSU [Associated Students of Stanford University] feel that the Third World communities themselves are better qualified than we are to determine who can best represent their concerns on this committee....For too long other people have been claiming to understand and represent the minority communities and have proven insensitive and inadequate; only the communities themselves can define their needs, and they therefore deserve the right to choose their own representatives. And, indeed, they want this right: At the senate meeting where we made this decision, all four student-of-color organizations brought numbers of students to lobby the senate; it was one of the largest public turnouts in years.[20]

Ms. Leyton's argument is a textbook invocation of multicultural relativism: "only the communities themselves can define their needs"—not even elected representatives in the Student Senate could do an adequate job. But Ms. Leyton does not explain why "all four student-of-color organizations"—blacks, Chicanos, Asians, and American Indians—are the only "Third World communities" deserving special representation on the powerful committee. It is true that "they want this right," but she offers no limiting principle to explain why other groups (religious minorities, for example) that also wanted such a right were not granted a similar degree of cultural autonomy.[21] Why did the Baha'i, for instance, who also requested autonomy, not receive special attention? More generally, if minority issues affected the whole community, then why didn't the whole community deserve to have input on the UCMI? An even more basic difficulty involved the attenuated connection between minority groups and Third World cultures. Were members of minority groups who never had lived in the Third World (and most Stanford students, whatever their race, have not) still entitled to a vote within their communities? It seemed unlikely that demographics alone could provide answers to these questions.

In the academic context, the multicultural principle of judging groups according to their own standards suffers from similar shortcomings. Consider, once again, the debate over the canon: It is certainly possible and may be highly desirable to study books from non-Western cultures. But a truly relativistic reading list is impossible. At some point criteria must be selected to determine which books from which cultures are read. These judgments, naturally, are imposed upon all cultures which offer competing criteria. As in the case of the UCMI, multiculturalists claimed to solve this problem with "proportional representation," a criterion seemingly based on objective demographic facts, rather than subjective judgments: Each culture (or, in the American context, each ethnic or gender group) should be studied in proportion to its numbers; each group, in turn, should be allowed to choose its own great works. On the surface, the rhetoric appears to have a certain degree of internal logic. But this illusion of coherence occurs only because, like Ms. Leyton's argument, the demographic facade simply dodges a deeper level of foundational questions, all of which require value-laden answers:

- *First, which groups (or cultures) count in the multicultural world?* If it is said that they all do, then it may be asked: What are relevant criteria for distinguishing groups? Are Americans of Irish or Italian backgrounds multicultural groups worthy of "proportional representation?" Are Japanese and Chinese Americans distinct groups, or are they lumped together in the category "Asian American?" Are homosexuals a group? Are conservatives? More abstractly, since there seems to be no limiting principle, why are chess players not a group? Answers to these questions are critical, because the central tenet of multiculturalism is that groups must be evaluated on their own terms. If groups are not correctly defined at the outset, then crucial resources (for example, required books, admission slots, and teaching positions) will be allocated improperly. These definitional problems with multiculturalism can become quite complex: If both women and blacks, for instance, are distinct multicultural groups, then do black women fall into two categories or are they treated as their own group?

These questions are not merely academic; sometimes they take concrete form. In May 1993, for instance, the Stanford Irish American Student Association formed. Like other ethnic groups on campus, the organization demanded the creation of an introductory course that would explore "its" issues—in this case, Irish American issues, from the mid-19th-century Irish migration to America to modern-day IRA terrorist bombings in London.[22] "Most Irish-Americans have been assimilated into the white mainstream, but they have a unique history and culture that many of them are ignorant of and that have been pretty much ignored by the academic world," Chip Curran, a sophomore, told the *San Francisco Chronicle*. "We want to raise the awareness on campus that there are other non-English groups that have had a major impact on the building of America," explained Chip, a double major in economics and African and Afro-American Studies.[23]

Curran's proposal caused a schism among the ranks of the *Stanford Daily's* editorial writers, who split over the proposal in unusual side-by-side editorials. Each group believed that it was arguing consistently from multicultural principles. One side favored the course, invoking the logic that had already been used on behalf of new race and gender studies requirements. Stanford "owes its students a wide variety of classes that incorporate different backgrounds, heritages and viewpoints," they wrote.[24] The other group opposed Curran's proposal, wondering if Irish American studies might not be an "ethnic error."[25] In other words, the multicultural correctness of Curran's proposal hinged on how one arbitrarily weighed and defined cultural differences. While the University eventually rejected Curran's proposal, it never addressed the deeper quandary the proposal raised about multiculturalism's definitional vagaries.

- *Second, how are differences between groups to be resolved?* Even assuming that workable criteria for defining groups can be determined, what does one do when the desires of these groups conflict? If two groups are acting in a manner consistent with each one's own standards, what set of external standards exists to arbitrate disputes? "Proportional representation" is not a sufficient answer unless both groups already agree to this standard, an unlikely possibility if the parties seek more than a partial victory. Even if multiculturalists concede that this might be a theoretical problem, but claim that it is one that can be worked out in practice through compromise, they still cannot explain what to do with groups that reject compromise altogether. Who is to say uncompromising groups are wrong?

This confusion arises whenever multiculturalists must choose between the conflicting views and desires of different groups. The preferred group almost always seems arbitrarily selected, because no explicit rationale is offered to justify the choice. To the dismay of football fans and school patriots, for instance, the university in October 1993 cancelled the annual Big Game Bonfire, a century-old tradition, in order to protect the habitat of tiger salamanders.[26] Once thought extinct from the San Francisco bay area, the salamanders had recently been rediscovered in the lake-bed site of the scheduled bonfire. The administration overlooked the fact that the salamanders had survived 100 such bonfires, and pandered to environmentalists and animal rights activists seeking to end the celebration. In this case, multiculturalists preferred environmental extremists over football fans.

The problem of irreconcilable groups can even be internalized by individuals. In a widely discussed editorial in the *Stanford Daily* in the fall of 1992, for instance, columnist Andrea Park described the ritual clitorectomies performed by some African and Middle Eastern cultures, but stopped short of condemning the barbaric practice.[27] As a feminist, Park despised the oppression of women and wished to condemn the custom; but after much soul-searching, Park wrote that she realized she could not judge other cultures by her own standards:

> How can I argue against a culture I haven't tried to understand? Is it relevant that I, an outsider, may find the practice cruel? As hard as it is for me to admit, the answer is no. To treat the issue as a matter for feminist outrage would be to assume that one society, namely mine, has a privileged position from which to judge the practices of another.[28]

Park had arbitrarily cast her lot with African and Middle Eastern cultures instead of feminists, even though there was no principled reason for her to do so. As a result, she apologized for a heinous form of ritual torture.

- *Third, how are differences within groups to be resolved?* If Chicanos, for instance, have a special "perspective" to share, and if indeed most Chicanos can be found to agree on a particular issue, such as the grape boycott, what does one do with dissenters in the group who hold contrary opinions? How does one determine which view is truly the "Chicano perspective," or which book is truly the "great Chicano work"? Groups can be defined in such a way as to preclude large degrees of heterogeneity, but intragroup differences cannot conceivably be eliminated altogether. Which individuals within groups count?

One possible answer is to let the larger faction within the group have its way—"majority rules." Curiously, a number of *minority* activists have advocated this standard. For instance, prominent black scholar and Yale law professor Stephen Carter, a Stanford graduate who gave the university's commencement speech in 1994, has questioned the worthiness of black conservatives to speak for the group, because they are few in number: "Oh, there are neo-conservative intellectuals with black skin, but, as we have already established, they lack any claim to blackness other than biological. They have forgotten their roots. They may look black, but they are not, we might say, the black people who matter."[29] In Professor Carter's view, black conservatives—a minority of all blacks—are not truly "black," because they lack the proper political consciousness. They are thus unfit to speak for the group.

But "majority rules," however indirectly the claim may be articulated, is an inadequate solution to the problem of intragroup difference. Why, for instance, is it appropriate to impose democracy (a Western standard) on groups and cultures that have never embraced the principle?

Moreover, if minority groups in general do not have to abide by the will of the majority group, then why should dissenters within a group have to be judged by majoritarianism?

The simplistic definition of multiculturalism provides no answers to any of these foundational questions. The OMD's messianic statement of purpose lacks sufficient substance to provide a blueprint for the multicultural world. It lacks judgments about which groups should count (and which ones should not), which members within these groups should count (and which ones should not), and which groups should trump other groups. Demographic facts alone cannot tell us which demographic facts should matter.

Multiculturalism as Ideology

Stanford's multiculturalists have so much in common with one another that they rarely, if ever, consider these foundational questions about multiculturalism. They generally agree which issues are important and how to address them, and, therefore, never realize the extent to which their underlying values really animate the agenda. If Stanford's activists did not derive their values from a common source, however, a unified effort to "transform" the university would not have been possible. Every multiculturalist would have had a different idea of which groups deserved proportional representation, which minority books truly represented the "perspectives" of their traditions, and which groups were privileged over others in disputes. This much diversity would have been too much: President Kennedy's "great experiment" would never have gotten off the ground.

If there exists an Ariadne's thread running through the multicultural maze, it appears to be this: Most of the multicultural faculty and administrators were student activists in the late 1960s, and many of the multicultural students emulate their adult role models from the earlier wave of protests. CIV professor Barry Katz summarized the attitudes of the multicultural generation:

> We felt—and I say we because I was of that somewhat rebellious generation myself—we felt like we needed systems of thought that would help us answer what seemed to us then to be very critical questions: Why were U.S. troops in Vietnam? Why were the urban ghettos in America blowing up every summer, and for that matter, why were there ghettos in the first place? Why was the American power structure so uniformly white, male, old, and rich? And just to make sure that nobody took these

> questions personally, we set fire to a few police cars and occupied a few administration buildings, shut down a couple of dozen universities, and things like that.[30]

Many of Stanford's multiculturalists share Professor Katz's radical past and identify with his "systems of thought." In Stanford's recent Centennial yearbook, for instance, Dean of Student Affairs Michael Jackson, a student senator at Stanford during the 1960s, described the formative role that decade played in the development of his thinking and revolutionary politics:

> I was clearly becoming more political. I wasn't a Panther per se, but I supported what the Panthers were doing....At the time I thought, "Society is really going to change—it really is going to get better. Poverty is going to be wiped out. There's going to be equal opportunity across the board—in education, housing, and access to government." I was going to be part of the change....The war dragged on. People became disillusioned. We didn't have the political or social levers to bring about *massive cultural change*. The young people were not the elected leaders, nor the captains and queens of industry, nor were they the heads of universities or foundations. *They weren't the professors and the teachers*....Frederick Douglass said there is no progress without struggle. As I enter my fourth decade, the struggle continues unabated.[31] (emphasis added)

In a Centennial yearbook photograph of Dean Jackson, taken in 1969, he is the picture of radical chic, sporting an unkempt Afro and wearing brightly colored bell-bottoms. Now, some 20 years later, the well-groomed dean could be seen strolling the campus, chatting with students, his hair coiffured, his double-breasted suit neatly pressed.[32] Having never left campus, many of the 1960s activists now are the professors and teachers. Their "unabated" commitment to the "struggle" has finally paid off. They still occupy administration buildings—only now they *are* the administration. They finally hold in their grasp the political and social "levers to bring about massive cultural change."

Activists of the 1960s like Dean Jackson and Professor Katz advocated "massive cultural change" because they believed America to be a country hopelessly divided by race, gender, and class. Only revolutionary reform, they argued, could correct a long history of oppression. Professor Katz's "uniformly white, male, old, and rich" establishment, they believed, had structured the "system" to reward itself and limit the success of minorities and women. The 1960s activists "struggled" to destroy this "system" and thereby end all forms of discrimination, and also to redress the "subordinated" groups that had been excluded from positions of power in American society. By the 1990s, their American proletariat had come to include, among others, blacks, Hispanics, American Indians, Asian Americans, homosexuals, and women, along with the poor and the working class.

To be certain, today's multiculturalists do not advocate exactly the same policies as the earlier generation. Some of the nuances and differences are significant, and will be explored in more detail later. But, as a rough first approximation, if one wishes to make predictions about how multiculturalists will derive their values, one need only take a poll of unreconstructed 1960s radicals. The radical answers are going to be quite close to the multicultural answers. The younger generation of student protestors usually sympathizes with these values, and in many cases is even nostalgic for the earlier era, whose activism continues to serve as a role model for its own. "People of my age look back on the 1960s as a time when youth had a voice," explained 21-year-old senior Tim Choy, a resident of Potter House, Stanford's "1960s" theme dormitory.[33]

This implicit (but rarely enunciated) frame of reference can answer the foundational questions the more simplistic definition of multiculturalism could not. First, multiculturalists solve the definitional problem (who counts?) by automatically choosing the so-called subordinated groups that comprise the American proletariat. Within this framework, the multiculturalists next solve the problem of intergroup differences by automatically favoring the more subordinated group (or simply ignoring the concerns of nonsubordinated, or "superordinated," groups). Lastly, minority individuals who do not adhere to the radical politics of their group's leaders are considered "sell-outs,"[34] or in Marxian rhetoric are suffering from a "false consciousness." Multiculturalists may thus ignore such dissonant opinions.

This approach does not deal with every contingency or solve all theoretical problems. Most multiculturalists, if pressed to rank and compare the subordinated groups against one another, would have no easy answers. But in practice such contrasts often can be avoided and the multicultural framework can provide answers to most of the issues that are confronted. For example:

- Chip Curran's proposal for an introductory Irish American studies class was never implemented because Irish Americans are not one of the multicultural groups that count. Although Chip invoked the same reasoning that had been used to justify race and gender studies requirements, Stanford's leaders sided with the opinion that such a study would constitute an "ethnic error."

- The Student Senate granted special representational privileges to the "four student-of-color" organizations, and not to the others groups that may have sought them, because these four organizations, unlike the Irish American Student Association or the Baha'i, are the multicultural groups that count. The values underlying Ms. Leyton's argument now come into focus: Whether any minority students have lived in the Third World is irrelevant. The four minority organizations are "Third World communities" because they share with the Third World a putative history of oppression (or cultural imperialism) by establishment American society.
- If we accept the characterization of radicals that America is hopelessly flawed by racial division, then their race-conscious remedies become more attractive. As the primary multicultural groups, racial minorities cannot be evaluated by whites. The choice, moreover, between minorities' and nonminorities' perspectives favors that of minorities, both as a matter of redress and because their historical condition has given them a special insight (*gnosis*) into race relations in America. For both these reasons, the Faculty Incentive Fund provides special grants to departments that hire more minority faculty.
- "Psychological coercion" means rape because the radical feminist agenda claims that men should be solely responsible for the consequences of any sexual intercourse with women. In multicultural terms, one may reach this value judgment by preferring the perspective of (historically victimized) women over men. Those females who do not agree with this conclusion may be discounted as suffering from a "false consciousness," as, presumably, they have not overcome the conditioning of male-dominated society. Indeed, some feminists have gone so far as to suggest that such females should not even be viewed as women, an argument analogous to the suggestion that black conservatives should not be considered "black."
- Grapes are politically incorrect fruit that must be excised from the cafeteria menu because the United Farm Workers (UFW) labor union claims that California's grape pickers are exploited by the people for whom they choose to work. The UFW, formerly led by the late Caesar Chavez, is part of the new left political coalition, and thus carries weight with Stanford's multiculturalists. This multicultural value is reached first by privileging the perspectives of poor Latino workers over those of rich white employers, and second by privileging the radical members of the Latino group (labor union leaders) over common workers (who, in spite of the

boycott, continue to report for work). Although Stanford's dining services now import grapes from Chile, many occupants of Casa Zapata still deprive themselves of grapes and grape juice in symbolic observation of the protest.[35]

- Enjoying collegiate football, with all of its connotations of Americana, is not one of the highest priorities of political activists—particularly in contrast to the importance of undoing historical injustices (both real and imagined) to American Indians. Fans cheering with cardboard axes might remind Indians of the "tomahawk chop" and offend them. Therefore, students are not permitted to engage in such activity—even though Stanford's axe is merely a symbolic trophy without connection to anything Indian.

In terms of a theory of group-based relations, multiculturalism, as it is publicly defined, has almost no empirical content and seems to be little more than wishful warm fuzziness. But when the value judgments of the American left are used to define the proper parameters, multiculturalism becomes transformed into a comprehensive and detailed worldview. Nevertheless, there is nothing obvious or necessary about these particular answers to the foundational questions. The multicultural resolution is *contingent*, and acquires a facade of legitimacy only because of widespread agreement on the underlying system of values on the part of all those leading the multicultural revolution.

In practice, only a relatively small vanguard drives the "transformation" of the university—tenured radicals such as Professor Katz, administrators such as Dean Jackson and Ms. Parker (Director of the OMD), and succeeding generations of student activists, such as Tim Choy, Stacey Leyton, and the grape-boycotting residents of Casa Zapata. But the multicultural movement encounters little resistance because the rest of the campus generally shares (or, at least, discerns nothing very wrong with) its underlying values.

Polls consistently show that the Stanford community is overwhelmingly left-of-center. In 1984, 71 percent of voters in the Stanford precinct, comprised almost entirely of the Stanford academic community, chose Walter Mondale over Ronald Reagan for president, despite landslide nationwide electoral and popular vote victories for President Reagan. In 1988, 78 percent of Stanford precinct voters supported Michael Dukakis over George Bush, again in marked contrast to the majority of the American people.[36] Even more strikingly, in 1994 Stanford senior Aman Verjee went to the local Registrar of Voters and conducted an extensive survey of political party affiliation among Stanford faculty. He found that the faculty of the major humanities departments are far more Democratic than the nation as a whole. (A similar 1986 study by Hoover Institution Fellow George Marotta produced almost identical findings.) Of the professors registered to vote, Verjee's study found that over 80 percent were Democrats and less than 10 percent were Republicans. A number of the core humanities departments had no Republican professors at all:[37]

Department	Democrats	Republicans	Other
Economics	21	7	0
Political Science	26	4	1
Psychology	20	0	1
History	22	2	0
English	31	2	1
Anthropology	15	1	2
African and Afro-American studies	12	0	0
Sociology	11	1	1
Feminist Studies	5	0	0
Law School	23	4	3

The partisan bias revealed by Verjee is not unique to Stanford, a fact which suggests that multiculturalism is motivated by similar values on other campuses. In a 1989 survey of faculty politics at colleges and universities across the country, commissioned by the Carnegie Foundation for the Advancement of Teaching, 70 percent of professors identified themselves as liberal or moderately liberal, 12 to 15 percent as moderately conservative, and only 3 or 4 percent as conservative.[38] The single demographic fact most significant to multiculturalism may be that the professoriate of today's academies are almost uniformly on the left of the political spectrum.

In practice, multiculturalists simply are demanding more—and with greater immediacy—of what a large segment of the university community already supports. As a result, the administration cannot convincingly tell activists "enough." Any admonishment would be like that of an alcoholic parent telling his children not to use drugs; the message simply is not credible. President Donald Kennedy, the former head of the Food and Drug Administration during the Carter administration, was no exception to this rule. Having used the office of the Stanford presidency on behalf of pet political causes—including public support for Michael Dukakis's presidential campaign and a denunciation of the military's ban on homosexuals—he could not convincingly resist multicultural calls for even more extreme politics.[39] Admittedly, by the end of his 12-year tenure, President Kennedy hinted that the multicultural experiment had perhaps grown beyond his control: "I do believe I gave it support. I also tried to give it some restraints. From time to time I indicated a worry that multiculturalism would become a kind of political ideology of its own."[40] But like so many of Stanford's educators, President Kennedy could criticize multiculturalism only by criticizing himself. And so, a sharper criticism would have been unimaginable—even if, in his last few months in office, he finally suspected what many others had known all along: President Kennedy's "bold experiment" had never been scientific; ideology had always biased its results.

Rather than involving a new and innovative approach, then, multiculturalism really depends upon and reinforces the community's preexisting values. The multicultural rhetoric could be used, just as readily, by a diverse array of other causes, in the name of rehabilitating other "victims"—entrepreneurs by critics of the nanny state, victims of crime by conservatives concerned with law and order, baby seals by those committed to animal rights. One could, just as readily, imagine universities setting aside resources for self-made millionaires, people who have been mugged, or pet owners—on the basis that the members of such groups share in some special *gnosis*.

To take but one more hypothetical example, if Stanford were pandering to Islamic fundamentalists—rather than to 1960s radicals—one could imagine identical rhetoric. From Teheran to Tripoli, militant Muslims have demanded that Western culture must go because it is oppressing their traditional societies. But an Islamic victims' revolution would differ significantly in the details. Instead of extolling the writings of Aime Cesaire, a revamped CIV might study the sayings of the Ayatollah Khomeini and Moammar Khadafy's *Green Book*. Religious litmus tests could be used to hire faculty with the *gnosis* necessary to present a perspective that does not suffer from an "Occidentalist" bias. The University's Committee on Minority Issues might be comprised of representatives from the four "multicultural" groups that would count—Sunnis, Shias, Ishmaelis, and Druze. Instead of grapes, an Islamic focus house might boycott hot dogs. And organizations from Hamas to Hezbollah might be extolled as the new vanguard, leading the way for others to follow. Obviously, Stanford's multiculturalists are not engaged in an Islamic *jihad*. But this example drives home an important point: Underneath a glossy veneer of open-ended and utopian rhetoric, multiculturalism depends upon very specific values to operate, and at Stanford the values that inform this process happen to be the radical values of the 1960s.

Indeed, the impossibility of a value-free multiculturalism should have been evident at the very outset, during the Western Culture debate. The protestors did not really believe that all cultures were equal, as they reserved a special condemnation for the West. To the extent that Western culture (both as a historical reality and as learned in Stanford's former freshman course) rejected relativism in its search for transcultural truth, it was the culture the multiculturalists had to reject. In committing themselves to cultural relativism over Western universalism, the multiculturalists made their first value judgment. In so doing, their pretensions of neutrality were also rejected and replaced with a different set of values.

Multiculturalism as Conformity

Yet multiculturalism is not exactly the same thing as a radical political program, since, at least on a superficial level, it is about something quite different. On a superficial level, multiculturalism seems to involve a theory that describes groups of people, the decision making within these groups, the interaction between these groups, and the possibilities for special insights by some groups. The multicultural rhetoric about "diversity" and "interactive pluralism" is not unimportant, because it serves the critical function of deflecting attention from the underlying value judgments.

This dual track (ostensibly concerned with "diversity," while in reality pushing an agenda) runs through much of the multicultural state. The agenda normally remains implicit, but sometimes can become quite explicit. The job description of Stanford's Multicultural Educator involves glimpses of both. At first, the description lists the usual banalities: The Educator must promote pluralism, which "encompasses the full range of human variety, including differences of race, class, gender, sexual orientation, disability, national origin, religion, ideological views, and other differences of background and belief."[41] But then comes the real job description: Stanford requires that the Educator be careful about making the multicultural agenda too explicit, because "if students believe that the institution is trying to remake them, inculcate ideas, and push an agenda it will be easier for them to resist educational efforts and avoid personal commitment to increased understanding."[42] A better summary of what multiculturalism is all about would be difficult to find. The OMD signals would-be applicants that there is more to multiculturalism than just "pluralism," for the job also requires the Educator to "remake [students], inculcate ideas, and push an agenda"—albeit an agenda that must remain beneath the surface (both in practice and in the job description itself), lest students "resist educational efforts" and "avoid personal commitment" to the new regime. With the arrival of more than 1,500 ideologically diverse freshmen each year, such "educational efforts" are required to induce enough "personal commitment" that consensus may be maintained on the values necessary for multiculturalism to operate.

These underlying values, and the "educational" efforts of Stanford's multiculturalists to enforce them, come to the fore in many contexts. One highly illustrative example that is worth exploring in more detail involved a series of events that occurred in the fall of 1988 in "Ujamaa," Stanford's black culture theme dormitory, named after the Swahili word for "cooperative living." On the early evening of September 29, 1988, Ujamaa House was the site of a remarkable conversation, whose three principal participants were two white freshmen, Gus Heldt and Ben Dugan, and a black sophomore, B. J. Kerr. According to the "Final Report on Recent Incidents At Ujamaa House," that would be issued in January 1989 by a select panel appointed by President Kennedy, the discussion's topics included black influence on music, black life in Africa, and the state of race relations in America.[43] B. J. informed the students that "all music is black" and that "all music listened to today in America has African origins—beats, drums, and so forth." A white bystander asked, "What about classical music? Beethoven?" Undeterred, B. J. declared that Beethoven also had been black—he had read it in a book in the Ujamaa library. Ben and Gus were incredulous. B. J. expressed displeasure with Gus and Ben for doubting. The idea that Beethoven had been black "was so far from their own truth," he declared, that the two freshmen "could not accept it."[44]

The following evening, Ben noticed a Stanford Symphony recruiting poster featuring a picture of none other than Beethoven himself (in the poster, Beethoven appeared white). Inebriated, Gus and Ben used crayons to color in the Beethoven flier with the stereotypical features of a black man—brown face, curly black hair, enlarged lips—and then posted the flyer on a "food for thought" bulletin board adjacent to B. J.'s door. The black residents of Ujamaa did not consider the satire amusing. B. J., who had lectured other people on Beethoven's blackness just several days earlier, was particularly flabbergasted: "I couldn't believe anybody would do that. You see things like that in the movies or on TV. It's the kind of thing someone would do in their room and joke about but it didn't seem like anyone would be bold enough to put it on a door."[45] One of the black resident assistants (RAs) in Ujamaa added that the flyer was "hateful, shocking. I was outraged and sickened."[46] Overnight, with the most minute shift in inflection, the symbolic significance of the claim that Beethoven was black had changed 180 degrees—from a source of multicultural pride to a point of multicultural derision.

Ben and Gus's satire was certainly in bad taste. But B. J.'s words and the two white students' drawing had said precisely the same thing. Nevertheless, the fact that these students were of different races made B. J.'s expression legitimate and the white students' something of a crime. A black student who said that Beethoven was black was bolstering racial pride, while white students doing the same—with the "wrong" intentions—were racist rabble-rousers. To the multiculturalists, for whom truth is subjective, the accuracy or falsehood of the original claim was irrelevant. Because "subordinated" groups are not subject to criticism by "superordinated" groups, the relevant issue was not what was said, but who said what to whom.

On October 16, an emergency house meeting was called to discuss the Beethoven flier. An Ujamaa "teaching assistant" (TA) had succeeded in extracting a confession from Gus by warning him that "people are really angry," "people are really suspicious of you," and there are people planning "to beat the hell out of you." According to the Final Report, "We asked T/A Brown if in fact there were residents planning to beat up [Ben] and [Gus]. He said no; this was a ruse to get [Gus] to tell the truth."[47]

If Gus's confession was extracted by intimidation, the emergency house meeting resembled a show trial. Ujamaa's residents had been discussing the matter among themselves for the previous two weeks, and the atmosphere was highly charged. Gus attempted an explanation: He had been disturbed and offended to find that people cared so much about race at Stanford, and he thought the focus on "ethnic differences" was counterproductive. Gus suggested that the poster had been attempted as "food for thought," educational, and "avant-garde" art.[48] Ujamaa's residents, however, were not interested in an art lesson, much less the suggestion that their focus on race—of which the show trial was but the latest instance—was excessive. A resident interrupted Gus's speech: "You arrogant bastard, how dare you come here and not even apologize. I want an apology."[49] Gus's flip reply indicated that he remained unrepentant: "1, 2, 3, we're sorry."[50] The "apology," needless to say, was inadequate, and some of the residents began to demand that Ben and Gus be removed from the Stanford dorm system. Ron Hudson, an assistant dean of student affairs, suggested rather lamely that it would be good to keep the two freshmen in the dorms so they could receive a better multicultural education.[51]

The din of the crowd quieted as B. J. rose to speak. Noting that Dean Hudson's suggestion was silly, B. J. stated that Ujamaa's residents should not educate the two freshmen because "this all came about because [black Ujamaa residents] were trying to educate [these two] about African history [in the first place]." It would be a waste to educate persons with "such dogmatic racism who came to Stanford with eighteen years of belligerent ideology," and he "shouldn't have to pay $20,000 to educate white people about racism" in his own home.[52] B. J. concluded that the proper remedy would consist of throwing the culprits out of the dorm.

In the course of his speech, B. J. had become more and more emotional. There are conflicting accounts of what occurred next, but observers interviewed for the university's Final Report generally agreed that towards the end of his speech, B. J. started to gesticulate wildly, lunged violently at the two white freshmen, and, seeming to have lost his mind, collapsed on the floor. According to the residence staff, when people caught B. J. "he was groaning and flailing his arms"; it "seemed as if B. J.

had lost his mind"; he was "not in control of his actions" and was carried out of the lounge to his room by about six students, while he was "crying, screaming and having a fit."[53]

B. J.'s tantrum was only the beginning of the end of the house meeting. The university's Final Report describes the pandemonium that broke loose next:

> As many as 60 students were crying with various degrees of hysteria. At least one student hyperventilated and had to be assisted in breathing. According to R/F Brooks there was "utter chaos." People were "crying, screaming," "hysterical" and "distraught." R/F Weiss said that there was "mass chaos," "people were holding hands and crying, tears were running down," the "staff was running around trying to collect people." She compared the scene to the mass hysteria that occurred when the [space] shuttle exploded or the U.S. exhibition air show in Germany where a group of planes simultaneously crashed. R/F Brooks told the staff "to make sure no one was alone." R/A Johnson reported that "one woman was jumping up and down saying this is not fair." She "herded" crying persons into her room which was a "wreck," "bodies everywhere."[54]

Multicultural diversity has its limits, and at Ujamaa events had moved far beyond the breaking point. Two freshmen, at Stanford for only a few weeks, had done nothing more than poke fun at multiculturalism with a satirical flier. In the subsequent days, the flier's significance became exaggerated to the point where it caused an entire dorm to have a collective nervous breakdown. Since the administration was unwilling to tell Ujamaa's minority residents (members of a privileged multicultural group) that they had overreacted, Ben and Gus had to be found guilty of instigating the entire episode. They were blamed for the "painful experience" and were removed from university housing for the remainder of the year.[55] The fact that Ujamaa's residents were largely responsible for blowing events out of all proportion was conveniently overlooked in the cathartic hunt for scapegoats.

As unfortunate as the entire episode was for Ben, Gus, and the other residents of Ujamaa, the incident is still useful for its instructional value. For multiculturalism to "work," some groups of people must defer to other groups of people. Within each group, some persons are "correct" (while others are "sell-outs"), and so on. Ben's and Gus's actions undermined multiculturalism on almost every level: They challenged a claim made by a representative of a favored group, they renewed the challenge with a flier, and (perhaps worst of all) they refused to confess to their crimes in front of a crowd that desperately needed reassurance. Because Ben and Gus were partially *right* in what they had said (that is, Beethoven was not black), their challenge could not be dealt with in a rational or intellectual manner. Rather, the residents of Ujamaa restored consensus by demanding the literal expulsion of the two nonconformists. Ben and Gus had to go because the multicultural community requires (as the substitute for objective truth) widespread agreement on underlying ideological values. At the same time, their punishment would also serve as a warning and deterrent to other would-be contrarians. Incidentally, the question of whether Beethoven actually was black, around which much of this debate ostensibly had revolved, was never resolved or even addressed.

Much as with the Western Culture debate, the details of the Beethoven incident gradually would fade, but as a putative racist episode it would provide the justification for additional "sensitivity training" sessions, more multicultural workshops, and new regulations on conduct. Speaking at a "Rally Against Racism" several weeks later, undergraduate Cheryl Taylor cited the Ujamaa episode as symptomatic of widespread oppression of blacks. The genesis of a new multicultural myth was well under way:

> By now, y'all must have heard about the Ujamaa incident—the racially defaced Beethoven flyer....This is a big deal; in the context of American society, these incidents are truly racist. They weren't just isolated incidents committed out of ignorance; rather, they were deliberate actions committed in response to the Res Ed. focus on diversity. In effect, these individuals sent a message to Stanford, and all communities of color[:] "we're sick of this cultural diversity bullshit that's being shoved down our throats. Your cultures are not legitimate—they don't mean shit to us—they have no place in this University—Niggers, we will put you back in your place.["] Well, they've been kicked out of the dorm and we are here today to say that no one is going to stand in our way as we fight for justice and respect.[56]

Close up, the OMD's effort to forge "harmony, unity, and equity" begins to appear far less benign. Certainly, Ujamaa achieved a "unity" of sorts by collectively expelling the two freshmen. But this unanimity comes at a high price, as scapegoats are made of those (and there will always be some) who do not conform willingly.

In practice, multiculturalism will tend towards either relativism or conformity, depending on whether one stresses the silly slogans or the hidden agenda. There are many instances where multiculturalism is relativist (or merely confused), for the simple reason that multiculturalists often have not probed their own rhetoric about diversity very deeply. But the Beethoven incident is a reminder of the widespread agreement that exists on certain basic values and that will assert itself very powerfully whenever "diversity" is pushed beyond rather narrow limits.

As we will show in the next two chapters, political activists have used the multicultural vehicle to effect sweeping change at Stanford. From areas such as the curriculum to extracurricular life, from faculty hiring to student admissions, from speech codes to long-range planning, the ambiguities of a simplistic (or relativist) multiculturalism have been resolved in favor of a number of radical policy objectives. On this level at least, multiculturalism represents a spectacular success for the American left, one that may not have been possible without the existence of this extremely enthralling, and confusing, idea.

On a deeper level, however, the need for a misleading idea like "multiculturalism" represents a colossal failure for the radical left. The need to engage in word games rather than an honest discussion of the real issues suggests that such an honest discussion would not lead to results that fit the desired agenda. In this respect, multiculturalism is a symptom of the retreat of the 1960s left, of its unwillingness—indeed, its inability—to participate in the marketplace of ideas that is the hallmark of a successful university and of a healthy society. As we will suggest in the second half of this book, multiculturalism may represent the last effort of a failed system of beliefs that could no longer be rationally supported—and that therefore required a conceptual framework that encourages its practitioners to retreat into a sort of cultural and intellectual regionalism, and, like the Ujamaa residents who suffered a collective nervous breakdown, perhaps to stop thinking altogether.

Notes

1. Lisa Koven, "Gerhard Casper: Man of the Year," *The Stanford Review*, January 4, 1993.

2. Colleen Krueger and Cathy Siciliano, "Diversity a source of campus vitality; Stanford students enhance their education with multiculturalism," *The Stanford Daily*, September 23, 1993.

3. David Sacks, "Departments Paid Bonuses for Minority Hiring; Affirmative Action Vital to Perpetuation of Multiculturalism, Says OMD," *The Stanford Review*, November 4, 1991. The OMD was moved from the second floor to the first floor after it was chastised for insensitivity to people in wheelchairs.

4. *Ibid.*

5. Sharon Parker, *Affirmative Action Plan For Stanford University*, October 16, 1991. The Plan was released by the Office for Multicultural Development and approved of by University President Donald Kennedy.

6. *Ibid.*

7. "DK welcomes freshmen to 'real world': 'Pluralism experiment must succeed,'" *Campus Report*, September 27, 1989. The article reprinted Donald Kennedy's September 22 welcoming speech to freshmen.

8. *Ibid.*

9. Parker, *supra* note 5.

10. Andy Dworkin, "Concern mounting over loss of billets," *The Stanford Daily*, May 24, 1994. According to *The Daily*, over the last five to ten years, the departments of French and Italian, German, Spanish and Portuguese, and Slavic Languages have lost a combined eight billets for tenure-track faculty—an approximate drop of about 20 percent in the number of faculty billets. An administrative merger between the French, Italian, Spanish, and Portuguese departments also decreased support staff for languages. Budget cuts to the humanities focused on the language departments, reported John Etchemendy, a university official. In addition, Stanford closed its popular program in Salamanca, Spain, and overseas studies programs in Paris and Florence were scaled back. *See* Thomas Wasow, "Many factors contributed to the closure of Stanford's Tours program," *The Stanford Daily*, November 13, 1990. The total capacity of Stanford's overseas centers has decreased by more than 200 "student quarters"—the number of total terms spent by students abroad—since 1984. *See* Sarah Katz and Romesh Ratnesar, "Report indicates concerns about Overseas Studies," *The Stanford Daily*, January 7, 1994.

11. Parker, *supra* note 5.

12. Menchu's speech was announced by an advertisement in *The Stanford Daily*, November 22, 1991. In addition to the Office for Multicultural Development, the list of sponsors included the Center for Latin American Studies, Casa Zapata (the Chicano/Latino dormitory), the Department of Spanish and Portuguese, El Centro Chicano, Innovative Academic Programs, Comité Unidad Guatemalteca, Stanford's Memorial Church, the Ho Fund, and the Institute for Research on Women and Gender.

13. Miranda Doyle and Holly Hacker, "Cabinet sends new sex assault rules back for revision," *The Stanford Daily*, November 1, 1991.

14. Like the *Affirmative Action Plan For Stanford University*, Sharon Parker also drafted the *School Plans for Faculty and Graduate Student Recruitment 1991-1994*, which was released by the Office for Multicultural Development and signed by University President Donald Kennedy and Provost James Rosse. *See* Sacks, *supra* note 3.

15. Beginning in 1987, the campus Chicano community demanded that the university no longer serve grapes or grape juice. Senior Julie Martinez explained that the boycott was an effort to protect California's grape pickers from carcinogenic pesticides: "It's a battle of wealthy grape growers and poor farm workers," said Martinez. "Who's the university going to listen to?" For activists like Martinez, not taking a side was equivalent to taking the side of the "wealthy" growers. President Kennedy encouraged the students, telling them "to let Food Service see that [grape] use is lower." *See* Erin Martin, "Short meeting disappoints Chicanos," *The Stanford Daily*, November 19, 1987. *See also* Delia Ibarra, "What grapes mean to me," *The Stanford Daily*, April 4, 1991.

16. "For the Record," *The Stanford Review*, November 25, 1991.

17. *Final Report Of The University Committee On Minority Issues*, March 1989.

18. The word is the OMD's. It comes from an article the OMD distributes to promote multiculturalism and overcome the "legacy of deep-grained monocultural thinking in the United States." *See* Joan Steinau Lester, "The Multicultural Organizational Change Process: Seven Essential Components," *Black Issues in Higher Education*, February 15, 1990.

19. This conception of multiculturalism is common at universities across the country. A good example is the Multicultural Curriculum Development Grant Program at the State University of New York at Binghamton. Peter Wagner, the university's Provost and Vice President for Academic Affairs, announced the program's inception in a December 18, 1989, memorandum: "Traditional curricula have been largely Eurocentric in emphasis, particularly in general education. Even

individual courses in which culture, ethnicity, gender, and race should be irrelevant to content may be affected by judgmental modes of thought and presentation, or by cultural disincentives....The intent of this program is to nurture and encourage the creation of a curriculum that is fundamentally multicultural, one that does not favor any specific cultural, ethnic, or racial group, and that assures parity in such other areas as religion and sexual preferences."

20. Stacey Leyton, "Minority panel selection justified," *The Stanford Daily*, October 16, 1987.

21. Indeed, in the very same issue of *The Stanford Daily*, someone made precisely this point: Would the Baha'i, for example, have reason to feel discriminated against because they were not one of the "Third World communities" that counted? *See* Koleman Strumpf, "Minorities not always diverse," *The Stanford Daily*, October 16, 1987.

22. Bill Workman, "Stanford Irish Americans Want Own Course," *The San Francisco Chronicle*, May 5, 1993.

23. *Ibid.*

24. *Ibid.*

25. *Ibid.*

26. Skip Schwartz, "Big Game Bonfire canceled to protect salamanders; Annual event would 'undoubtedly cook' recently returned animals," *The Stanford Daily*, October 8, 1993.

27. Andrea Park, "Non-Western feminism," *The Stanford Daily*, December 1, 1992.

28. *Ibid.*

29. Ed Malone, "Graduation speaker's works contradict 'conservative' label," *The Stanford Review*, April 4, 1994.

30. Barry Katz, *Campus Report*, August 8, 1986.

31. Michael Jackson, quoted in *The Stanford Century*, Stanford Alumni Association, 1991.

32. In March 1995, Dean Jackson left Stanford to become vice president of the University of Southern California. *See* Martin Yeung, "Speeding the process: New dean of students will be chosen by end of quarter," *The Stanford Daily*, May 22, 1995.

33. Theresa Johnston, "Focus Houses Offer Students Culture...and the '60's," *Stanford University News Service: Stanford Story Source*, December 1992.

34. One independent-minded black freshman revealed in *The Stanford Daily* that the leaders of the BSU indeed branded dissenters as "sell-outs." He wrote: "The BSU should not label blacks who criticize them as 'sell-outs.' If 'selling out' can be defined as not helping the black cause, then those who refuse to listen to constructive criticism are the true 'sell-outs.'" *See* Michael Jones, "Freshman criticizes Black

Student Union's agenda, leadership," *The Stanford Daily*, May 29, 1992.

35. Jim Luh, "Few eateries serve grapes," *The Stanford Daily*, May 6, 1994.

36. *See* Martin Anderson, *Imposters in the Temple* (New York: Simon & Schuster 1992).

37. Aman Verjee, "Does Stanford engage in political discrimination?" *The Washington Times*, January 9, 1995.

38. Anderson, *supra* note 36.

39. *See*, for instance, Grace Lee, "Anti-gay ROTC policy questioned by Kennedy," *The Stanford Daily*, May 20, 1992.

40. Michael Friedly, "Changing the Face of Stanford: Kennedy leaves behind legacy of multiculturalism," *The Stanford Daily*, May 27, 1992.

41. Heather Heal, "No budget cuts here: Stanford seeks new multicultural educator," *The Stanford Review*, January 19, 1993.

42. *Ibid.*

43. James Lyons, "Final Report on Recent Incidents at Ujamaa House," *Campus Report*, January 18, 1989. In the Final Report, aliases were used for the individuals involved, although their names were widely reported by the media at the time. Ben was referred to as "Alex," Gus as "Fred," and B. J. as "Q. C." Otherwise, the Report provides a highly detailed chronology of events. *See also* Bob Beyers, "Stanford Launches Investigation Of Worst In Series Of Racist Incidents," *Stanford University News Service*, October 17, 1988.

44. *Ibid.*

45. *Ibid.*

46. *Ibid.*

47. *Ibid.* The Final Report, interestingly, makes nothing more of the residence staff's dissembling. Apparently, coercive tactics were permitted if they furthered multiculturalism. Two ("superordinated") freshmen's defiling a flier and angering ("subordinated") minorities was an abuse of power; a university staffer's bullying of a student in his charge was not.

48. *Ibid.*

49. *Ibid.*

50. *Ibid.*

51. *Ibid.*

52. *Ibid.*

53. *Ibid.*

54. *Ibid.*

55. Eileen Walsh, "Freshmen Who Defaced Beethoven Poster Suspended From Student Residence Community for Two Quarters," *Stanford University News Service*, January 10, 1989.

56. Cheryl Taylor, speech at "Rally Against Racism," October 26, 1988. Her remarks were reprinted in "A Mandate for Change," October 26, 1988, a press statement printed and distributed by the Black Student Union, Movimiento Estudiantil Chicano de Aztlan (MEChA), Stanford American Indian Organization, and Asian American Students Association.

3

Educating Generation X

Of all the intensely politicized campuses in the republic—and there are many—Stanford is about the worst. Moreover, the politics that dominate are not simply the poisonous teachings of Marx, Lenin, the German mentors of Hitler or any of the other propounders of New Dawns this century. All those fanatics come across as teachers of genius and integrity compared with the infantile nitwits being taught on America's flagrantly politicized campuses.[1]

—Columnist R. Emmett Tyrrell, Jr.

I couldn't have taught this class 10 years ago," history professor Kennell Jackson declared to an overflowing classroom on the first day of the 1992 Spring quarter. "But people don't look at me like I'm crazy anymore—what history does has broadened considerably."[2] And Professor Jackson was not exaggerating. "Black Hair as Culture and History," his new upper-level History seminar, addressed how black hair "has interacted with the black presence in this country, and how it has played a role in the evolution of black society."[3]

Turning from the chalkboard, Professor Jackson asked whether anyone had experienced "A Black Hair Event" recently. One student piped up from the back of the room: "Juliette Lewis's cornrow hair at the Oscars." "That's a good one," Professor Jackson agreed, producing a picture of the actress from *USA Today*. "Any others? No? Well, look for next week."[4]

If not for Professor Jackson's earnestness, one might have mistaken the class for a parody of multiculturalism. The syllabus outlined the curriculum for the quarter:

April 1: Introduction to the Idea and the Unfolding of the Course
April 8: The African Conception of Beauty and the Place of the Face, Head, and Hair in the Conception of Beauty
April 15: Early Black Hair in America to the 1920s
April 22: The Birth of Straightened Hair: The Practice and the Cultural Ideas Surrounding This Development
April 29: New Ideas on Black Hair in the 1960s and the Rise of the "Afro" (with Some Cornrows and Some Braiding)
May 13: The Great Debate: The Legacy of the 1960s; Black Hair as Identity
May 20: The 1980s-1990s as Festival of Black Hairstyles: Fade-O-Rama, Braiding, and Dreadlocks
May 27: The Economic and Status Importance of Black Hair
June 3 and 10: Visits from Hairstylists[5]

In addition to discussing such topics as "the Rise of the 'Afro'" and "Fade-O-Rama, Braiding and Dreadlocks" with local hairstylists, enrolled students viewed the 1960s musical *Hair*, read Willie L. Morrow's *400 Years Without a Comb* and Dylan Jones's *Haircults*, and studied the lyrics of Michael Jackson's hit pop single "Man in the Mirror."[6]

Towards the end of the quarter, Professor Jackson engaged students in "The Great Debate"—the dilemma over whether blacks should "straighten" their hair or remain "natural." The "greatness" attributed to this debate (implying that one of the most important things a black student could think about is his hair) was an indication of just how far Professor Jackson and his multicultural followers had strayed from the color-blind "promised land" of Martin Luther King: They lived in a world where blacks were judged neither by the color of their skin *nor* by the content of their character, but rather by the straightness of their hair.

The absurd race consciousness of "Black Hair" is a testament to the extremes to which multiculturalism has taken the curriculum. The new thinking and new disciplines that loftily promised to "broaden horizons" and "open minds" in reality teach students banalities: that the Afro represents 1960s rebelliousness and that straightening one's hair is a symbol of cultural subordination. Rather than helping students to surmount superficial racial differences, the new curriculum has enshrined them in an attempt to make minority students feel good. In this respect,

"Black Hair" finds its niche as a self-help seminar: Disadvantaged students may experience a sense of dignity at Professor Jackson's discovery that African Americans were the preeminent wig makers of colonial America. Hairdressers, too, can take pride in their inclusion on Stanford's reading list. An academic climate once intended to foster individual thought now promotes group therapy.

As a practical matter, the rejection of objective academic standards has left trendiness as the only guiding principle. No one wants to seem less "tolerant" or "open-minded" than anybody else, so even a class as trivial as "Black Hair" must be enthusiastically welcomed. Professor Jackson, for one, certainly makes the subject matter sound important. Perspiration dripping from his forehead, he proclaimed, "Black hair has interacted with society, and today I'm trying to make it into a field. You wouldn't find the same interaction in Africa. You don't find the conflict—over whose hair should be what, in what dimensions." Moreover, he intoned, "The term itself is homogeneous. It allows people to avoid what black hair is. This is a very real issue, that there is this thing that we are assuming is called 'black hair.'"

Despite Professor Jackson's pretensions, few people in the "real world" truly believe that his class will improve the next generation of American minds—the group born roughly between 1965 and 1974, formerly called "twentysomethings" or "post-boomers," and now increasingly known as "Generation X."[7] Nevertheless, Professor Jackson is correct in his observation that "what history does has broadened considerably"—at least at Stanford. After creating new classes like "Black Hair," Stanford's multiculturalists have changed the university's "distribution requirements" (DRs) to mandate such classes for graduation. Moreover, they have revamped much of the more mainstream curriculum to incorporate elements found in "Black Hair"—the class's therapeutic function, its adulation of trendiness, its emphasis on victims and victimhood, and its radicalizing of differences. In the absence of objective standards to prune these classes from a coherent curriculum, not one but a number of curricula, each supporting some professor's personal agenda, have sprung up like weeds in the garden of higher education and have choked off genuine liberal arts learning. The resulting effect is that the new curricula are ultimately empty. When everything is educationally important—and even hairstyles are worthy of study—nothing is educationally important. It has not taken long for Generation X to reach this unfortunate conclusion.

The Therapeutic Curriculum

It is often remarked that the most difficult aspect about Stanford is getting in. In the last decade this witticism has grown increasingly true.

Despite its well-earned reputation as a school with perhaps the most competitive admissions process in the country, classwork at Stanford in many ways no longer demands the intellectual equivalent of sweat. In March 1993, Stanford's Committee on Academic Appraisal and Achievement (C-AAA) undertook "a comprehensive review of Stanford's policies concerning grades and transcripts."[8] The impetus for the study was growing concern over the leniency of Stanford's grading system. Of all letter grades granted to students, about half were A's, 39 percent were Bs, only 10 percent were C's, and about 1 percent were D's.[9] Stanford had eliminated the "F" in the early 1970s, so students who flunked a class's minimum requirements simply received no credit for the course (NC), a mark which did not appear on their official transcripts.[10] The resulting grade distribution often warped incentives. "Stories abound on campus," reported the *Chicago Tribune*, "of students fearing they didn't do well on final exams, tearfully begging professors to 'fail' them—thus erasing any record that they took the course—to avoid a dreaded D or C."[11] Stanford changed the system slightly in 1994 (as explained in the final chapter).

In addition to the favorable grade distribution, Stanford also offers a number of grade sweeteners. Students may take classes P/NC (pass/no credit), an option under which they do not receive a letter grade for passing, but get a "+" on their transcripts.[12] Many students select this option in classes meeting DRs as it allows them to complete these graduation requirements with the least possible effort. For many years, students also had the option of "dropping" a class up to 24 hours before the final if they felt they were not doing well. Since the average grade at Stanford is an A-,[13] many students exercised this option as a precautionary measure against getting a C or even a B in a risky class. Even if a student fails to anticipate a low grade and remains in the class, he may retake the class if he is dissatisfied with his grade. Under this retake option, the new grade simply supplants the old one on the transcript.[14]

The Committee's study of Stanford's grading policies did not alarm the faculty so much as prompt a defense of grade inflation. The position of the status quo was best described by one faculty member: "The liberal transcript policies offer [students] a respite from demanding parents, fear of life-long failure, and ulcers....We need to address the emotional fabric of their lives."[15] In short, the desire to make students feel good trumped the need for academic rigor, not to mention the need to provide parents a return on their $100,000 investment.

The reaction of some professors indicated that they might even be willing to accept 100 percent grade inflation—or its functional equivalent, the abolishment of grades altogether—in order to promote student self-esteem. Writing to the *Stanford Daily*, education and psychology professor John D. Krumboltz and education professor Nel Noddings criticized the survey: "No mention was made of eliminating D grades, and yet it is clearly the fear of D grades that leads students to request an NC grade instead."[16] Of course, eliminating the D would only make the C that much more undesirable. In that case, the fear of C grades would lead students to request an NC grade instead. Over time, one would have to eliminate the C as well, and then the B. Indeed, Professors Krumboltz and Noddings reached the same conclusion:

> No questions were raised about the necessity of grading itself....No hints about modern evaluative techniques were mentioned. The questionnaire gave us the choice of maintaining the status quo or moving backward.[17]

If "moving backward" meant reducing grade inflation, "moving forward" would likely entail inflating grades further: "If we want to equip [students] to deal effectively with the unknown future," the professors concluded, "then we must teach and evaluate them in a way that motivates them for the rest of their lives."[18] Presumably, giving everybody high marks would "motivate" students in such a way. Not surprisingly, however, the inflated grading system has precisely the opposite effect. Students have little incentive to work hard and perform above average when the average grade is a high B or even an A. "Stanford has a really lax policy," complained Julie Makinen, editor in 1993 of the *Stanford Daily*, to the *Wall Street Journal*. "It isn't fair to the people who do really excellent work."[19]

The desire to boost the self-esteem of students, even at the expense of academic standards or of recognizing excellence, extends beyond the grading system. Stanford's Freshman English classes, once designed to develop reading and writing skills, have been reorganized to fit the new therapeutic agenda. Over half of Freshman English classes, which (like CIV) all 1,500 freshmen must take, require participation in the "Community Service Writing" project (CSW).[20] Instead of focusing on the basics, these classes assign freshmen to various "public service" projects—ranging from answering telephones at Stanford's Haas Center for Public Service to visiting East Palo Alto elementary schools.[21] Students also write grant proposals for their professors' favorite community service agencies, including homeless advocacy projects, AIDS support groups, and environmental action leagues.[22] According to a CSW informational flier, "Students report that the project fosters a 'can do' attitude. They see the inside of community service agencies, see what a difference one committed person can make, and make a real contribution to the community in their role as volunteer writers." This "can do" attitude, however, has been achieved only by sacrificing the original purpose of the Freshman English requirement—reading great literature and writing about it. One student reported that his final exam in Freshman English consisted of writing an elementary school physics test. "I certainly don't think it helped my writing in any way," he said.[23] According to Ken Fields, the Director of Freshman English, only one-third of Freshman English classes still involve writing essays on classical literature.[24]

A more literal example of the feel-good curriculum is Psychology 174, "The American Drinking and Drug Culture." More than 200 students packed the first day of class in Spring 1994, and Professor Elise Lennox's introductory comments hinted at the reason for the large turnout: "I don't think I ever have given anyone a C, if that helps with your course selection." Required work included a "multiple guess" final examination; a "written observation" of a "self help/support group meeting," such as Alcoholics Anonymous; and a group or individual project. Professor Lennox singled out an exemplary project from the previous year: "One woman copied some literature on alcohol and date rape, painted it on a sign, and hung it in White Plaza." The first class activity was not much more demanding: Students played "Spring Break Bingo," which required finding a different classmate to answer "yes" to each situation described in the squares of a "bingo" card. Squares (or situations) included: "Went to Mexico for spring break," "Did something really *stupid* over spring break," "Threw-up more than once over spring break," and so on.

According to the class syllabus, Psych 174 was to "explore the complex love-hate relationship that America has with alcohol, tobacco, and other drugs," and the course's own schedule provided perhaps the best indication of what this "love-hate relationship" might entail. While guest lecturer and drug expert Dale Gieringer spoke competently regarding the case for marijuana legalization, Professor Lennox claimed that "his position is that if we tax each joint two bucks we could pay off the national debt," and the course then concluded with a rambunctious "Class Party." Apparently, the 1993 class party had gotten a bit out of hand, and so, Professor Lennox announced, the 1994 party would have to be "substance-free." No event could better capture the essence of the feel-good curriculum than the spectacle she had intimated: students getting drunk studying "The American Drinking and Drug Culture."

The cause of group therapy explicitly takes center stage in Drama 113, "Group Communications," whose instructor Helen Schrader ("Helen" to the students) frequently begins class by announcing that "I'm not interested in facts—I care about how you feel."[25] According to the university's *Courses and Degrees* handbook, the purpose of Group Communications is to focus "on inter-personal processes of communication as they relate to inter-group experience."[26] Despite this rather formidable-sounding description, "Group Comm" (as it is known for short) is not a difficult class. The course has no books and no homework, and grading is attendance-based. Most students get an A simply for showing up (twice a week, for two hours at a time) and participating in discussions. The teaching assistants, upperclassmen who lead the discussions, also receive four units of academic credit, recorded as "Special Research" on their transcripts.[27]

On the first day of class, sign-up lists are passed around, with a different list for each multicultural group. To ensure the racial diversity that is deemed a necessary prerequisite for "group communication," the sign-up lists are apportioned by race: Once all the slots for white students have been filled, for example, no more white students may register for the class—even if there are still open African American or Hispanic slots.[28] In addition to the lists for whites, African Americans, and Hispanics, the class also has separate lists for Asian American, Native American, and "international" students. About 100 students enroll in Group Comm each Winter and Spring quarter; many more are turned away.

Group Comm does not meet in a classroom, but in Casa Zapata, Stanford's Chicano/Latino theme dorm. "The location is key," announced Helen on the first day of class in Winter 1993; Casa Zapata provided some sorely needed "cultural intervention."[29] A look around the dorm indicates what Helen means: Casa Zapata is organized around an explicit anti-Western theme, in the form of murals decorating the lounges and hallways. One depicts skeletons from the Third World pulling down Hoover Tower (of the Hoover Institution think tank, which symbolizes the "oppressive" forces of free-market capitalism); another resembles da Vinci's Last Supper, with revolutionaries substituting for the apostles (Che Guevera sits in Christ's place).[30]

With the proper setting established, the multicultural theater of Drama 113 could begin. The course is organized around a series of successive intra- and intergroup discussions. The group distinctions considered important are the usual ones: racial groups, genders, and economic classes (upper, upper middle, lower middle, and "working"—note the absence of the unmodified middle class). During the intragroup discussions, the various groups list adjectives describing themselves and the other groups, and formulate questions for the other groups. Then, in a highly stylized series of interactions, representatives from the various groups speak to one another, report their respective adjectives and questions, and pretend to be engaged in a normal conversation—although it is not, because everybody knows that everybody else in class is ("secretly") watching. The in-class antics, designed to promote trust, often bordered on the absurd: On the 1993 anniversary of Martin Luther King's death, Helen had the class stand up, hold hands, and sing "We Shall Overcome." Most students did not know the words, and just mouthed along: The appearance of conformity was enough.[31] In Winter 1994, Helen added a new feature: Each class ended with a 15-minute "affirmation" session, during which members of the class would thank each other for "affecting" them.[32] If one did not know better, one could easily mistake the class for a skit on *Saturday Night Live.*

The adjective most commonly used during class discussions, according to senior Nate Linn, who took the class in Winter 1993, is "oppressed." Nate described to us the overall tenor: "The adjectives people came up with to describe themselves were repetitive. There was little real communication—people did not dare ask one another hard questions, since you could never predict when there might be an incredible emotional outburst."[33] In one small group discussion in which Nate participated, students were told to reveal a significant maturation experience in their lives. One woman divulged that she had had an abortion, and, suddenly realizing that she had revealed this intimate detail to a room full of strangers, broke down crying. Such incidents apparently are not uncommon in the emotionally charged atmosphere of Group Comm.[34]

The discussions about economics represent perhaps the most revealing of the dramas staged in Group Comm. The big division occurs between the "lower-middle" and "working" classes on the one hand, and the "upper" and "upper-middle" classes on the other. Very few students identify themselves as upper class, and the two lower classes invariably accuse the upper-middle class students of attempting to hide the fact that they are really members of the upper class.[35] The truth of this accusation is a telling indicator of the dynamics of Group Comm: Students in the upper classes are described as "greedy," "self-centered," "spoiled," and "shiftless," whereas those in the lower classes are "oppressed," "hard-working," "community-centered," "family-centered," "sharing," and "co-operative."[36] The lower-class people want to go back and work in their communities, while upper-class individuals are depicted as selfish and rootless. At times, the lives of lower-class people appear so superior to those of the upper-class that it is unclear how the latter actually are oppressing the former. Simultaneously, however, the claims of economic exploitation are a significant component of the critique of the upper classes—their selfishness is making others' lives miserable.

This internal contradiction became explicit in a dramatic show-down during Winter 1993. A self-described working class student, junior Tamara Alvarado, spent five minutes discussing her economic deprivation as a child—how her family had not been able to afford any of the nice things wealthier people enjoyed, and how unhappy much of her youth had been as a result. Tamara was reduced to tears in retelling the story of her oppression. Trying to be helpful, an upper-middle-class person asked whether Tamara wanted her children to be members of the upper-middle class. Without a moment's hesitation, Tamara replied: "Absolutely not"; her children would grow up in a lower economic class as well. Several students responded: Then how could she be sorry for her own childhood? No one received an answer to that question, because the distraught young woman promptly ran out of class. The next day, Tamara read a prepared statement, in which all of her original claims were repeated. Nothing had changed; the poor community was still awful, but she still wanted to go back. This time around, though, the rest of the class did not ask any hard questions; instead, perhaps remembering Helen's aphorism "I'm not interested in facts—I care about how you feel," people just took turns affirming what she had said, and telling her how much better they now understood.[37]

For the patrons of Stanford's therapeutic curriculum, a concern for facts, logic, and important topics ranks below the desire to promote self-esteem, even if this spire of "self-esteem" is sloppily built atop a sand foundation of indefensible feelings and inflated grades. In this respect, classes like Group Comm and Black Hair provide precisely the wrong training for preparing minority students to redress the financial and power imbalances they perceive in society at large. Those who are taught to run away from hard questions will not even make it past their first job interview.

The Trendy Curriculum

Stanford's multiculturalists are not equal-opportunity esteem builders. As with the upper-class actors condemned in Group Comm, not everybody is allowed to feel good. Rather, plaudits are given only to those students and faculty who fit and accept multicultural values. New freshmen quickly learn which kinds of attitudes are likely to earn them obloquy and which their professors' approval, and adjust their behavior and classwork accordingly.

A good example is provided by "Peace Studies," an interdisciplinary class taught by faculty from the departments of Sociology, Political Science, Psychology, History, Education, and VTSS (Values, Technology, Science, and Society). As grades are based only on a take-home midterm and an open-book final, the 100-plus students who enroll each year count on an easy A. According to the course syllabus, Peace Studies, only half-jokingly called "PC Studies" by some students, defines "peace" as "(1) not war" and "(2) collaborative well-being."[38] The first definition is correct, and the second one is what the course spends all but two class sessions discussing.

In practice, the vague concept of "collaborative well-being" serves as a euphemism for a smorgasbord of the lecturers' pet policy choices—nationalized health care, government-guaranteed employment, transfer payments to inner cities, and so forth—all taught under the rubric of "peace."[39] On April 9, 1992, for instance, Peace Studies celebrated feminist values as a panacea for the world's problems. Professor Byron Bland explained that feminists "expose some fundamental attitudes and behaviors that cause war and violence and identify significant ways of promoting a more peaceful world." An assigned article maintained that men were to blame for conflict: "If we keep working with feminist peace policies, do not join the military, develop our 'women's logic,' continue to care for others, feel compassion, share power, and become more assertive," women might be able to change the world, "provided we do not copy men."[40] Added another class reading, "The feminist assumption is that gender division of work, pleasure, power, and sensibility are socially created, detrimental to women, and, to a lesser degree, to men, and therefore can and should be changed."[41]

While Peace Studies devoted much effort to theories only tangentially connected to the study of peace, far more conventional topics received only cursory attention. The curriculum largely neglected how and why real wars start and end, completely omitting World War I, World War II, the War for Independence, and other significant historical conflagrations. The Vietnam War and Gulf War were reviewed briefly, but only as they related to the "peace movement" and the (often unpacifistic) protests it staged. In the class's final lecture, entitled "Peace and You," the course's lecturers fondly recounted their own 1960s activism and exhorted students to join the "peace movement" and "to act responsibly and effectively on behalf of peace."[42]

Another trendy example is History 267, misleadingly named "The History of Rights in the United States." Forsaking a legal or even particularly historical approach, the Winter 1993 class never studied the Declaration of Independence or the Constitution, the original sources of rights in the United States. Instead, without considering any opposing views, the entire schedule extolled rights movements originating in the 1960s, with class readings centering on Professor Stewart Burns's own book, *A People's Charter*, a vigorous argument in favor of special group rights for racial minorities; the dust jacket identifies Professor Burns as "a political activist for many years."[43] According to an enrolled student, the teacher's "activist" views became well known within a few weeks, and none of the enrolled students continued to challenge the prevailing wisdom.

If professors have filled their classes with the trendiest political theories, students have mastered the game of telling the professors what they want to hear. As another example, consider the widely subscribed Anthro 1 class, "Introduction to Sociocultural Anthropology."[44] This five-unit course provides the foundations for those students who choose to begin a major in anthropology. As it also fulfills the DR in the social and behavioral sciences and can simultaneously be used to meet the non-

Western culture studies requirement, the course regularly enrolls upwards of 400 students. In Fall 1991, Anthro 1 centered on case studies of !Kung Bushmen, Canadian Indians, and Algerian peasants. The preferred mode of analysis followed the views of Professor Cheleen Mahar and her like-minded teaching assistants (TAs): !Kung culture had been destroyed by the pernicious influences of the West, Canadian Indians were oppressed and exploited by their government, and Algerian peasant culture could most usefully be analyzed in terms of the Marxist "subproletariat."

For the students of Anthro 1, it soon became clear that a good grade depended on a close adherence to the party line. Senior Mike Newman explained to us how the "go along to get along" mentality worked: "I didn't bother attending class or reading any of the books. It was enough for me to flip through the lecture notes, so long as I'd tell the TAs what they wanted to hear." Mike took the class on a pass/no credit basis, the option under which students who receive a passing grade simply receive a "+" on their transcript and no record is kept of those who fail. Indeed, he did not even think it necessary to be sober: "I completed the [take-home] midterm after returning drunk from a Halloween party. I found myself to be even more creative than usual."

Mike was not in much better condition for the final, he told us. His exam essay on !Kung culture merits some study, though not for its intellectual content:

> Three hundred years ago, the San, or Bushmen, occupied all of southern Africa along with the Nama. However, incessant conquests by Bantu and Dutch imperialists have pushed the San further and further into the Kalahari desert, leaving them only the land which the imperialists consider uninhabitable or unexploitable [grader's check mark]....
>
> As these resources were quickly depleted, more and more !Kung found themselves working for European farmers rather than attempting to maintain farms themselves. Of course, Europeans did not pay generously for this labor [check mark], providing a pittance that was hardly enough for a man to support himself, much less a family unit that was growing increasingly burdensome as the women no longer had anything to gather and the elderly no longer could pass on information that was rapidly becoming irrelevant [check mark]. Alienated from their traditional roles, many in the community began to lose the self-esteem that originated from the

> performance of these functions, a contributing factor to the alcoholism that ultimately gripped the community [check mark]....
>
> Obviously, the !Kung and other San peoples have not benefited from their exposure to Western "progress" [check mark]. To return to their former culture is at this point a geographical impossibility, but the modern world has brought them only starvation and despair. That white people actually expected the San to drop overnight a way of life stretching back numerous melennia [sic] in return for Western agriculture and the Judeo-Christian ethic demonstrates the cultural arrogance behind their oppressive practices, but the sad reality is that the San have accepted Western notions of their own inferiority [check mark]....

"I thought that I might have gone a little overboard with this answer, but I was wrong—the TAs just ate it all up," Mike noted. "It seemed as though they really liked it whenever I put negative-sounding phrases near the word 'Western.'" In his essay (which typifies the entire exam), the West is "imperialist," "arrogant," "providing a pittance," and "oppressive," and the non-Western !Kung provide the positive counterpoint: They are a culture with "traditional roles" that build "self-esteem," and naturally have nothing to gain from their "exposure to Western 'progress.'" The more black and white the analysis, the more favorable the TA's response; critical thinking and fine distinctions, apparently, could only hurt one's grade.

Keeping these priorities in mind, Mike also had to contrast a neo-Marxist with a more moderate analysis of the urban poor, and was certain to come out with the right answers:

> Bourdieu and Lewis present two different paradigms for understanding the phenomenon of urban poverty worldwide. Bourdieu's analysis is far more radical, arguing as does Fanon that the Algerian peasants he studied, and by extension all oppressed peoples, can achieve revolutionary consciousness and fight back, even though in reality the peasants often depend on their oppressors even as they curse them [yes (TA's comment)]....Lewis would have us believe that the poor don't mind their condition, thus assuring their inability to achieve revolutionary consciousness. Bourdieu's critique of the Algerian

> lumpenproletariat reaches a more sensible conclusion, that the oppressed resent their oppressors, but their dependency on them holds them back.

Although seemingly unrelated to a question regarding "the construction and expression of groups and personal selves," Mike felt that the invocation of a global environmental apocalypse would not hurt:

> Babcock's article on Helen Cordero's "Little People" demonstrates the connection between object and self. Cordero's created objects become an extension of herself, the clay people identify her and her connection as a human being to the earth [check mark]....Western man has a hard time understanding the connection of man to nature....One can only hope that we learn this before our planet is destroyed.

Mike denied believing any of the things he had written, but explained that it was the easiest way to ensure that he would pass the class and meet two of his distribution requirements. Even so, he was stunned to learn that his final grade in the course would have been an A. "My only regret was that I didn't take the class for a grade," Mike concluded.[45]

Those who questioned the prevailing orthodoxy were less fortunate. Senior Chris Aguas received a lower exam grade (a B, quite a low grade in a class like Anthro 1) for arguing that referring to the !Kung as "Bushmen" did not constitute an act of cultural imperialism (Professor Mahar had declared that "Bushmen" connotes something "primitive," and therefore creates an unwarranted imputation of cultural inferiority). Chris argued, consistently with multicultural principles, that the belief that the "primitive" is undesirable itself constituted a cultural bias: If one could not impose one's cultural standards on other societies, then how could one infer that the claim that something is primitive means that it is less desirable? This argument was apparently too sophisticated for the exam grader, who dismissed these observations with the conclusion, "But it's still wrong to call them 'Bushmen.'"[46] Although Chris Aguas may have understood anthropology better than Mike Newman, Mike Newman understood Anthro 1 far better than Chris Aguas.

In addition to classes like CIV, Freshman English, Group Comm, Peace Studies, and Anthro 1, multicultural trendiness pullulates throughout the major departments. The OMD promised "to integrate multiculturalism in" (not just append it to) all programs of the university, and it is in such central courses that the multiculturalists have pushed their views onto the greatest numbers of students:

- The class "19th-Century American History," taught by Professor Estelle Freedman, devoted one-half of its class time to a study of women, as they had constituted one-half of the U.S. population during that time. As a result of these priorities, the class did not have enough time to learn about the War of 1812.[47]
- Religious Studies 8, "Religions in America," a class that can be counted towards three different graduation requirements, devoted whole lectures to Shamanism, the Peyote Cult, and the Kodiak sect, but not one to the Catholic Church. When discussed at all, Christianity was viewed from a feminist or gay "perspective" through such works as "Jesus Acted Up: A Gay and Lesbian Manifesto," "A Second Coming Out," and "Beyond the Father: Towards a Philosophy of Women's Liberation."[48]
- Class assignments for Feminist Studies 101 have included writing (but not necessarily sending) "a letter to our parents coming out as a lesbian," according to Minal Hajratwala, a woman who took the class in 1991.[49]
- At Stanford's Education School, future junior high and high school teachers are taught how to integrate a watered-down multiculturalism into their curricula.[50]
- English Professor Regenia Gagnier had been scheduled to teach courses on Victorian political economy and 19th century fiction in Spring 1991. When the Persian Gulf War started, "Suddenly Victorian political economy didn't seem as relevant," she told the *Stanford Daily.* Instead she developed an undergraduate course and a graduate colloquium on the "Literature of War."[51]
- History 61 devoted an entire quarter to "Social Movements of the 1960s in California." The class studied "grassroots political activism and social turmoil stretching from student involvement in the Civil Rights Movement in the early 1960s to the early Gay Liberation Movement of the mid-1970s." Class readings included Black Panther David Hillier's autobiography and *Social Movements of the 1960s: Searching for Democracy*, by none other than Professor Stewart Burns (of "History of Rights" fame).[52]
- "Pop culture" is "gaining legitimacy as [a] supplement to course material," reported the *Stanford Daily* in 1993. English professor Seth Lerer's Arthurian literature class, for instance, watched movies such as *Monty Python and the Holy Grail, The Sword of the Valiant,* and *Excalibur.* David Schmid, a graduate student in Modern Thought and Literature writing a thesis on modern-day serial killers, also taught a Freshman English class, in which students viewed violent films such as *Deathwish* and *Colors* and listened to rap music.[53]

Not everything related to exotic peoples and social perspectives, however, is catnip at Stanford. A telling example of a class that could *not* be taught was "Nietzsche and the Apaches," proposed by philosophy professor Walter Lammi in the 1989–90 school year to the Innovative Academic Courses (IAC) program at Stanford.[54] At the time, IAC claimed to be seeking courses that would focus on "cross-cultural studies for multicultural education." Professor Lammi thought that his proposed course fit this ostensible set of requirements perfectly. One of the central issues of Nietzschean philosophy concerns questions of human nobility, and part of Nietzsche's argument is that the conditions for such nobility may be found among "primitive" or "barbarian" tribes. Professor Lammi noted how closely the historic reality of Apache culture had fit some of Nietzsche's abstract notions, particularly in its emphasis on martial values in the development of what Nietzsche considered the superior human soul, in its tough initiation rites, and in the tenacity, heroism, and sometimes cruelty of its warriors. The IAC director and Stanford's administration rejected Professor Lammi's proposed course out of hand. Because Professor Lammi would have discussed the warlike nature of Apache culture, including ritual torture, Stanford students might have generalized and reached some negative impressions about other American Indians and perhaps "people of color" as a whole. An administrator informed Professor Lammi that his course might undermine the struggle of minority groups against the dominant culture, and IAC director Margo Horn told him that his proposal was "bizarre," "offensive," and "certainly not consistent with the goals of 'education for difference.'"[55]

While "Nietzche and the Apaches" did not make the new curriculum, Comparative Literature 189, "Representing Sappho: the Literature of Lesbianism," abundantly met the criteria of "education for difference." Offered by the English department for the first time in Spring 1994, the class sought, in the words of Instructor Terry Castle, "to resexualize lesbian history."[56] Shakespeare's *As You Like It* was identified as a "loci classicus of lesbianism," and the remainder of the course readings were probed for "male and female representations of lesbian desire" and for "lesbianism as 'symbolist,' 'decadent,' 'modernist,' and 'utopian' literary motif."[57]

"Representing Sappho" is not some anomaly on the margins of an otherwise terrific Stanford education. At least three other classes explored similar themes—Feminist Studies 295, subtitled "How Tasty Were My French Sisters"; Comparative Literature 110, "The Politics of Desire: Representations of Gay and Lesbian Sexuality"; and Law 587, "The History and Politics of Sexual Orientation: Cross-Disciplinary Perspectives."[58]

In 1993, six new "dialogue tutorials" in "American Counterculture Literature" also promoted trendy sexual mores. Lecturer Keith Gandal told the *Stanford Daily* that he organized the program to explore "the idea of alternative ethics," a euphemism for radical 1960s-style experimentation: "You get a dose of [the Protestant capitalist tradition] growing up as a child," explained Gandal. "When you arrive in junior high, there's a new ethic of exploration and rebelling against your parents."[59] English lecturer Wilfred Koponen's tutorial, "Gay Novels and Gay Identity," spotlighted some of these "new ethics." One assigned reading, Alan Hollinghurst's *The Swimming Pool-Library*, featured the theme of pederasty. A brief excerpt from the book is highly illustrative of what passes for great multicultural literature:

> I was turning to leave when I spotted a lone Arab boy wandering along, hands in the pockets of his anorak, fairly unremarkable, yet with something about him which made me feel that I must have him. I was convinced that he had noticed me, and I felt a delicious surplus of lust and satisfaction at the idea of fucking him while another boy waited for me at home.[60]

"Gay novels offer insight into the construction of gay identity," Professor Koponen (himself admittedly homosexual) proclaimed.[61]

Another of Stanford's X-rated English classes is "Representing Sexualities: Whitman to AIDS." The syllabus warned that "Sexually-explicit materials, both hetero- and homoerotic, may be viewed and discussed in this class."[62] Scheduled readings included "A Posttransexual Manifesto" by Sandy Stone, John D'Emilio's "Capitalism and Gay Identity," Henry Abelove's "From Thoreau to Queer Politics," and Eve Sedgwick's "How to Bring Your Kids up Gay," in addition to two videos, *Voices from the Front*, by the militant homosexual group ACT-UP, and *Tongues Untied*, a pornographic gay film. Although the course catalog identifies the upper-level seminar (numbered English 187 D) as consisting of "scholarly and critical studies of literary texts,"[63] Professor Jay Grossman spent his first class session presenting an episode of the television comedy *Cheers* and then deconstructing the show as "homophobic." "This course I imagine, or like to imagine, will bolster anti-homophobic discourse," he explained. Such discourse also was bolstered, presumably, by the first reading assignment—several weeks of a cartoon strip in which a teenage character reveals that he is gay. For Stanford's English department, if the material is trendy enough, it does not even have to be literature.

When everybody defers to everyone else's judgement, nobody thinks for himself. And so, perhaps the most unfortunate aspect of the trendy curriculum is that it trains students to think with the herd rather than to think critically. The new curriculum may be described as the product of an echo effect, in which different people in the Stanford community, faculty and students alike, repeat one another's claims until so many people make the same claims that everybody starts to believe them. Such conformity can be psychologically overpowering, but it does not promise to yield the truth or to communicate anything significant.

Political science professor John Manley provided a particularly telling example in his Winter 1990 offering of Political Science 10, "Introduction to American National Government." Professor Manley devoted much of the course to critiquing American society as hopelessly marred by divisions of race, class, and gender. He particularly emphasized "institutional racism"—defined as the existence of social institutions that unconsciously reinforce racial divisions in our society. One class discussion on institutional racism culminated with Professor Manley's inquiry of his students: "How many of you attended high schools in which a majority of the students are white?"[64] The number of raised hands indicated that an overwhelming majority of the 200 or so enrolled students had. Here, then, if there could be any doubt about Professor Manley's claims, was the clinching piece of evidence: Only those students who attended predominantly white high schools in our society would ever get into good universities, whereas the rest of the students in our racially segregated school system would be denied the educational opportunity to hear political science lectures at Stanford. And this sort of racism was all the worse for its insidious character: Students, and American society at large, might not even recognize the existence of such unconscious institutional racism, at least not until they had been enlightened by educators like Professor Manley.

Whatever one's views on race relations in our society, the argument made by Professor Manley in Poli Sci 10 is simply an illogical assumption. On this occasion sophomore Jill Morganbesser broke his spell: "But, Professor Manley, since a majority of the high school students in America are white, wouldn't it follow that if our schools were perfectly integrated that you would expect *everybody* in class to have attended high schools in which a majority of the students are white?"[65] Professor Manley had no response to this obvious objection. So committed was he to attributing America's social ills to racism that the broad range of alternative reasons why most Stanford students had attended mostly-white high schools had never occurred to him.

The German philosopher Lessing defined dogmatism as "the tendency to identify the goal of our thinking with the point at which we have become tired of thinking." The ideological commitments of the multiculturalists have discouraged them from reflecting critically upon their controversial claims. In Professor Manley's case, facts that are evidence of integration instead point to racism. The resulting dogmatism has more in common with the contradictory logic of the Red Queen from *Alice in Wonderland* than with the ideal of a Western university:

> Alice laughed. "There's no use trying," she said. "One can't believe impossible things." "I dare say you haven't had much practice," said the queen. "When I was your age I did it for half an hour a day. Why, I've sometimes believed as many as six impossible things before breakfast."

The Victims' Curriculum

The characterization of Westerners as chronic oppressors ("colonial addicts," in Aime Cesaire's words) running through Group Comm, Peace Studies, and Anthro 1 is made more explicit in the many classes concerned with the "education for difference" described by Ms. Horn—that is, with focusing positively on those groups of people multiculturalists consider the "victims" of America and the West. In this spirit, Stanford's Faculty Senate expanded the university's requirements in Fall 1990 to include one course on race (misleadingly labeled "American Cultures") and one on gender.[66] The requirements were necessary, Peter Duus, chairman of the Faculty Senate Committee on Undergraduate Studies, told the *San Francisco Chronicle*, because CIV "did not go far enough in expanding Stanford students' knowledge of non-European culture."[67] Many of the new courses that meet the race and gender studies requirements are taken directly from departments like Feminist Studies, Afro-American Studies, Asian-American Studies, and Chicano Studies, which Stanford had established in the late 1960s in response to an earlier wave of protests.[68]

Enrolling upwards of 100 students each quarter, Linguistics 73 is one of the most heavily subscribed courses fulfilling the new race studies DR. Entitled "African American Vernacular English," the class is premised on the notion that inner-city slang (of the type heard in rap songs) is a legitimate dialect of the English language, deserving scholarly attention rather than derision. "AAVE is not just a 'careless' form of speech in which 'anything goes,'" explained the course syllabus.[69] In Winter 1993, course activities included attending sermons at two predominantly black churches in Palo Alto (where students were advised to "dress nicely and bring two collections") and presenting research projects at an all-day "AAVE happenin'." Students viewed such films as *Do the Right Thing*, *Putney Swope*, or *Daughters of the Dust* each Friday, and could earn extra units if they tutored an African-American student in East Palo Alto. Typical of the class readings was a transcript of an interview with Foxy Boston, a 13-year-old from East Palo Alto:

> F: Ahm, an' if duh boys ain' up on duh scoop dem girls be goin', (sucks teeth) "Boy you bettah wake up an' smell dat caffeine!" (laughter)
> D: Smell what?
> R: Caffeine. You know as in coffee?
> F: Up on duh scoop. An' you know, sometimes dey be sayin' ahm, like if a boy say, "Girl, wha' choo talkin' about?" She go, "You don' know what Ah'm talkin' 'bout? Boy you bettah wake up an' smell dat big Sanka brand! Like that tell 'im like that....say "Oh so you tryin' to clown or so you try to dis' me or some'pn?[70]

The gender studies classes hardly provide much better preparation for life after graduation. Director of Feminist Studies Sylvia Yanagisako, who was instrumental in pushing the Faculty Senate to accept the new requirement, defined feminist studies as the study of "how all institutions and relationships are shaped by gender...gender is not just what men and women do, it is a system, it is the culturally created differences between men and women."[71] This definition avoids the most important question, however—namely, what fraction of differences between men and women are biological in origin and what fraction are "culturally created." Rather, this formulation adopts an extreme answer to a very complicated question: For feminists like Professor Yanagisako, there are *no* "natural" differences between men and women—*all* differences are culturally created.

This rather dubious premise drives the structure of the program: According to Professor Yanagisako, feminist studies investigates "how societies create gender differences as part of gender inequality." For Stanford's feminists, all societies in which gender differences are manifest—that is, all currently existing societies—must have artificially created these differences, often with the intent of oppressing women. Consequently, any area of society in which such differences still exist must be unjust. The resulting political program has a revolutionary and utopian dimension: Only a society radically different from our own will be able to eliminate all gender differences.

Professor Yanagisako indicated that even a field as seemingly apolitical as athletics involves such unjust differences: "Money is directed into men's athletics, not into women's. Thus, it is not surprising that men tend to be the ones who excel in athletic disciplines."[72] Even these very brief observations suffer from two very significant mistakes—of the sort that are endemic to almost all of the pseudoscientific claims made in feminist studies. First, Professor Yanagisako's observation is not completely accurate factually: There are some sports (volleyball, for example) in which women's teams receive considerably more funding than men's. Second, and more important, correlation does not prove causation: It may be the case that money is directed into men's sports *because* men are the ones who excel in certain athletic disciplines. Only if one assumes that there are no natural differences—that men and women would perform equally well in football if they received equal funding, or that if enough money were poured into women's sports they would become as popular as men's football or basketball—could one infer that every difference is *caused* by the cultural bias.

For some of Stanford's feminists, the suspicion that unjust gender differences have shaped Western society extends to all fields.[73] Consider, for example, just those Feminist Studies classes meeting the new gender studies DR in Spring 1994. Anthropology 154, "Creation/Procreation: A Comparative Study," investigated "the gendered aspects of cosmological or religious systems" and studied biology "as sexual politics."[74] Anthro 250, "Gender and Nationalism," explored the thesis that nationalism and other forms of "hegemony" are male creations that oppress women.[75] Linguistics 154, "Language and Gender," sought to find "differences between the speech of females and the speech of males, and to relate these findings to characterizations of women and men and their respective places in society."[76] The class also explored the "embedding of power in language," "linguistic authority," "meaning-making rights," and "the reproduction of male power and the male perspective in language."[77] Feminist Studies 135, "Women and Organizations," searched for "women's cultures that are not male-defined" and "a definition of female personhood that is not ultimately dependent on the exercise of male power and approval."[78] The class also maintained that capitalism, industrialism, and bureaucracy are "male strategies of organization."[79] Finally, History and Philosophy of Science 160, "Gender and Science," asked in what ways science is "gendered" and what a "feminist science" might look like.[80] History professor Estelle Freedman, who has taught the class, explained that because most scientists have been men, much of science has been warped by a "male perspective."[81]

The demands for a "female science," "women's organizations," and a special "female perspective" point to a contradiction that permeates all of feminist studies. If there are no gender differences and men and women are completely fungible, then it would not matter who is doing what: The fact that all of the physicists of the 17th century, for instance, happened to be men should not discredit the theory of gravity. Nor is the revolution of Earth around the Sun sexist because the scientist who discovered this fact, Copernicus, happened to be a man. Had women studied these matters, presumably they would have discovered the same things. Feminism's egalitarian rhetoric does not square with its multicultural gnosticism.

Along these lines, it is worth noting that women happen to teach the overwhelming majority of these gender studies classes. Now, if there are no natural differences, then the very funding of these programs would be evidence of unjust gender discrimination—albeit one that favors women. By the very criteria feminists have defined, are we not long overdue for more of a "male perspective" on feminist studies?

In practice, of course, gender (or any other multicultural) studies do not require a great deal of internal coherence, because they are not concerned with truth. Rather, for the activists pushing these programs, the most important feature of these courses is that they suggest a political realignment in American society. Political theory is the major component of the gender studies classes, and it is here that the agenda becomes most apparent. A random and cursory glance through some of the books used for feminist studies courses produces the following insights into the human condition:

> If the professional rapist is to be separated from the average dominant heterosexual, it may be mainly a quantitative difference.[82]

> Women's struggles must be directed immediately against male dominance. In order to do this...women must forsake heterosexuality, which divides women from each other and ties them to their oppressors....[W]omen's bodies are socially constructed. Nothing about women is 'natural': women are made not born....[In the] new society, there will be only persons: both women and men will have disappeared....[F]eminism is the theory and lesbianism is the practice.[83]

> The future: Artificial parthogenesis, egg fusion, and cloning; if developed, these techniques would produce children from women's eggs without the use of sperm....[S]ome of us would be glad if they became available. One woman said: 'I have a real longing for egg fusion because I am in a deep and long-term relationship with a woman and would love to have a child which comes truly from both of us...I do yearn to create a new being with her from the start.'[84]

> Ardent feminists are convinced that ['qualified'] is a contemporary euphemism for penis, and in a high proportion of cases they are absolutely right....Here are some no-no's:....Never reveal what salary you are making....If the agency recruiter or prospective employer insists that you give this information, lie....Put down the salary that men in equivalent jobs make if you know it; otherwise, add approximately $10,000 to what you got paid.[85]

If one did not know better, one might think that these texts were a satire of feminism, or the product of some malicious stereotype—so preposterous are the claims that they make. But these feminist writings and ideas are not unrepresentative of much of what passes for scholarship in this area. The passionate hatred of men, the utopian demands for an elimination of all gender differences, the (totally inconsistent) demands for a uniquely female perspective, and the belief in widespread gender discrimination are the core of the new gender studies curriculum.

If there is something to be learned from the new race and gender requirements, then perhaps it concerns the futility of multicultural victimology. Ironically, the basic tenets of multiculturalism should make it impossible to determine who victims are in the first place. This problem is caused by the necessary involvement of a third party: Besides the victim and victimizer, there must be a person assessing the victimization itself, the one awarding victim status. But multiculturalism denies the possibility of individual objectivity. In its view, each group is jostling every other for position in a giant power struggle, where the judgment of every individual is colored by his membership in, and allegiance to, a particular group. According to multiculturalism, it should be impossible to find impartial third parties to assess victim status. Because every individual seeks to promote the interests of his group, the very act of assigning victim status must also be seen in the context of a larger intergroup power struggle. The group that successfully obtains victim status—and the privileges of redress and proportional representation this status confers—may be seen as a victor in this power struggle. And yet, if it is a victor—that is, if it is a powerful group—then, by definition, its members can no longer be the "victims."

The details of the passage of the new race and gender DRs perfectly illustrate this internal contradiction. The supporters of the race DR, which revolves around "systematically discriminated" minorities, claimed that the requirement was needed to remedy these groups' lack of institutional power and their consequent exclusion from curricular decisions. The proposal identified African Americans, American Indians, Asian Americans, Hispanic Americans, and Pacific Islanders as such discriminated groups. Irish Americans, Slavic Americans, and Mormons did not make the list of those with victim status, even though all of these groups have in fact experienced some discrimination in America's history. Not surprisingly, before a Faculty Senate meeting to evaluate the new requirements, several dozen students protested outside.[86] According to a *Stanford Daily* poll, only 39 percent of the overall student body supported the new race studies requirement, and even fewer—only 31 percent—supported the gender studies requirement, but both changes passed anyway.[87] Apparently the groups who had successfully lobbied for the new requirements were not as deprived of institutional power as they claimed.

The very establishment of well-funded minority studies departments ironically demonstrates that many self-proclaimed "victim" groups possess institutional power quite disproportionate to their numbers. In recent years, the Stanford administration has launched more than a dozen different programs benefiting minority and women students and faculty:[88]

- The Undergraduate Scholars Program pairs minority students with faculty mentors to complete and publish research projects. The program also invites six minority scholars to campus to speak and hold workshops with students.
- The Stanford Center for Chicano Research (SCCR) Graduate and Undergraduate Mentor Program similarly sponsors research projects and pairs Chicano students and faculty.
- The Chicano Fellows Program provides funds for graduate Chicano fellows and visiting professors.
- The American Indian Summer Institute Program provides special instruction for incoming American Indian freshmen "to ease their transition from high school to the Stanford environment."
- The Graduate Program for Aspiring Law Teachers, sponsored by Stanford Law School, identifies and supports minority law school graduates seeking careers in teaching law.
- The Irvine Dissertation Fellowship Program assists "promising minority graduate students during critical stages in their development as professors."
- The Field and Summer Research in Latin America Program, sponsored by the Latin American studies department, aids blacks and Latinos in their pursuit of master's and doctoral degrees.
- The Master Tutor Program and Minority Student Outreach and Tutor Development Program train minority tutors and also provide special tutoring for minority students.
- The Lalarza Prize for Excellence in Chicano Research helps "to identify and recruit the most promising [Chicano] students for graduate study, and to introduce them to the rewards of an academic career."

- Other programs include (but are not limited to) the Physics Department Recruitment and Retention Program; the Martin Luther King Papers Faculty Development and Mentoring Program; and the Stanford Teacher Education Program (STEP), which seeks "to contribute directly to the preparation and credentialization of ethnic and minority teachers for California schools."

In addition, reflecting perhaps the latest trend in preferred victim groups, special scholarships have recently been endowed for homosexual students.[89] Racial quotas have even been applied to the purchasing of goods and services through the university's centralized procurement department, including the Stanford Shopping Center (a university property). As part of the policy, departments receive a booklet listing established minority, women, and disabled vendors in a variety of goods and services. The policy influences $10 to $15 million spent annually on smaller purchases by departments.[90]

The bulk of these affirmative action programs are directed at faculty recruitment, and closely resemble the CIV hiring clause, which urges "that race, ethnicity, and gender be considered as factors in the hiring of new faculty." Consider the *Stanford Daily*'s explanation of the hiring clause:

> The spirit of the hiring clause is not to simply consider a faculty applicant's pigmentation, accent, surname or chromosomes in their evaluation. What is meant is to consider the applicant's ethnicity, race and gender as it applies to their intellectual and academic perspective.[91]

Like CIV, race and gender studies depend on the notion that minorities and women have a special knowledge about the contemporary situation. As the *Stanford Daily* notes, however, not every minority person possesses the perspective necessary to teach minority studies. Not just any minority or female faculty would be good for the new curriculum—pigmentation, accent, surname, or chromosomes are ***not enough***. Only those with the proper "intellectual and academic perspective" need apply. Of course, since the "academic perspective" sought by CIV, race studies, and gender studies is a multicultural one, the most qualified minority or women faculty—that is, those with the correct "academic perspective"—will be multiculturalists. Those minority persons who have the "special perspectives" needed for the new curriculum will, by definition, share the requisite left-liberal bias. In the name of "diversity," race and gender studies departments have brought to campus a group of faculty almost monolithic in its thinking.

As "subordinated" minorities, moreover, these special recruits will enjoy at Stanford a privileged perspective that is not subject to review or criticism. This unchallengeable perspective enables the transmission of multiculturalism, which in turn justifies separate race and gender studies departments, new race and gender DRs, and more recruitment programs. Multicultural victimology and race and gender studies reinforce one another, and provide cover (as well as money and jobs) for the same political movement.

The Radical Curriculum

In a number of the new classes, radical politics—camouflaged elsewhere as therapy, trendiness, or redress—move to the center. All pretense of objectivity is dropped. Particularly notable among the latter were the Innovative Academic Courses (IAC) and Student Workshops On Political and Social Issues (SWOPSI) programs, which ostensibly were concerned with enabling people from the surrounding community to teach Stanford classes on issues that would not otherwise be covered. After a reorganization in 1992, many of the courses were transferred into departments like Feminist Studies.[92]

Most of the SWOPSI and IAC courses provided three to five units of credit towards graduation, and many of them required students to engage in explicitly political activities. The classes often received "mixed reviews," reported the *Stanford Daily*, as students criticized them for "being too liberal or too subjective by professors."[93] IAC Director Margo Horn proudly admitted as much: "I think that what people teach reflects politics."[94]

Consider the three-unit "Issues in Self-Defense For Women," one of the more reasonable-sounding of the SWOPSI offerings, which later became a feminist studies class. Surprisingly enough, the class has remarkably little to do with physical education for women (there is a reason it is not offered through Stanford's athletics department, which offers a range of karate, judo, and other self-defense classes). Instructor Alyson Yarus explained: "It is less important that we teach individuals in our classes how to defend themselves than it is to change society."[95] Yarus said the class was an important step toward a "feminist utopia," which would end sexism, starvation, classism, and hierarchy.[96] "I guess a feminist utopia is probably a socialist world," she explained; "I am a socialist at heart." Jae Choi, another member of the Women Defending Ourselves Collective that teaches these classes, echoed these priorities: "What we've got right now is shit. We need to show people that there is an alternative....Stanford provides lots of people who will be in positions where they can influence. The more they are aware of issues like this, the more they can influence."[97]

Because of the need to comply with federal regulations that prohibit gender discrimination at universities receiving federal funding, the feminist studies department was forced to add a new men's section in 1993—a prospect about which the instructors were not enthusiastic. Choi explained: "The purpose of the class is empowerment....It wouldn't make much sense to teach that to men who already control all of the power."[98] The separate and unequal men's section did not include "assertiveness training" or "physical defense techniques," but still kept the readings, such as *This Bridge Called My Back: Writings By Radical Women Of Color*, a book that won a prize from the Before Columbus Foundation.[99]

Perhaps the most unfortunate consequence of the self-defense class is that it leaves women technically and physically unprepared to deal with real-life assault situations. Instead of teaching women the holds, moves, preventive measures, and familiarity with weapons necessary to protect themselves from aggressors, the course seeks to give women a false sense of "empowerment" through a feminist ideology that does nothing to overcome the natural disadvantages in strength, size, and quickness that women face when confronting men. One hopes that the women who got A's in the course will not be emboldened to walk by dark alleys.

The intellectual mischief of the multiculturalists is not limited to the classroom. At academic conferences and in academic journals, many of the same ideas—regarding the evils of the West, the need for 1960s-style activism, and the push for a new society, all couched in talk about victims and oppressors—are recycled *ad nauseum*. A complete review of the state of multicultural scholarship is beyond the scope of this book, but an examination of two of these academic conferences at Stanford—each billed as major events and sponsored by the university—will provide a representative sampling of the new thinking.

"Talking 'Terrorism': Ideologies and Paradigms in a Postmodern World" was one of a series of conferences organized as part of the University's centennial celebration in 1988 and was sponsored by the Stanford Humanities Center.[100] In the lobby of Stanford's Cubberley Auditorium, conference attendees were confronted by videos showing pictures of rioting Palestinians, marching Sandinistas, Chinese Red Guards, and Winston Churchill holding a gun. Viewers were encouraged to read Noam Chomsky's *The Real Terror Network*, a book with the thesis that the United States government is behind virtually all of the world's suffering and violence. The conference proceeded on an even more extraordinary premise: "Terrorism" is a word devoid of meaning—merely a label attached to people with whom one disagrees (unless, of course, one disagreed with the West; in that case terrorism *did* exist and referred to acts perpetrated against the Third World by capitalist Western societies).

At this conference, Edward Said, a representative of the PLO, delivered the keynote address. Mr. Said informed his Stanford audience that American actions throughout the world were offensive to decency and morality, and concluded that it is treasonous for any person with intellectual integrity to work for the U.S. government. Christopher Hitchens, another outspoken critic of American policies, compared the word "terrorism" to "witchcraft" in its lack of real meaning. Hitchens suggested that both terms served purely as tools to discredit certain people, as part of a "state strategy of propaganda."[101] For Hitchens, as for the other participants, the only proper use of the word "terrorism" was "the use indicated by Chomsky in *The Real Terror Network*" (that is, in reference to the United States government).[102] Hitchens's speech was followed with a performance by Ulrich Preuss, the former legal counsel to Germany's Baader-Meinhof gang. Preuss attempted to locate the "essence" of terrorism in "meanings and symbols," while downplaying its violent dimension. Preuss declared that terrorism is superior to other acts of violence because of its "political quality," and lamented "the unsupportable gulf between what the terrorists know to be the right order and the means to achieve it." He ended by elevating terrorism as a sort of "political theology."[103]

Even the most violent kidnappings, tortures, and murders could be effaced as "political theology" or dismissed as something nonexistent like "witchcraft," so long as the object of this violence was the West, its citizens, and its governments. At the same time, even the most seemingly nonviolent activities, like trade between First and Third World countries, could be transfigured into the imaginary "terrorism" of Western capitalism. In some respects, this seeming paradox—that the word "terrorism" referred to something nonexistent and simultaneously was something perpetrated by the West—holds a key to understanding multiculturalism. Stanford's activists had declared that "Western Culture's got to go," and the "Talking 'Terrorism'" conference provided one blueprint for how such a liquidation might be effected. Western civilization could be eliminated more readily if bereft of the will to resist terrorists or if it could be brought to turn on itself by locating and eliminating the supposed "terrorism" that constituted its very being.

In contrast with "Talking 'Terrorism,'" the conference entitled "Women of Color and the Law" sounded positively benign. Organized by Stanford Law School in the fall of 1990, this symposium sought to explore the challenges facing "women of color" in the American legal system. The prestigious *Stanford Law Review* lent its support, printing a special edition of the conference's major speeches.[104]

The conference's keynote speech was delivered by Angela Davis, professor of history of consciousness at the University of California, Santa Cruz, and the quadrennial vice presidential candidate of the American

Communist Party. She set the tone for the conference:

> There is something about the way in which Western society has constructed the law that evokes a sense of dread in me. Although I was never quite able to summon up enough courage to consider studying the law, I do know that many who have entered the legal profession with the express purpose of doing battle against injustice have found the philosophical principles underlying the social function to be hopelessly biased. Personally, I have always found *the law* to be one of the most terrifying dimensions of the social order.[105] (emphasis in original)

Most of the remaining speakers were even more radical than Davis, as the *gnosis* enjoyed by "women of color" became an excuse for a series of explicitly political sermons. Sharon Parker, Director of Stanford's OMD, who like Angela Davis and most of the conference's other speakers held no law degree, spoke on "Understanding Coalition," while Evelyn Nakano Glenn, professor of Asian American and women's studies at the University of California, Berkeley, entitled her historical lecture on the work of women "Cleaning Up/Kept Down."[106] Not all of these lectures were open to the general public. At various points in the proceedings, all those who were not "women of color" were asked to leave Kresge Auditorium—because only "women of color" could possibly "understand" whatever would be said next.

Typical of the performances was that of Haunani-Kay Trask, a Native Hawaiian who works at the Center for Hawaiian Studies at the University of Hawaii. An activist who hopes to see Hawaii declare independence from the United States, Trask began her presentation with a personal introduction that emphasized her revolutionary credentials:

> Aloha mai. Aloha mai. I am Haunani Kawekinohaleakala, descendent of the Pi'ilani line of the Maui and the Kahakumakaliua line of Kaua'i. I greet you as an indigenous woman, as an American-subjugated Native, as part of a non-self-governing people—Hawaiians—and as a Polynesian member of the pan-Pacific movement for self-determination that has been growing in our part of the world for the last thirty years....Who we are is determined by our connection to our lands and our families. Therefore, our bloodlines and birthplaces tell our identity....This is who I am—not what I do or where I work—but who I am—lineage and residence.[107]

She exalted the culture of Native Hawaii as radically antithetical to the evil West: "Those of us committed to the recognition of our nationhood have evolved away from identification as Americans and, in many ways, despise all that is 'American.'" Trask continued to describe her "interdependent and wise society:"

> As in most indigenous societies, there was no money, no idea or practice of surplus appropriation, and no value storing or payment deferral because there was no idea of financial profit from exchange. Therefore, no basis for economic exploitation existed in pre-*haole* Hawai'i....[P]eople living in each ahupua'a had access to all the necessities of life...forest land, taro and sweet potato area, and fishing grounds.[108]

One may wonder how much Trask actually would have enjoyed living in the idyllic paradise she describes. For with her Marxist rhetoric regarding the exploitation of "surplus" value in Western culture, Trask unwittingly acknowledged part of the truth: Only capitalist Western societies have a problem with the exploitation of surplus value because such societies are the only ones that produce much surplus value to be exploited. Digging for taro roots and fishing for seafood are quite different from the kind of work one imagines people do at the Center for Hawaiian Studies—a center whose very existence requires more surplus value than Native Hawaiian culture ever generated.

The focus of Trask's tirade, however, was more limited than the West generally. Almost everybody agreed with her about the evils of Western civilization, and so, to distinguish herself, Trask had to come up with a somewhat narrower set of targets. Most implausibly, she suggested that Western liberals (of the sort putting on the "Women of Color and the Law" conference, presumably) were a particularly big stumbling block to Native Hawaiian self-determination. Full of sound and fury, Trask continued: "In particular, Natives must beware of white liberals, particularly lawyers, anthropologists and archaeologists, and other scientists and technicians. These people's interest in Native Hawaiians is often self-serving—it is motivated by professional aspirations" or by "some personal/psychological problem, such as guilt about being part of an oppressive white ruling class in a stolen Native country."[109] Cooperation with white liberals, she said, should be limited to immediate goals; in the long term, after all, Trask hoped to throw 80 percent of the present-day Hawaiian population—those who are not Native Hawaiians—off the islands. If Native Hawaiians and non-Native "liberals" worked too closely with one another, they might become friends. Such friendships would be an obstacle in the coming revolution:

> For myself, as a Native nationalist, the only long-term coalition I could ever participate in would be with other Native people: first, my Polynesian relations, the Maori and Tahitians and Samoans; then other Native peoples, like Indians and Aborigines; and then, Third World peoples....To the extent that coalitions take us away from our people or divert our energies, they are a waste of effort and may actually be detrimental to us. In the nascent stages of a struggle, coalitions with non-Natives may work. At later, perhaps more developed stages—when Natives are asserting their sovereignty, for example—coalitions may not work.[110]

After the conference, law professor Mari Matsuda, herself a Japanese American from Hawaii, exulted that the "Women of Color and the Law" conference "*was* coalition."[111] Matsuda, for one, did not appear particularly upset about her expulsion from Trask's future paradise. And, for that matter, she had little reason to worry. The struggle was still in its "nascent stages," and all of the participants (Matsuda and Trask included) agreed on the most immediate goal: The common enemy, which provided the glue to cement the alliance of "women of color," was the West itself.

The Empty Curriculum

The radical conferences, Black Hair, race and gender studies, the new CIV courses, and "political action" programs like SWOPSI and IAC—all promote an "education for difference" of sorts. Each class examines a different persecuted minority group, a different episode of injustice, a different "socially constructed" oppression, and so on. But, cumulatively, the new humanities curriculum provides students with a solid background only in minutiae. Never once questioning their fundamental assumptions, dozens of professors, aided by students, spend their entire careers poring over ephemeral literature, minor historical records, or marginal sociological studies. After all this effort, it is hardly surprising that even the most banal of observations, when found or imagined, becomes transformed into unchallengeable confirmation of the most esoteric theories imaginable.

In this vein, the class experiments conducted in Psychology 116, "The Psychology of Gender," a heavily enrolled class meeting the gender studies DR, prepare academically inclined students for the type of research they might expect to complete along a multicultural career track. One group research project, passed out to the class in Spring 1994 by Professor

Laura Carstenson as an exemplar, studied "Gender Discrepancies in Pizza Consumption." The students described their cutting edge experiment:

> We observed couples eating at a local pizza restaurant (Applewood Inn) and recorded the number of slices each individual consumed. The intent of the study was to show that men and women eat more when in the company of a same-sex partner than with an opposite-sex partner. The effect was expected to be greater for females than males because of issues related to body-image and societal gender-based etiquette rules. Toppings, age of each individual, and observed relationship were recorded.[112]

The group found that "gender discrepancies exist not only in quantity, but also in rate of consumption." Of course, even if the results were accurate, they have almost no significance whatsoever, because they may be interpreted in a number of different ways. While a feminist researcher might interpret them as confirmation of the widespread oppression of women, one could just as readily conclude that it is men who are really oppressed because they are pressured to eat more than women. Or, perhaps these differences in pizza consumption reflect nothing more than natural physical differences between men and women. When even pizza can confirm multicultural dogma, it is unlikely that anything could disprove it.

In many respects, multicultural fieldwork recalls the "science" of phrenology (also known as craniometry), which reached its zenith in the late 19th century. Phrenologists believed that even the smallest variations in brain sizes were highly predictive of human intelligence. And so, upon this thin reed, the most laborious of experiments were conducted. Skulls and brains across races were measured lobe to lobe to justify theories of racial superiority (then fashionable in academic circles); numerous data of length, width, and volume were diligently recorded and analyzed. The leading American anthropologists J. W. Powell and W. J. McGee even made a wager over who had the larger brain, the winner to be decided by a measuring after their deaths.[113] Modern medicine has since shown phrenology to be without foundation, but for a long time its practitioners managed to convince themselves of their own assumptions with carefully designed experiments.

The new multicultural phrenologists think they can reduce the world to a few simple variables—if not brain size, then perhaps black hairstyles and pizza toppings. These simple and banal observations, in turn, are embedded in elaborate theoretical frameworks, which do all the "work" to yield the desired results. The multicultural paradigm always takes precedence over the evidence, and ensures that the desired conclusion will be reached. This curious, almost symbiotic juxtaposition of banal simplicity and Byzantine complexity was encapsulated, for instance, in the self-described purpose of "Post Neo-Colonialism and Identity Politics," a graduate-level anthropology course (the following description, it is worth stressing, comes from the introductory syllabus *explaining* the purpose of the course):

> This course attempts to sort out the significance and mobilization potential of a new jumble of cultural practices located in the terrain that calls for yet paradoxically refuses boundaries. This terrain is situated in the borderzone between identity-as-essence and identity-as-conjuncture, and its practices challenge the ludic play with essence and conjuncture as yet another set of postmodernist binarisms.
>
> Much work on resistance has been response-oriented, reacting to the Eurocenter by occupying either the essence pole or the hybrid pole. The course stakes out this new terrain, where opposition is not only responsive, but creative. It is a guerrilla warfare of the interstices, where minorities rupture categories of race, gender, sexuality, and class in the center as well as on the margins, and where such ruptures intersect with and challenge the late 20th century murky overlap between nationalism(s) and imperialism(s).
>
> The course examines the strategies of theorizing this hodgepodge of everyday experience and its textual representations. It scrutinizes new units of analysis that transcend and resist national boundaries through their creative articulations of practices which demonstrate possible modes of corroding the Eurocenter by actively Third-Worlding it. It explores the processes through which identity and place become multiple as they are actively forced into constantly shifting configurations of partial overlap.[114]

The pretentious terminology ("Third-Worlding" the "Eurocenter"!) may sound impressive until one realizes that it means very little—just the same old anti-Western themes, dressed up in neologisms. As with phrenology, the ornate research techniques and convoluted lingo simply mask a substantive emptiness. Instead of clear and rational discourse, one sees a wholesale retreat into a sort of fanatical obscurantism.

In spite of multiculturalism's widespread implementation, it is difficult to gauge just how much direct intellectual impact the doctrine has had on the current generation of students—Generation X. While multicultural educators succeed in radicalizing a number of students, many others become so alienated by the multicultural ideology that they actually become more conservative. Comments and public statements on behalf of multiculturalism may significantly overstate the actual level of agreement, because most students understand that tolerance and open-mindedness are not great multicultural virtues.[115] Like Mike Newman in Anthro 1, they value good grades and choose to regurgitate politically correct answers—it is not especially difficult. And many students who buy into multiculturalism will be disabused of these notions soon after graduating, since many multicultural claims—like Professor Manley's in Political Science 10—simply do not withstand close scrutiny. The ferocity of multiculturalists may be a sign of weakness, not strength: If their claims could survive in a competitive marketplace of ideas, the multiculturalists would have no need to exclude all other perspectives to convince students that they are right. To have a lasting effect, multicultural education would seem to require a monopoly that multiculturalists do not (yet) enjoy in American society at large.

Nevertheless, these observations do not render multicultural education any less catastrophic. For the major impact is indirect: While indoctrinating the new generation with ephemeral ideologies, multiculturalists simultaneously are wasting some of the best years of America's brightest students. The lost opportunities to study some of the West's great thinkers, to address the enduring questions in philosophy or religion, or to inform one's thinking about public policy or contemporary issues are not replaceable. The multiculturalists do not discriminate in this regard; they exact a steep price from liberal and conservative students, believers and heretics alike. Even most students who feel cheated by multicultural education do not know what they have missed. Of course, many suspect that there are more important issues than the "Great Debate" (over black hairstyles). They know that terrorism is real, unlike witchcraft. Some students do not even believe that multiculturalists are asking any of the important questions, or that *any* of the answers proposed by people like Aime Cesaire happen to be right. But this awareness of one's ignorance is not the end of education: It is only the beginning. Most students have only the vaguest notion of what some of the alternatives might be—what Socrates, Jesus, or Jefferson said that might be relevant to the contemporary situation. They have only a minimal understanding even of the ideas that built the American regime. Most have not read John Locke or Adam Smith, much less *The Federalist*, Alexis de Tocqueville, or Abraham Lincoln. Many students sense this "presence of absence," but after years of multicultural education lack either the will or the rudimentary knowledge necessary to correct this loss.

Multiculturalism's failure to sustain the minds of students with anything more nourishing than the intellectual equivalent of junk food comprises a significant part of the betrayal many members of Generation X feel towards the baby boomers who preceded them. The terms and icons most frequently associated with Generation X, from angry rock lyrics to sloppy "grunge" dress, connote a curious combination of angst and apathy—towards both their own futures and the causes for which the earlier generation agitated. This mix of emotions is curious because one would not expect truly apathetic people to feel anxiety about anything. Much of Generation X's angst may be attributed to the "presence of absence" it feels—students intuit that something is missing, but have not been taught quite enough to realize what that might be. Generation X may not know who Caliban and Prospero are, but it has the ineffable feeling that perhaps it *should*.

Most of the time, however, apathy reigns. For undergraduates out of step with the campus *zeitgeist*, the more common reaction to multiculturalism is cognitive nihilism: Because the multiculturalists are wrong, it appears that nobody is right. Since Stanford and the universities for which it is a model have made education and multiculturalism practically equivalent, the rebellion against multiculturalism becomes a revolt against learning itself—there seems little point to the whole endeavor when university studies involve little more than indoctrination in the multicultural agenda and a parroting of the party line. If multiculturalists are right to say that the inanities of Group Comm or Lee Iacocca's "Car Buyer Bill of Rights" are the most important things to study, then there really would be nothing significant to learn. And this conclusion is reached by a significant number of students (many of whom we knew) who have had enough of multicultural education; for these students, the danger is not that they will become disciples of multiculturalism, but that they will get turned off the life of the mind forever.

While critics of the 1960s often accuse that turbulent decade's youth of being nihilistic, the moniker more aptly describes much of our generation. Now as then, 1960s-style activists at least believe in multicultural causes—even if, sometimes, multiculturalism represents nothing more than what is trendy. Generation X, by and large, has rejected even multiculturalism, sometimes because its members keenly sense the essential emptiness, but usually because they simply are uninspired by waning ideas. Of course, a number of young radicals do agitate for multiculturalism, but these students really are the last products of the previous era, yearning for the days when social activism will again become popular and widespread, often sharing more in common with their faculty and administrative backers than with their apathetic peers. While many members of Generation X view multiculturalism coolly, however, they simultaneously have failed to restore or embrace the tradition multiculturalism supplanted. Like Cesaire's Caliban, who asks to be called "X" because he has been stripped of his identity, "Generation X" has been labelled as such because it neither possesses a distinctive identity nor can even remember when it had one. It is the deracinated result of multicultural upheaval.

Nihilism is not really an alternative to multiculturalism, however; it is merely the culmination of a confused and often destructive body of ideas. If our generation is to find the meaning it seeks, it must look outside the multicultural wasteland. A truth which transcends the conventions of multiculturalism, if it exists at all, must be embedded in the only set of perspectives rejected *a priori*—in the ideals and values of Western civilization. At a minimum, the following would seem certain: The most powerful critique of the radical ideology that animates the multicultural state has been made by Western thinkers—economists, historians, philosophers, writers. The most comprehensive alternative to the current crisis will be found not in far-away lands and distant cultures, but right here at home, in the traditions and intellectual currents that have shaped our own world. Before this study has been conducted properly, Generation X will rightfully feel betrayed by its elders.

Notes

1. R. Emmett Tyrrell, Jr., "Students' Rights Trampled at Stanford University," *The Stanford Review*, January 4, 1993.

2. David Sacks attended the class and took lecture notes. *See* David Sacks, "The Cutting Edge of Multiculturalism," *The Wall Street Journal*, July 29, 1992. Professor Jackson responded in a letter to the *Journal*, in which he defended the course as a "very important scholarly interest." Professor Jackson wrote: "Black hair in America is a huge issue, encompassing themes from economics, cultural history, aesthetics, fashion and, obviously, ethnic identity. Black hair deserves legitimate scholarly attention because it has been such a presence in the personal and collective quest of blacks for a place in American society." *See* Kennell Jackson Jr., "Unsnarling the Black Hair Issue," *The Wall Street Journal*, August 21, 1992.

3. *Ibid.*

4. *Ibid.*

5. *Harper's Magazine* reprinted much of the course syllabus. *See* "Fades, Braids, and Grades," *Harper's Magazine*, October 1992.

6. Sacks, *supra* note 2.

7. "Generation X" is named after Douglas Coupland's novel by that name.

8. Gail Mahood, "Summary of Findings and Perspectives on Stanford's Transcript and Grading Policies," Committee on Academic Appraisal and Achievement (C-AAA) March 29, 1993. *See also* Martin Anderson, "Academic currency's devaluation," *The Dallas Morning News*, June 4, 1993.

9. *Ibid.* (Percentages of letter grades are calculated from the overall grade distribution, which also includes nonletter grades.)

10. *Ibid.*

11. Carol Jouzaitis, "Easy College A's Become Rampant; Critics: Excellence Gets Lost," *The Chicago Tribune*, May 4, 1994.

12. Mahood, *supra* note 8.

13. Vivien Wang, "Universities grapple with grade inflation," *The Stanford Daily*, May 11, 1994. According to *The Daily*, by 1992–93 the percentage of A's had grown to 51 percent.

14. Jouzaitis, *supra* note 11. *The Chicago Tribune* interviewed Eric Bannasch, a 20-year-old from Sarasota, Florida. Bannasch was considering repeating a physics class in which he received a low grade: "I don't want to take it again," said the sophomore engineering major, "but I feel pressure to because no one else will have a C on their transcript. It will bring my grade-point [average] down."

15. Mahood, *supra* note 8.

16. John Krumboltz and Nel Noddings, "Questionnaire's bias leads to inaccurate survey results," *The Stanford Daily*, April 9, 1993.

17. *Ibid.*

18. *Ibid.*

19. Suzanne Alexander, "Trophy Transcript Hunters Are Finding Professors Have Become an Easy Mark," *The Wall Street Journal*, April 27, 1993.

20. Lisa Koven, "Frosh English focuses less on basics, more on service projects," *The Stanford Review*, November 16, 1992.

21. *Ibid.*

22. In her Fall 1991 Freshman English class, for instance, Professor Susan Wyle handed out a list of nonprofit groups for which students could write newsletter articles. (The authors obtained these syllabi, as well as many others, from a student in the class.) These groups are all left-liberal causes: The Hunger and Homeless Action Coalition of San Mateo County, which works "towards long-range solutions to the problem of homelessness through public education and advocacy"; The Homeless Agency Project (HAP) of the Bar Association of San Francisco, which exists in part "to educate the homeless community (and their advocates) of the protections offered by disability statutes"; Ellipse Peninsula AIDS Service, "a not-for-profit agency committed to helping individuals who are HIV infected, their family members, loved ones and friends"; Bay Area Action, which "works locally to achieve the Earth Day 'Agenda for the Green Decade'"; Mid-Peninsula Citizens for Fair Housing, which, upon complaint, "may dispatch trained volunteer 'testers' to gather evidence of illegal discrimination"; and The Environmental Protection Division of the City of Palo Alto, which "educates" the public about "environmental issues."

23. Koven, *supra* note 20.

24. *Ibid.*

25. Interviews with Jason Sugarman (class of 1994), who was a senior when he took the class in Winter 1994, and Nathan Linn (class of 1993), who was a senior when he took the class in Winter 1993. David Sacks also kept a daily log of class activities when he took the class in Winter 1993.

26. Stanford University, *Courses and Degrees*, 1993–94.

27. Interviews, *supra* note 25.

28. *Ibid.*

29. David Sacks, Group Communications Daily Log, January 5, 1993.

30. Roberta Chavez, "Murals reflect culture, conflict," *The Stanford Daily*, April 20, 1992.

31. David Sacks, Group Communications Daily Log, January 19,

1993.

32. Interviews, *supra* note 25.

33. *Ibid.*

34. *Ibid* Linn, Sugarman, and Sacks all observed instances where participants became so upset during the course of the discussions that they fled the room.

35. *Ibid.*

36. *Ibid* For the most part, upper-class students dare not suggest any negative adjectives about the lower classes. Linn noted that during one upper-middle-class intragroup discussion, however, one person indicated that he thought members of the lower classes might be "dirty." Even this observation was too heterodox. In the subsequent intergroup discussion, another upper-middle-class person confessed that someone had had this horrible thought: She had been so traumatized, she told the class, that she "almost had to leave the room."

37. *Ibid.*

38. "Peace Studies," Course Syllabus, Spring 1992.

39. David Sacks took the class in Spring 1992. These prescriptions can also be found in the lecture notes, which are transcribed and distributed by a service of the student government.

40. "Peace Studies" Class Reader, Spring 1992.

41. *Ibid.*

42. Syllabus, *supra* note 38.

43. James MacGregor Burns and Stewart Burns, *A People's Charter: The Pursuit of Rights in America* (New York: Knopf, 1991).

44. Interviews with Michael Newman (class of 1992) and Christopher Aguas (class of 1992). David Sacks took the class in Winter 1994.

45. *Ibid.*

46. *Ibid.*

47. Interview with John Abbott (class of 1992).

48. Jack Guerrero, "Bearing the PC Crucifix: 'Religions in America,'" *The Stanford Review*, April 25, 1994.

49. Minal Hajratwala, "Sexuality, Feminism, Ethnicity: The Makings of My Bisexuality," *Aurora*, May 1991.

50. Education classes 246 A, B, C, and D offer "Secondary Teaching and Multicultural Education Practicum." *See Courses and Degrees*, *supra* note 26.

51. Susan Jackson, "Effects of Gulf War felt in the classroom," *The Stanford Daily*, April 9, 1991.

52. David Goldberger, "Social Movements of the 1960s in California," Course Syllabus, March 31, 1994.

53. Solveig Pederson, "Pop culture gaining legitimacy as supplement to course material," *The Stanford Daily*, February 1, 1993.

54. Walter Lammi, "Nietzsche, the Apaches, and Stanford: The Hidden Agenda of Education for Difference," *Academic Questions*, Summer 1991.

55. *Ibid.*

56. Interview with Michael Petras (class of 1997). The class also explored "the paradox central to Western-Anglo-male cultural phenomena," announced Professor Castle—a supposed fascination with lesbianism (an "important trope in Western culture") but an overt rejection of homosexuality.

57. Terry Castle, "Representing Sappho: Readings in the Literature of Lesbianism," Course Syllabus, March 29, 1994.

58. Adam Ross, "'How tasty were my French sisters?' Lesbianism and politics in cross-cultural feminism," *The Stanford Review*, April 19, 1993. Adam Ross, "Gay issues permeate curriculum; Sexuality politics and gender at issue in comp lit class," *The Stanford Review*, April 19, 1993. Matt Hulse, "History and Politics of Sexual Orientation," *The Stanford Review*, February 7, 1994.

59. Kris McNeil, "The 'ethic of rebelling': New seminars examine counterculture literature," *The Stanford Daily*, February 8, 1993.

60. Richard Castanon, "Dialogue tutorials might compromise academic goals," *The Stanford Review*, January 25, 1993.

61. *Ibid.*

62. Jay Grossman, "Representing Sexualities: Whitman to AIDS," Course Syllabus, Spring 1994.

63. *Courses and Degrees*, *supra* note 26.

64. Interview with Jill Morganbesser (class of 1992).

65. *Ibid.*

66. Diane Curtis, "Stanford Now Requiring Ethnic, Sex Role Studies," *The San Francisco Chronicle*, December 13, 1990.

67. *Ibid.*

68. Romesh Ratnesar, "Reform nothing new to undergraduate education," *The Stanford Daily*, November 1, 1993.

69. Matthew Meskell, "Say What···African American Vernacular English class puts a new spin on linguistics," *The Stanford Review*, January 25, 1993.

70. *Ibid.*

71. Jennifer Bryson, "Expansion of feminism draws fire," *The Stanford Review*, April 1989.

72. *Ibid.*

73. *See* Stanford University, *A Woman's Guide to Stanford*, 1993–94. Stanford distributes the guide to new female students each year. The book explains: "For centuries, women in Western cultures have been excluded from academic life. Precious few women have been given the

opportunity to pursue intellectual interests, and thus the founding fathers of academia were just that: fathers. The bias that results from this male domination is evident throughout academia. Even supposedly scientific and unbiased subjects such as biology and psychology have long been based on male thought and male subjects, to the exclusion of women's experiences."

74. Carol Delaney, "Creation/Procreation," Course Syllabus, Spring 1994.

75. Purina Manekar, "Gender and Nationalism," Course Syllabus, March 30, 1994.

76. Penelope Eckert, "Language and Gender," Course Syllabus, Spring 1994.

77. *Ibid.*

78. Susan Krieger, "Women and Organizations," Course Syllabus, Spring 1994.

79. *Ibid.*

80. Joan Fujimura, "Gender and Science," Course Syllabus, Spring 1994.

81. Bryson, *supra* note 71.

82. Susan Griffin, "The Politics of Rape," in *Made From This Earth: An Anthology of Writing* (New York: Harper & Row, 1983).

83. Alison Jaggar and Paula Rothenberg, eds., *Feminist Frameworks: Alternative Theoretical Accounts of the Relations Between Men and Women* (New York: McGraw-Hill, 1984).

84. The Boston Women's Health Book Collective, *The New Our Bodies, Ourselves: A Book By and For Women* (New York: Simon & Schuster, 1982).

85. Betty Harragan, *Games Mother Never Taught You* (New York: Warner Books, 1981).

86. Karen Ho, "New Course Requirements Approved," *The Stanford Review*, June 3, 1991.

87. Geoff Goldman, "Few support DR proposal," *The Stanford Daily*, November 29, 1990.

88. "Diverse Strategies to Boost Minority Professoriate Under Way at Stanford," *Stanford University News Service*, September 16, 1988.

89. Robert L. Jamieson Jr., "Gay couple bequeaths scholarship for homosexual students," *The Stanford Daily*, February 28, 1991.

90. David Sacks, "Departments Paid Bonuses for Minority Hiring; Affirmative Action Vital to Perpetuation of Multiculturalism, Says OMD," *The Stanford Review*, November 4, 1991.

91. "Keep the Spirit," *The Stanford Daily*, May 24, 1988.

92. Maryellen Driscoll, "Innovative academics gets mixed reviews," *The Stanford Daily*, February 14, 1989.

93. *Ibid. The Stanford Daily* explained that a controversy arose in Fall 1988 over a SWOPSI course entitled "Animal Rights or Wrongs: a case for animal rights." Some faculty, particularly from the Biological Sciences Department, "objected not to the topic of the course but to its slanted presentation by its instructors, who were both local animal rights activists."

94. *Ibid.*

95. Stephen Russell, "Fem 110 may violate Title IX," *The Stanford Review*, January 19, 1993.

96. *Ibid.*

97. *Ibid.*

98. *Ibid.*

99. *Ibid.*

100. Joel Shurkin, "International 'terrorists' are less violent than their predecessors, researcher says," *Campus Report*, February 10, 1988.

101. David Gress, "'Talking "Terrorism"' at Stanford," *The Stanford Review*, April 1988.

102. *Ibid.*

103 *Ibid.*

104. *Stanford Law Review*, Vol. 43 no. 6, July 1991. Most of the speakers had never before written articles for a law journal, and the *Stanford Law Review's* staff spent more than two years cleaning up essays—putting citations in the proper format, working with a quarrelsome group of people, and even trying to find cites to support wild and unsubstantiated charges. As a result, publication of the issue was delayed until January 1994.

105. Angela Davis, "Keynote Address: Third National Conference on Women of Color and the Law," *Stanford Law Review*, July 1991.

106. Sharon Parker, "Understanding Coalition," *Stanford Law Review*, July 1991. Evelyn Nakano Glenn, "Cleaning Up/Kept Down: A Historical Perspective on Racial Inequality in 'Women's Work,'" *Stanford Law Review*, July 1991.

107. Huanani-Kay Trask, "Coalition-Building Between Natives and Non-Natives," *Stanford Law Review*, July 1991.

108. *Ibid.*

109. *Ibid.*

110. *Ibid.*

111. Mari Matsuda, "Beside My Sister, Facing the Enemy: Legal Theory Out of Coalition," *Stanford Law Review*, July 1991.

112 Brant Schelor, et. al., "Abstract: One Slice or Two? Gender Discrepancies in Pizza Consumption." Professor Laura Carstenson handed out the paper on the first day of Psychology of Gender in Spring 1994.

113. According to Stephen Jay Gould, "The dissection of dead colleagues became something of a cottage industry among nineteenth-century craniometricians." For an account of the rise and fall of craniometry, *see* Stephen Jay Gould, *The Mismeasure of Man* (New York: W. W. Norton, 1981).

114. Smadar Lavie, "Post Neo-Colonialism and Identity Politics," Course Syllabus, Spring 1994.

115. One indicator of actual student opinion is provided by Stanford's annual student government elections. In most years, the multiculturally correct "People's Platform" won these elections, although it rarely drew over 55 percent of the vote. More moderate candidates consistently received over 40 percent. On many specific issues, the multiculturalists fared far worse; for example, students registered opposition to proposed speech restrictions by a margin of nearly 2 to 1 in the spring of 1990. And during the 1991 elections, the politically centrist "Students First" slate actually wrested control of both the executive and legislative branches of Stanford's student government.

4

The Engineering of Souls

Stanford is a trendy place and it responds to trends. Its shameless self-congratulation about this is sufficient to render it ridiculous in the eyes of serious people no matter what their political persuasion.[1]

—Professor Allan Bloom

The residents of Roble Hall were eating dinner one evening in April of 1989 when nine intruders, dressed in camouflage, wearing masks, and brandishing weapons, burst into the cafeteria. While some of these guerillas pointed their guns at startled undergraduates, two others lifted English professor Ronald Rebholz and senior Sarah Fandell from their seats. The head of the squad engaged the attention of witnesses, condemned the targets as campus "subversives," and then abducted the two.[2]

Only later would alarmed observers learn that the kidnapping was part of a series of "guerrilla theater" actions known as "Project Awareness," staged by kidnappers and kidnappees alike. The *Stanford Daily* reported the next day that the Project was staging mock kidnappings all over campus to demonstrate the way that citizens allegedly were being abducted by some Latin American governments.[3] In Wilbur dorm, some student diners became so convinced that one of these kidnappings was real that they overpowered the kidnappers and "rescued" the kidnappee.[4] Such terror had been precisely the point of the demonstration, Project members explained, because only through such "genuine confusion and fear" could residents come to "understand" the group's message.[5]

Project Awareness's consciousness-raising efforts dramatically illustrate that multicultural education is not limited to the classroom and other formal academic settings. President Kennedy's bold experiment was to create—first at Stanford and then beyond—"a new kind of community." This new community would succeed only if it were populated by a new kind of citizen. In order for Stanford to create (and then graduate into society) this ideal multicultural person, the ideas and values advocated in class would need to be implemented, in an even more immediate way, in the day-to-day living arrangements of students.

If need be, this transformation would proceed dormitory by dormitory, and as the residents of Donner Hall learned, sometimes even room by room. When the freshman dorm residents returned from Spring Break in 1991, they received quite a shock. The walls of the basement pool room (the dorm's main recreational area) had been splattered with graffiti. Samples from three of the walls included: "Bush sucks cock"; "Liberation '91" (with a machine gun); 1960s peace symbols; and other specimens of art and paint splatters.[6] The fourth wall was covered with more graffiti: "Peace flamers suck granola"; "Stormin' Norman '96"; "If a woman says no, she means yes—J.J.R."; and American and Confederate flags.[7]

Before Spring Break the dormitory had asked a group of students to repaint the peeling walls of the pool room. These volunteers decided to redecorate the room with "graffiti art" and covered three walls with the first set of slogans and "art," mostly protests against the Gulf War between the United States and Iraq, still raging at the time. The committee left several cans of paint in the room. A second group of students, which one member described as "a bunch of conservatives," decided to add some graffiti of their own—putting the second set of slogans and "art" on the remaining wall. The quote from Jean Jacques Rousseau ("J.J.R.") was added in order "to cause a little uproar among the liberals," according to one person involved, who said he learned the quote in CIV.[8] More than "a little uproar" followed. In a subsequent third round of graffiti, one resident scrawled "Rednecks must die," apparently in reference to the members of the second group. Other students proceeded to splatter the entire room with paint, including the pool table and some of the heating pipes. Donner's students returned from Spring Break to a new pool room and a new multicultural trauma.

As at Ujamaa during the Beethoven incident, Donner's residence staff convened a special house meeting shortly after these events. Resident assistant Adrian Miller, a senior, explained that the meeting attempted to discern what constituted "art." The incident "brought up the whole issue of First Amendment freedom of expression," he said, "but some of the words were offensive to a lot of students and we've got to take that into consideration."[9] Resident fellow Linda Paulson, a Stanford English professor, was one of those offended by the second round of graffiti: "I was saddened that it was in my house. It was violent and it was a congregation of violent sentiments that were coupled with anti-female sentiments and I just didn't know that people in my dorm felt that way."[10] Christine Nash thought the (phase two) graffiti had "sexist undertones" and showed "blatant disrespect." "I am angry that I live with these people," she said.[11] Added resident Laura Battaglia, "A majority of the people here are outraged. That's men and women."[12]

These same residents, however, were not upset at the characterization of the president of the United States as a homosexual (an attack, presumably, on President Bush and not on homosexuals). Nor were they appalled at the call to kill "Rednecks" or to settle differences with machine guns. The focus of their anger was somewhere different. Led by the resident fellow and staff, Donner's residents blamed the four conservative students (the "Donner Four," as they became known on campus) not only for the content of their graffiti (phase two), but for the entire mess (all three phases). Although the Donner Four claimed not to have taken part in phase three, which caused the greatest amount of physical damage, at one point it was even suggested that they should pay the entire $3,000 clean-up bill: Because only their writings were deemed "offensive," only they should pay damages.[13]

As in many free-speech cases, the (Donner) majority's attempt to punish a minority for "offensive" speech is problematic. Even though the liberal students were "offended" by the "conservative" art, the conservative students could just as plausibly have claimed to be "offended" by the "liberal" art. To an outside observer, the reciprocity appeared almost perfect: It would seem difficult to single out either side for all the blame in the series of escalating events that ended in the trashing of the pool room. If anything, the liberal graffiti had been marginally more bawdy: While quoting Rousseau may be construed as condoning violence against women, "Rednecks must die" explicitly calls for violence. "Peace flamers suck granola" obviously denigrates antiwar activists. But some antiwar activists do eat granola, whereas the liberal students' allegation of presidential fellatio was an *ad hominem* attack unalloyed by truth or humor.

In recent years, radical activists have justified funding and support for controversial art on the basis that such art is needed to challenge people's fundamental assumptions about the communities and society in which they live. This argument was advanced, for instance, by Stanford's commencement speaker in 1992, Kirk Varnedoe, who is a director of the Museum of Modern Art in New York City and a prominent voice in the arts community: "Art may be at its most powerful—and most uncomfortable for authoritarians of all stripes—when it orchestrates perplexity, fails to conform to what you already know, and instead sends you away temporarily disoriented but newly attuned to experience in ways that are perhaps even more powerful, because they are vague, rogue and indeterminate."[14] The episode in Donner suggests an interesting twist on this line of reasoning.

Even though all three phases of the Donner "art" could be justified on such grounds, the graffiti of phase two—which offended, shocked, and challenged the greatest number of people—would seem to have been the most successful under this conception of "art." To Stanford's multiculturalists, the claim that "Bush sucks cock" was nothing new or even very interesting, but the idea that "Peace flamers suck granola" was truly novel and unheard of. Instead of being delighted in the challenges presented by the "conservative graffiti art," however, Donner's multiculturalists were outraged and angry: For America's arts community and Stanford's multiculturalists, the purpose of art is to attack the fundamental assumptions of *other* people. Of course, nobody—neither multiculturalists nor anybody else—ever really likes art that challenges and undermines their most fundamental and sacred assumptions about the world. The events in Donner served as a timely reminder that the multicultural definition of "authoritarians of all stripes" is not the only possible one.

The Donner incident points to broader issues than just the multicultural definition of art, however. The very fact that such an episode occurred in the first place—that a dormitory committee considered blatantly political graffiti appropriate for a common recreational area—underlines the point that multicultural education is pushed as aggressively in student residences and other informal settings as in the classroom.

Residential Education is the name for the university division that runs Stanford's student housing, and its self-characterization indicates that "Res Ed" is far more concerned with promoting "multicultural experiences" than taking care of housing logistics.[15] "Our charge as resident fellows and resident assistants is, primarily, to be educators—to bridge the gap between the classroom and the daily lives of students," explained Evan and Ann Porteus, resident fellows in Roble Hall. "We attempt this education in a variety of ways—organizing programs focused on social and political issues, multiculturalism, issues of sexuality, issues of race, gender and class, etc."[16] To facilitate this "programming" (the term is Res Ed's), most residences have one resident fellow (RF), typically a member of Stanford's faculty, and several resident assistants (RAs), juniors and seniors who also live in the residences. In recent years, Res Ed also has added "program assistants" and "theme assistants" to plan additional workshops and multicultural events.[17] "In the absence of a critical number of minority faculty, in the absence of a curriculum on minority experiences in the United States, Residential Education has, for the past decade, been providing students with this exposure through films, lectures and group discussions," boasted Cecilia Burciaga, RF in the Casa Zapata dorm. "Other universities have a housing office or a dorm office. We have Residential Education."[18]

Stanford's "theme" dorms, residences in which the RFs and RAs organize programming around a particular set of political issues, provide a clue as to what this education entails. Robinson House was the feminist studies theme dorm until the departure of its RF, when it became the new environmental theme house. Murray House explores "modern thought and literature," and Lantana House is the "community service" dorm.[19] Potter House's "1960s" focus was proposed by its RF, history professor Clay Carson. According to *Campus Report*, "Programming ranges from the fun—a 'Name that Tune' contest with hits from the '60s to '90s—to discussions about presidential politics, civil rights, the origins of the ecology movement, the women's movement, and gay and lesbian activism."[20] By contrast, one would find it hard to imagine, even in 20 years, a "1980s" theme dorm, replete with workshops on bond trading and discussions about Reagan's foreign policy *vis-à-vis* the "evil empire." Theme dorms transmit only those ideas and values—environmentalism, feminism, '60s radicalism—stamped with the multicultural seal of approval. Inauspiciously, Alice Supton, director of Res Ed, promised the *Stanford Daily* in 1993, "I envision all upper-class houses with resident fellows will eventually have some sort of focus."[21]

Indeed, Res Ed already extends multicultural classroom discussions into almost every informal dormitory setting. During the late 1980s and early 1990s at Stanford, dorm speakers and Res Ed activities included the following:

- Joan Baez, the peace activist and singer, spoke about her work during the protests of the 1960s.
- Another speaker devoted his lecture to a discussion of the CIA's drug experiments on humans in the 1950s, and used this as a springboard for an indictment of the entire U.S. military.
- A Rastafarian leader informed his audience in Branner (Stanford's largest freshman dorm) that President Reagan corresponded to the Antichrist foretold in the Bible ("Ronald Wilson Reagan equals 666").
- A graduate student writing his research thesis on patriarchal behavior in animated films condemned Disney's *The Little Mermaid* as "sexist" and "phallocentric."
- A dorm-based discussion on feminism culminated in an attack by one of the RFs on women who chose more traditional roles as mothers and did not pursue careers. She had not done so, and could not imagine why other women might.
- A Nicaraguan activist told Roble Hall residents how wonderful conditions had become after the Sandinista revolution. With considerable glee, he noted that once-wealthy Nicaraguans had lost just about everything (they no longer had money for "jewelry" or "fur coats"); the impoverishment of the upper classes justified

the economic decline of the country as a whole.

- Ex-model Anne Simonton offered a more Puritanical twist. A self-described "radical feminist" who tours Stanford's residences year after year to talk about the exploitation of women, Simonton maintains that traditional female roles border on the pornographic: "I felt like a prostitute as a model," she told an audience in Branner. "I was selling my body, and my agent seemed like a pimp. The only difference was, modelling was legal."[22] She quit modelling after she became convinced that she was indirectly promoting violence against women, and argued that even ordinary media advertisements are "demeaning to the female integrity" and encourage men to beat and rape women.[23]
- Congressman Bill Gray spoke about his work in pushing liberal Democratic policies. When one of us suggested that some nonliberal speakers might be desirable for the sake of balance, the RF responded that he did not know of any that he could approach.

Most people who choose to become RFs are ideologically committed to the multicultural experiment, and they select RAs whose devotion to the cause is even more vigorous. "There are people who are going to feel it's being rammed down their throats," explained Jae Choi, an RA in Robinson House. "We have to respect this as RAs, but we know that we're not going to appease everyone."[24] Marie Leggon, a senior who worked at Twain House, echoed these attitudes: "I'm a strong advocate of pluralism....To some people, I was seen as too adamant, too opinionated, almost militant."[25] Such sentiments hardly reveal a residence staff out to create a sense of ease and elan for 17-year-old freshmen away from home for the first time. Res Ed Director Alice Supton's attempt to justify this "militancy" was more of an admission: "We think that some white male students felt targeted by the campus environment last year, which was very aware of white male privilege."[26] Evidently, white males were not so "privileged" that they enjoyed immunity from the unpleasant "targeting" efforts of their RAs.

The motivating sentiments of Marcus Mabry, an RA in Donner Hall during 1987–88, are not unusual: "Driving my decision to remain here [as an RA] was the idealistic belief that I could make a difference. As a black man who is also a feminist, I felt I could open some eyes, broaden minds and attack some 'isms.'"[27] Describing the tactics used at Donner Hall to enlighten freshmen, Mabry explained his mission and the difficulties he faced: "Once RAs posted a magazine ad that showed only a woman's legs and the line, 'Pantyhose for men.' We found the ad offensive and asked students to comment; many men didn't see the problem. I tried soft sells like putting up cartoons of episodes in African American history in the bathroom stalls, but some people complained, 'I can't escape this multiculturalism stuff anywhere.'"[28] When hallway bulletin boards and even bathroom stalls become vehicles for transmitting the truths of multiculturalism (clearly not one of the "isms" Mabry was trying to "attack"), it should hardly strike Mabry as odd that some of Donner's residents felt that it was everywhere. Nonetheless, Mabry was correct in characterizing cartoons in bathroom stalls as "soft sells"—for that is what they were in contrast with such dorm-based activities as graffiti painting and mock kidnappings.

Of course, bathroom stall cartoons, the Donner graffiti, and even the mock kidnappings are all relatively harmless. In general, these kinds of "awareness" efforts are more nuisances than anything else; they do not wreck lives. But these efforts do bespeak the multiculturalists' desire to effect a radical values transformation—in the words of Lenin, to be "the engineers of souls." "We promote certain basic values," admitted Dennis Matthies, RF at Otero House, a freshman dorm. "Some of these values are at odds with prevailing conditions in our society."[29] Beneath a veneer of tolerance and open-mindedness, Stanford's Res Ed program acts as much *in loco parentis* as did old-style university proctors.[30] But whereas old-style universities promoted the values of the parents in whose place they acted, today's Stanford is promoting a very different set of values often the sorts of values many parents spend 18 years trying to make sure their children do *not* absorb. "In our experience you have to be there pushing at the extremes in order to produce a modicum of change," declared RFs Evan and Ann Porteus.[31] And there are other areas where the consequences of such extremism can be far more devastating.

On a very general level, multiculturalists are seeking to promote two distinct sets of values. Each set has its own points of vulnerability. But the most interesting aspect of these two sets of values is that they are contradictory. One set advocates, with almost religious fervor, the benefits of sexual exploration and, more generally, liberation from traditional Western norms. Another set of values demands prudery and ascetic self-denial, a new kind of Puritanism in many ways more restrictive then the original. While each set of values is flawed in its own way, the more revealing question is why Stanford's leaders simultaneously advocate a theology of liberation and a new Puritanism. At bottom, both sets of multicultural values share a least common denominator, and it is this underlying similarity that resolves the apparent paradox.

Liberation Theology

In October of 1993, Jason Allen married Terry Rouman in Stanford's Memorial Church. While the university regularly makes the Church available for the weddings of graduates, their ceremony was something of a first. Jason and Terry are both men.

"We were kissing and people in the street just stood with their mouths hanging open. Somebody yelled, 'That's disgusting,'" Allen, smiling, told the *Stanford Daily*.[32] Associate Dean Diana Akiyama, who presided over the Church's first homosexual marriage, explained that her personal decision to conduct the "commitment" ceremony (Memorial Church no longer uses the term "wedding") was based on her acknowledgement that doing so would be "politically risky, but theologically compelling."[33] Dean Robert Gregg added that the Church staff "wanted to focus on what we were about religiously....We had talked about what we thought would be the right kind of response in terms of justice, compassion and our service to the community. We agreed that [Terry Rouman and Jason Allen's] relationship warranted that kind of support."[34] The church ceremony made an important political statement, Mr. Rouman explained, because his "non-gay friends would see [the ceremony] as equal to their weddings."[35] Indeed, out of their sympathy with Rouman and Allen's ideological goal, the church's clerics not only ignored the fact that no major religion approves of homosexuality; in their eagerness to complete the ceremony, they also waived regular fees for use of the church (more than $1,000) and bypassed normal procedures (a six-month wait), thereby giving the homosexual pair preferential treatment over a long list of heterosexual couples.[36] Dean Akiyama more accurately could have described her support of the ceremony in reverse—theologically risky, but politically compelled.

The homosexual marriage in Stanford's nondenominational Memorial Church angered a number of religious groups on campus.[37] But, for multiculturalists, the choice between insensitivity towards homosexuals and insensitivity towards religious groups is hardly a choice at all. "We had a first," Akiyama boasted of the ceremony; "there will be a second."[38]

Stanford's first homosexual wedding is only one of a number of cases where multiculturalists privilege the concerns of relatively few homosexuals over those of larger numerical majorities, whether they involve religious groups or the heterosexual student population at large, often in the name of personal liberation:

- The Office of Residential Education aggressively recruits homosexuals for RA positions. Res Ed even advertises in the *Stanford Daily* for this purpose.[39] Director Supton explained that Stanford's residences needed "RA's who will promote openness to issues of sexuality and sexual preference."[40] Ken Ruebush, for instance, stated in his application that he was homosexual and got the job, which pays $4,500 per year (plus free housing).
- The Gay and Lesbian Alliance at Stanford (GLAS) and Res Ed coordinate dorm-based discussions, in which homosexual activists seek to promote "alternative lifestyles." Every year each fresh-

man dorm is visited by a panel of homosexual speakers, and these panels are almost never balanced by contrasting viewpoints.[41] GLAS also holds weekly "Queer Be-Ins" at the Coffee House, in which homosexuals take over the campus's most popular hang-out.[42]

- The University has placed the "Gay Liberation" statue, depicting gays and lesbians caressing each other, near the campus's centrally located Quad.[43] By contrast, a statue commemorating Stanford's founding family waits by a dumpster in the university's maintenance yard because "there is no place to put it." The statue of Leland, Jane, and Leland Jr. Stanford "is not sympathetic to current sensibilities," said a university curator.[44] Indeed, moral sensibilities have not so much changed at Stanford since its founding as have been inverted.
- GLAS receives financial support over and above other organizations. In 1988, the homosexual community was bequeathed its own university-sponsored community center. The Lesbian, Gay, and Bisexual Community Center (LGBCC), a department of Student Affairs, receives University funding, staff time, equipment, office space, and the resources of the Office of the Dean of Student Affairs.[45]

The university is also willing to tolerate excesses by members of the homosexual community that would never be tolerated in any other group. In men's bathrooms throughout campus, but particularly in libraries and the history department, holes have been drilled between the walls of toilet stalls to facilitate "anonymous bathroom sex." One Green Library employee described a restroom in the South Stacks of the library as a "horror story," with homosexual graffiti covering the walls. Students who use these bathrooms are often solicited for homosexual sex.[46] David Bianco, a homosexual activist well-known on campus, described one such encounter in a 1990 *Stanford Daily* article:

> "Doug" was barely a teenager when he saw the man in the next bathroom stall tap his foot. Curious, he tapped his own foot back, and before he knew it, the man had gotten on his knees and was caressing Doug's leg. Although he found his first sexual partner "basically by accident," Doug, now an undergraduate, looks back at that incident as the first time he was able to express his lifelong attraction toward other men. As Doug grew older, anonymous bathroom sex became an addiction. Whenever he felt he could not "handle it," he recalls, the following scenario ensued: "I go to this one bathroom and

> sit in a stall. I tap my foot and wait to see if they tap back, as a signal. Typically Doug and the other man would engage in mutual masturbation and occasionally oral sex underneath the stall. Doug was swamped by emotions each time he had an encounter. "I felt guilty, ashamed, depressed—I was nervous, scared of the danger, angry with myself." He came to Stanford assuming that the gay community on a college campus would be more open about sexuality and that he could be accepted as a gay man for the first time. He quickly sought counselling and "came out" for the first time.[47]

Apparently unwilling to anger members of the homosexual community, the university has failed to reseal "glory holes" in a number of the campus's public bathrooms, despite the discomforting effect on people seeking to use toilets for more prosaic purposes.[48]

The university's advocacy of homosexual causes is just one of a larger set of decisions and policies inextricably linked to judgments about personal morality—questions involving interpersonal relationships, family values, and sexual mores. In many ways, the multicultural left has extended the sexual revolution of the 1960s, to the extent that liberation from traditional moral restraints is now exalted as a kind of salvation—hence Dean Robert Gregg's assertion that the homosexual marriage "focus[ed] on what we were about religiously." Traditional notions of morality are at best *passé* and at worst oppressive, multiculturalists have concluded, because the people who invented these norms failed to consider the special needs of minorities with "alternative lifestyles."

A central tenet of the new liberation theology, illustrated by the account of "Doug," is that guilty feelings are much worse than the acts provoking them. Multiculturalists eschew guilt as the consequence of an incomplete liberation from Western biases. In the name of freeing individuals from these oppressive restrictions (so that people can finally "be themselves" and "do their own thing"), multiculturalists have eliminated traditional male-female distinctions and declared that other sexual restraints have got to go. One university residence now even has coed group showers, for instance, and the University's Tuesday Night Flicks shows a number of X-rated movies, including the sadistic *Salo,* which is advertised as one of the most disturbing films ever made and features torture and child molestation.[49]

To facilitate the new morality, Stanford funds numerous contraceptive "education" programs. The AIDS Education Project promotes the "Safer Sex Shoppe," which sells students contraceptives and gives many more away for free at dorm-based "RubberWare" parties, in which students are encouraged to "play" and "experiment" with various kinds of sexual devices.[50] In 1987, the Project distributed 9,000 condoms in two hours.[51] The Cowell Student Health Center also distributed condoms subsidized by the Stanford administration and student government, and, in conjunction with Stanford's psychology department, the Center taught students to become "Contraceptive Peer Counselors" for academic credit.[52] Both the AIDS Education Project and the Cowell Center justified their subsidies on the disingenuous grounds that many students could not afford to pay the market price of 50¢ a condom.[53] In 1988, Res Ed also set up condom dispensing machines in every dormitory.[54] These machines were not particularly successful, though; most students could get contraceptives for free elsewhere.[55]

Just in case these "education" efforts are insufficient, however, there is also the "Condom Rating Contest." This annual event distributes packets of condoms to students, along with pamphlets and ballots.[56] In 1989, student organizer Daniel Bao claimed that "people are going to have sex anyway. It's like handing out shoes to people who don't have them....If people insist on being sexually active, then we should be sensitive to that and advise protection."[57] The details of the contest, however, suggest that it involves more than a welfare-like distribution of condoms "to people who don't have them." The pamphlet exhorted the contestants to "try out these condoms by yourself, with a partner, or partners. Be creative. Have fun. Enjoy." The ballot asked participants to rate each of seven condoms by smell, taste (Bao: "Some people like to taste them"), appearance, sensualness/comfort, lubrication, and sense of security. Even on a very superficial level, such "festive foolery" goes well beyond merely educating people about contraceptive options.[58]

Ostensibly, multicultural sex education is predicated on the notion that there are vast numbers of people who are sexual ignoramuses. In the case of AIDS, some multiculturalists actually suggest that the absence of their education will cause people to die unnecessarily. These claims notwithstanding, the truth of the matter is that very few of today's college-age Americans do not know how women become pregnant or how people may contract AIDS—and those few who do not know these things are definitely not attending Stanford. Hence, if the only purpose of these "awareness" campaigns were to "educate," they would not really be necessary. Efforts like the "Condom Rating Contest" have a very different goal, however. Despite claims of value neutrality, their purpose is to promote a very specific set of values. For instance, Assistant Dean of Student Affairs Michael Ramsey-Perez, an admitted homosexual, declared that "abstinence is simply not a viable option, nor has it ever been....A condom, used properly and in conjunction with spermicides, is about as safe as you're going to get."[59] When the university promotes casual sex and an assistant dean refuses to recognize alternatives, the net effect is to declare that conceptions of sexual conduct that do not conform to the new liberation theology are wrong.

It is worth noting that all of these efforts have not had a positive impact on the level of AIDS, unwanted pregnancies, or abortions at Stanford, relative to American society at large. More than 100 Stanford women still have unwanted pregnancies each year, of which about 90 percent end in abortion. The resulting abortion rate at Stanford is about twice the national average.[60] And as for AIDS, the rate of death at Stanford is perhaps four to five times that of the relatively "uneducated" society at large.[61]

In addition to the sexual mores of the 1960s, the multiculturalists have, in many cases, also embraced that generation's liberated attitudes towards drug use. To take but one of the more blatant examples: In 1991, the Bridge, Stanford's counselling center, hosted a two-day conference entitled "Linking the Past, Present and Future of Psychedelics." But instead of advising students about the dangers of drug use, this conference celebrated the drug counterculture of the 1960s. Attendees were greeted by television monitors filled with swirling patterns, videos created specifically to stimulate visual sensations during LSD trips.[62] Booths in the lobby offered drug-inspired art and distributed articles advocating the use of drugs. One of the pieces indicated that "hemp [can] be used as an alternative fuel source, thus ending the American dependence on foreign oil."[63]

Drug gurus Timothy Leary and Robert Wilson promoted the salutary effects of psychedelic drugs with even greater conviction. Lecturing the 500-person audience, Wilson held up an apple and declared, "This is your brain." He subsequently dropped the apple, adding, "This is your brain after it's been hit by stupid uninformed TV commercials on drugs."[64] Timothy Leary attempted to provide more of a philosophical grounding:

> The use of hallucinogens was suppressed in feudal society because [knowledge of the power of the mind gained through psychedelic drugs] is incompatible with a society that depends on there being one God....The whole theory of "know thyself" came from a bunch of Greek philosophers hanging around and getting high. They had a lot of secret rituals that involved psychedelic plants.[65]

Leary argued that contemporary use of illegal drugs is a critical ingredient of a therapeutic "shamanistic environment." More specifically, Leary suggested that such an environment should consist of people using

"LSD and ecstasy to set up a hypnotic trance state, and then listen and dance to music for five or six hours. Sex, drugs, and rock'n'roll—that's what it's all about."[66] One may only speculate about what kinds of advice the Bridge offers students behind *closed* doors.

An indispensable ingredient of the multicultural theology of liberation includes the liberation from Western religion and its mores. This liberation takes many forms, but as with the CIV reading list, the unifying theme involves the yearning for a new religion to replace the old. This new religion may involve little more than an ideological commitment to social or political trends, as in the case of the homosexual wedding. In other instances, however, the discomfort with traditional religious expression becomes more explicit, as the new multicultural religion becomes transformed into a religion of antireligiosity.

A good example involves the transformation of Stanford's church. Memorial Church reopened in the fall of 1992, after earthquake repairs, as a very different institution. The university failed to replace the Bibles, which had been removed—leaving empty holders on the backs of 100-plus pews.[67] Money was not the problem—the extensive renovation had cost millions of dollars, the custom-made wooden chairs in the side chapel cost about $1,500 apiece, and the church also had bought an expensive new speaker system. Nor were the books even damaged in the earthquake. The church staff simply believed that, while homosexual marriages were "theologically compelling," Bibles were not. Although the church retains stained-glass windows depicting Christ and some of the Christian saints, the church's leadership is not entirely comfortable with that remaining vestige either: One speaker devoted a sermon to denouncing these icons on the grounds that they made the church less inclusive.[68] In a few years, at this rate, the church may experience a fate similar to that of many such buildings in the former Eastern Bloc: a sports auditorium, a repository for condom dispensing machines, or perhaps a museum of multiculturalism.[69]

Memorial Church's new mission focuses on social and political work, pursued with evangelical zeal—for example, writing sexual harassment policies on campus, organizing divestment efforts from South Africa, and providing sanctuary for potential conscientious objectors during the Persian Gulf War.[70] The new religion comes complete with new rites, totems, and holy places—and even pilgrimages to visit some of these places. In 1987, for instance, Thomas Ambrogi, then Acting Dean of the Church, in conjunction with the Reverend Herb Schmidt, the official campus Lutheran pastor, and graduate student Emily Goldfarb, organized a trip to reconstruct the National University in El Salvador, which had been damaged by an earthquake several months earlier. Stanford's Public Service Center helped 14 student participants raise $1,000 each, advertised as covering the costs of travel, room, board, and reconstruction materials. AGEUS, a student group with links to the Marxist FMLN guerrillas, who were then attempting to overthrow the Salvadoran government, hosted the Stanford delegation.[71] During the 10-day trip, the only earthquake relief occurred during a lunch break by regular construction workers; according to one participant, it was "little more than a photo opportunity."[72] Many of the student participants were genuinely surprised by this turn of events, as they had expected to do real relief work. Instead, they received a series of one-sided presentations, given by AGEUS, on the political situation in El Salvador. Law professor Thomas McBride summarized what happened: "The educational purposes of the trip may have been affected by efforts to indoctrinate or use the Stanford students as a propaganda symbol."[73]

The efforts of the official campus ministry closely resemble the social engineering pushed through the curriculum and Residential Education. A similar fanaticism seems to animate all of these drives; the only difference, perhaps, is that the religious dimension becomes more explicit in the case of Memorial Church's clerics. But even in the case of Stanford's nonclerical multiculturalists, the degree of ideological commitment seems to require something like a religious leap of faith.

The push for the new anti-Western religion extends well beyond Memorial Church. Every year, the holiday season becomes the occasion for a ritualized attack on Western religious traditions. *Stanford Daily* columnist Ashley Ryan's invocations about the evils of Christmas trees were not atypical:

> [M]any non-Christians feel alienated by having such a symbol in their residences....The Christmas tree must go....As Stanford sees itself as a leader in the struggle for multiculturalism, it needs to reach out and modify itself to the different religious communities on this campus.[74]

Ryan's reference to "multiculturalism" resonates strangely: Why would it not be more "multicultural" to include decorations from all religious traditions represented in a dorm, rather than from none? As with the debate over Western Culture, the multicultural regime never opts for genuine pluralism. The preferred solution always involves a community of belief that excludes the West.

Christmas trees do not represent a logical stopping point for these annual denunciations. At Stanford, almost any reference to the Judeo-Christian West is now experienced as *per se* oppressive and may invite reprobation. Even dorm gift givers (students who are paired up with others during the holiday season to give gifts) are no longer called "Secret Santas"—that reminded residents of Santa Claus, another symbol of

Christian oppression. The onetime "Secret Santas" have been renamed "Secret Snowflakes" or even, in one dorm, "Equally Accepting Nondenominational Gift Bearers." In the process, even a totally innocuous symbol of goodwill acquired a negative ideological connotation. If nothing else, one cannot help but wonder what sort of a childhood some of Stanford's multiculturalists must have had.

The New Puritanism

Given the stress the university places on the value of personal liberation, one might expect students to enjoy an unrivaled degree of freedom in personal matters—freedom to form social liaisons and to join different groups, freedom to explore a wide variety of sexual practices and partners, even the freedom to indulge in illegal drugs without fear of punishment. The multicultural academy would seem a world without restraints.

But liberation and freedom are not identical. As the multicultural treatment of religion indicates, the need for some to be liberated (from traditional mores or from Santa Claus, for example) implies a corollary need to restrict others' freedom (to use bathrooms unmolested or to display Christmas trees, for instance). And there are other areas where multicultural liberation limits rather than expands the freedom of students—where students' desire to have fun is given far less free rein than much of the rhetoric would seem to require.

Two closely related examples involve Stanford's troubled fraternity system and the dismal dating scene.[75] Once home to over 40 fraternities, the university has in recent decades reduced the fraternity presence to less than 10 houses.[76] (There are no housed sororities.) Less than a quarter of students now "go Greek," but despite declining numbers the system has remained the center of campus social life, with fraternities and sororities hosting parties open to the entire campus almost every weekend. Nevertheless, despite these parties' ability to facilitate social interaction and to increase "knowledge of the power of the mind" (to borrow Timothy Leary's words) through a liberation from sobriety, they have become a regular focus of attack.

In 1988, a "frat crackdown" began, as Fraternal Affairs Adviser Joe Pisano promised that he would take a "be good or be gone" tone with fraternities.[77] Since then minor infractions or even incidents unrelated to house activities have become cause for obloquy and quarter-long probations, as Stanford's administration has declared war on fraternities:

- In 1992, the Delta Kappa Epsilon fraternity received "a sharp warning" when an unknown assailant set fire to a tree outside their house and instigated other dangerous acts against members of the fraternity. While a similar attack on the homosexual or black community centers probably would have prompted an immediate university investigation, the fraternity was warned that if the danger continued, it would lose the house.[78]

- In 1992, the Sigma Chi fraternity was placed on social probation following a party in which its "Robin Hood" decorations were preposterously declared a "fire hazard."[79]
- In 1988, the University Task Force on Fraternities and Sororities effectively sought an end to the fraternity system by attempting to prohibit the "subjective selection" of students for housing.[80]

While alumni outcry has precluded outright elimination of housed fraternities, the university has prohibited unhoused fraternities from building new homes.[81] Since many fraternities are able to raise money from their national charters, the move would actually save the university money by reducing its housing obligations. Nevertheless, in a 1992 issue of the *Inter-Fraternity Council Newsletter*, Dean Michael Jackson censured fraternal housing, writing, "The notion of students excluding others from access to certain university housing for subjective reasons is one which the University does not seek to foster beyond what has already been grandfathered into the University's housing system."[82] Of course, there is no similar problem preventing Ujamaa or other ethnic theme houses from allocating housing based on "subjective reasons."

The animus against the Greek system, and the attempts to eliminate it, accompany more informal stigmatization of Greek students, with the usual hysterical denunciations. Thus, junior Jessica Bar attacked fraternities for sexism in a 1992 letter to the *Stanford Daily*. "Women, wake up!" she wrote. "These men for whom you are starving yourselves are the same ones who objectify you and dehumanize you, who judge you on the basis of your looks and condemn you for showing any signs of insurgency."[83] According to Matthew Moran, a black Inter-Fraternity Rush Chairman, members of the Black Student Union, MEChA (the Latino student group), and the Office of Residential Education dissuade freshmen from joining the Greek system.[84] Arturo Armenta, a member of both the Latino community and the Greek system, agreed that MEChA leaders "not only influence students to avoid Rush, they ingrain the idea that to become Greek is to become 'racist, sexist and homophobic.'"[85] Partly in response to "challenges from campus groups and the administration," sororities and fraternities in 1989 began to require that new members "attend workshops focused on discussing racism, sexism and homophobia."[86]

At first glance, the stigma attached to Greek social organizations is puzzling. Social interaction between men and women, of the kind found at campus-wide fraternity parties, date functions, or other Greek mixers, would seem like an absolutely necessary precondition for any kind of sexual revolution. But the need to liberate victims from the forces of oppression supposedly embodied in fraternities (racism, sexism, and homophobia) trumps such practical concerns. Multicultural opposition to the Greek system perfectly illustrates that the flip side of liberation for some (anti-Greek racial minorities, women, and homosexuals) is reduced freedoms for others (Greeks and those who attend Greek functions). For every social barrier removed in the name of liberation, Stanford's administration often imposes new restrictions elsewhere.

The new Puritanism sometimes manifests itself in open hostility to the dating scene. In 1987, for instance, Stanford's RAs and RFs started banning parties in which roommates would find one another blind dates. These parties represented a prime social opportunity for timid dorm residents to meet other students, to mix with the opposite sex (in short, to get a date), and to develop important social skills. Indeed, such events would seem essential if thousands of university-subsidized condoms are not to go to waste. But RA Jerilyn Mendoza explained that such events were baleful because they were based on heterosexual social interaction, which is "very uncomfortable to people who are gay and aren't out of the closet."[87] However innocuous a behavior may be, the new Puritans can rule it impermissible if it conflicts with the need to liberate protected minority groups.

Perhaps the most blatant contradictions between the values of liberation theology and the new Puritanism occur in the realm of sexual conduct. Multiculturalists are not always the defenders of sexual spontaneity on campus. Beginning in the fall of 1991, the Stanford community learned a great deal about the need to limit a new phenomenon called "date rape" when the university proposed a new sexual conduct policy. The policy was proposed after the release of an 18-month study by the Stanford Rape Education Project, which concluded that sexual assault was more pervasive at Stanford than most would have thought possible. On the basis of 70 questions asked each of 1,250 students, the study concluded that 26 percent of undergraduate women and 33.5 percent of graduate women had been sexually coerced. The numbers shocked even outside of Stanford: the *San Francisco Examiner* luridly headlined its article on the report "Date rape common on Stanford campus—33% of females forced to have sex."[88] According to the Rape Education Project's survey, not only had one in three women at Stanford had "full sexual activity when they did not want to," but one in eight men had been forced to have sex against their will. The numbers implied that sexual assault was vastly more common at Stanford than in the nation as a whole. (By contrast, an FBI study of 59,000 households conducted at the same time concluded that one in 1,000 women were raped each year.)[89]

As if to punctuate these numbers, a high-profile sexual assault case hit campus in the fall of 1991. Just as the proposed sexual conduct policy was spotlighting the date-rape problem, a 17-year-old freshman woman accused senior Stuart Thomas of sexually assaulting her in his dorm room (the name of the woman was withheld because she was a minor at the time of the incident). Within a few days, the news was all over campus: "Student reports sexual assault in Stern Hall room," "Reported rape stuns Stern Hall residents," announced front-page headlines in the *Stanford Daily*.[90]

After the concurrent shock of the rape statistics and the accusation of date rape faded, it soon became clear that the details of both were less concrete than initially publicized. In the Thomas case, it was soon discovered the young woman did nothing she did not consent to. She admitted to drinking eight shots of liquor under her own power. More important, the woman also told police that she never felt "any intimidation, fear, or threat" from Thomas. She consented to the act of sexual intercourse—twice—as well as to oral copulation. Her participation was active (according to the police report, she rubbed his back as he undressed her), and indeed, at one point while she was undressed she borrowed his robe, walked downstairs to the women's bathroom, and then returned to his second-floor room to continue the session.[91]

Upon reviewing the evidence, the district attorney realized that no jury would convict Thomas of rape and instead sought the lesser count of "illegal sex with a minor," or "statutory rape" (which does not involve the issue of consent, only age). Although Thomas was clearly guilty of serving alcohol to an underage woman and taking advantage of her resulting lack of judgment, there was no sexual assault. Had the incident occurred just a few weeks later, after the woman's eighteenth birthday, there would have been no case at all. Understandably, however, the woman regretted the whole incident afterwards. She, as much as Thomas, had accepted the multicultural dogma that "people are going to have sex anyway" and that "abstinence is simply not a viable option."

The particular symbolism of this incident, involving a victimized woman who complained about a white male, posed a poignant catch-22 for Stanford's multiculturalists. It was ideologically impossible for them to side with the man. But siding with the woman would require calling into question the kinds of promiscuous attitudes they advanced in so many other contexts.[92] After all, nothing happened between Thomas and the woman that was not encouraged by Timothy Leary and Dean Ramsey-Perez. Taking either side would undermine their political coalition. Given the extreme publicity this incident received, however, it could not just be swept under the rug. The multicultural coalition required a solution that would put the blame squarely on Thomas (the white heterosexual male) but would not require a rethinking of the broadly held attitudes about the desirability of the sexual revolution.

Stanford's multiculturalists solved this dilemma by shifting the focus of the woman's sexual assault charge. The woman told police that she had felt a "certain coercion" due to Thomas's size and "the smooth, persuading manner" in which he talked to her, and that her judgment was impaired due to the alcohol he had served her.[93] If the emphasis was placed on these circumstances, the sensational charge that the woman had been "coerced" into sex could overshadow the fact that she had consented. Since "coercion" was synonymous with rape, the rape charge against Thomas could still be justified (even if the district attorney did not prosecute), and it would thus be possible to avoid confronting the underlying moral questions. Careful observers, however, noted that this usage of "coercion" required a certain linguistic legerdemain. The definition of the word had subtly changed from meaning physical force to meaning nothing more than verbal persuasion.[94]

The Thomas case provides a microcosm of multicultural thinking about rape. In the Stanford Rape Education Project's survey, as in the Thomas case, the devil was in the details of its definition of "date rape," which told a somewhat different story than the shocking headlines. Eighty percent of the women and 93 percent of the men claiming to have been coerced into sexual activity did not label their experience as "rape." Only 10.6 percent of women who had been sexually coerced "definitely" considered their experience to be rape, and only 2 percent reported the incident to police.[95]

According to Rape Education Project spokeswoman Vivian Vice, "Women had been raped who really didn't even know they had been raped."[96] Dr. Alejandro Martinez, director of Stanford's Counseling and Psychological Services, explained this phenomenon by claiming that because most of these instances involved an acquaintance, it might be difficult for the victim to make sense of the situation. "It's ambiguous to them," Martinez stated. "They feel bad, but they don't know what they feel bad about."[97]

A more likely explanation, however, is that the other 89.4 percent did not understand the multicultural definition of "rape." In the Stanford survey, persistent argumentation alone was considered sexual assault. The survey never actually asked whether students had ever been raped, leaving that judgment to the organizers of the Rape Education Project, who presumably knew better. Instead the students were asked:

> Have you ever engaged in full sexual activity (defined as vaginal, anal or oral intercourse) with someone when you didn't want to because you were overwhelmed by his or her continual arguments and pressure? Because he or she

> gave you alcohol or drugs? Because he or she threatened or used some degree of force (twisting your arms, holding you down, etc.) to make you?[98]

Thus, a woman who does not consider herself a rape victim, but who regrets having been talked into engaging in sexual activity, qualifies as a rape victim. Once again, the Thomas case provides the model: His crime—seducing (or "coercing") a woman who was later regretful—fit the multicultural definition of rape precisely, even if it did not at all fit the legal definition. When verbal pressure means coercion and coercion means rape, then the number of rapes will become as large as the number of seductions that are later regretted.

The university's new sexual conduct policy is predicated upon the Rape Education Project's expansive definition of rape. The policy declares, "Sexual assault by force or coercion, including deliberate coercion through use of drugs or alcohol, is absolutely unacceptable at Stanford University." An employee of the Dean of Student's Office said that coercion could constitute "verbal pressure without threat" or being "belittled, shamed, or pressured, either verbally or emotionally" into an unwanted situation.[99] Doug Dupen, deputy director of Employee Relations and Human Resources Services, who had helped write the new policy, noted that the prohibited coercion was broader in scope than the category of "coercion through drugs or alcohol," and even suggested that it might include "a moonlit night on the beach."[100] President Kennedy further managed to blur distinctions by noting that "yes" might mean "no," when there was "even a hint of coercion" or a loss of normal capacity could be detected.[101]

One critic of what he calls the "rape crisis movement" is UC Berkeley professor of social welfare Neil Gilbert. Professor Gilbert notes:

> The estimates of sexual assault calculated by feminist researchers are advocacy numbers, figures that embody less an effort at scientific understanding than an attempt to persuade the public that a problem is vastly larger than commonly recognized....Under the veil of social science, rigorous research methods are employed to measure a problem defined so broadly that it forms a vessel into which almost any human difficulty can be poured....Among those who practice social advocacy, this is known as "consciousness raising" and is deemed a respectable function of advocacy numbers.[102]

While preventing sexual assault is a laudable and serious goal, the Rape

Education Project unfortunately has succumbed to the temptation Professor Gilbert described. Its findings are "advocacy numbers," not real facts.

The rape crisis movement transmits its exaggerated fears to freshmen yearly. One of the most carefully orchestrated orientation programs is "Sex in the '90s," a series of skits on health issues and rape prevention with such titles as "Nonoxynol-9," "The Right Time," and "The Party Zone."[103] In 1992, organizer Kathy Zonana announced to the audience that one out of every three Stanford women, and one out of every eight Stanford men, had been raped—perhaps in the hope that frequent repetition might make these numbers more credible.[104]

One telling skit even portrayed the morning after a "multicultural" date rape. The rapist did not realize he had committed rape the night before until he talked about the event to a friend. Similarly, the victim realized that she had been raped only after discussion with a confidant. "It must have been the alcohol," they both conclude. At the end of the skit, the victim was escorted to the hospital, and the confused rapist was left to ponder, and regret, his folly.[105]

Of course, it is ludicrous to believe that anyone who had been forcefully violated would not know it and bear physical marks. But since a multicultural rape charge may indicate nothing more than belated regret, a woman might "realize" that she had been "raped" the next day or even many days later. Under these circumstances, it is unclear who should be held responsible. If the alcohol made both of them do it, then why should the woman's consent be obviated any more than the man's? Why is all blame placed on the man?

The actions of campus feminists raised a similar question when, in addition to enacting a new sexual conduct policy, they launched a major effort to change the university's set of rules governing student conduct. Law professor Deborah Rhode sought to lower the threshold of proof for violations like rape from "beyond a reasonable doubt" to "by clear and convincing evidence."[106] Whereas the former standard requires a jury to be 99 percent sure of the defendant's guilt before convicting, the new standard would have required only about 60 to 70 percent certainty. For Professor Rhode and other activists, the solution to the crisis would require the increased prosecution and conviction of heterosexual males, even if the probability of falsely convicting innocent students would increase significantly.

Indeed, the purpose of the rape crisis movement seems as much about vilifying men as about raising "awareness." A pamphlet released by the Rape Education Project and distributed to freshmen begins to explain just how radical the manufacturers of the rape crisis are:

> Rape mythology is so pervasive that many men who

> participate in gang rapes or acquaintance rapes do not understand that they have committed rape. Assuredly, some of this is feigned ignorance, but perhaps some men don't understand the degree to which they have defined their sexuality as a need for unlimited sexual access. Too many men confuse sex with domination and control....Not all men rape, but a potential partner in a relationship can not assume that any man is incapable of rape.[107]

According to the rape crisis movement, all men have been socialized to be potential rapists, while most (if not all) women have been socialized into accepting a "culture of rape," in which they are nothing but objects of sexual abuse by men. Since women are trained to submit to men, no possibility of consent exists for one of the parties, and rape becomes intrinsic to all heterosexual relations. Because men are the oppressors and women are the victims, all the blame can be shifted to the former. Concludes Stanford feminist Adrienne Rich: "Only through lesbianism and complete rejection of men can women reclaim their self-esteem and control over their own lives."[108]

The rape crisis movement's ideological embrace of lesbianism is a point at which the new Puritanism and the new liberation theology meet. The new Puritanism is a bizarre kind of overreaction to some of the failures of the sexual revolution. As in the case of 1960s activists, multiculturalists claim that people should be liberated from the sexual restraints of the Western tradition. But when this liberation does not produce an erotic utopia of untrammeled satisfaction, Stanford's social engineers seek to avoid responsibility for some of the negative results—more unwanted pregnancies, more abortions, a greater number of AIDS cases, and above all, more instances of regret. So instead of blaming a failed ideology, they blame these problems on a mythical "culture of rape." This rape culture supposedly socializes men to be aggressors and women to submit helplessly.

This solution is highly imperfect, even for the multiculturalists. For if the only way to avoid confronting some of the difficulties with their sexual revolution is by infantilizing women, then it is not clear how the multiculturalists have helped women make any progress. If women are socialized to make irrational choices, as multiculturalists maintain, then why should any woman, including Adrienne Rich or Deborah Rhode, be given a serious hearing? Similar questions arise in the sexual realm. How do we know that women who regret having sex have not just been "socialized" (by Stanford's rape educators?) into thinking that they did not really "consent"? For that matter, if men are no less "socialized" than women, then why should they be held any more responsible?

By blaming interpersonal problems on a "culture of rape," the rape crisis movement misses the trees for the forest: The problem, to the extent there is one, is primarily on the level of the individual choices that are made in particular instances—like those of Stuart Thomas and the 17-year-old woman. But when individuals are simply "constructs," and their crimes and faults are blamed on society, every individual mistake vindicates the multiculturalists' *a priori* condemnation of the West and reaffirms the need for sweeping social reform. Stanford's social engineers believe that if they can just mix the right formula of programs, consisting of some combination of condom distributions, X-rated movies, and rape reeducation perhaps, then a sexual utopia will follow. Because all such recipes deny the reality of individual choice and the place for individual responsibility, their attempts to build a heaven on Earth produce even greater unhappiness.

The Multiculture

Long before the Stanford administration ever had heard of Stuart Thomas, the case of Allan Cox exposed where its heart really lies. Cox had been dean of Stanford's School of Earth Sciences since 1979, and was internationally known for developing theories of plate tectonics and continental drift. On January 27, 1987, Cox biked down a steep mountain path, raised his uncovered head over the handlebars, and smashed into a large tree. He died immediately, and the coroner later ruled the incident a suicide. Cox had learned four days earlier that the parents of a retarded 19-year-old boy had filed charges against him for allegedly molesting their son over the past five years. One of the parents had been Cox's graduate student during that time. The child had to undergo therapy, for which Cox agreed to pay just before his death.[109]

From the way Stanford's leaders vilified a 22-year old senior for a one-night stand with a woman (who was only a month away from 18, and in full possession of her faculties), one would think they would wholly cast out a dean who spent five years secretly molesting the teen-age mentally handicapped son of his graduate student. The highest levels of the administration, however, not only pardoned Cox's behavior, but glorified him. A crowd of 1,000 heard President Kennedy attest to the deceased pederast's "fineness":

> Reverence for nature, love of the land, respect for people. These are the qualities that stood out in Allan. Those of us who knew him know his fineness, know his compassion and commitment to others, and know that a generous and sensitive regard permeated all his human relationships. We loved him; we trusted him; and we still do.[110]

Stanford's leaders subtly shifted the blame to those members of the Stanford community who were not understanding or sensitive enough to Cox. Acting President Jim Rosse stated, "I do not believe he was capable of doing anything that could harm another human being."[111] Psychology professor Albert Hastorf, former provost, resolved that we should be more "sensitive," "understanding," and "supportive of each other."[112] Vice Provost Raymond Bacchetti told the *San Jose Mercury News*, "The complexity of human nature wrapped up in all of this we will never have any way of knowing."[113] Most outrageously of all, Stanford established the Allan V. Cox Medal to celebrate "Cox's vision of the potential for faculty-student partnership at a research university and his contributions at many levels of making the potential a reality."[114] Every year, faculty and graduating seniors receive a request to nominate a worthy colleague for the Allan Cox prize.

While Allan Cox was seen as complex but ultimately worthy of a medal, no such status was accorded Stuart Thomas. His everyday promiscuity—of the sort that the university encourages in numerous ways—was execrated. At the very least, this double standard suggests that multiculturalists are not really concerned with protecting people from sexual abuse. So if some sex at Stanford is good and other sex is bad, then what makes the difference? The answer is that sex—like religion, art, and gender relations more generally—has itself become a vehicle for the attack on the West. Sometimes, this attack takes the form of "liberation"—the promotion of homosexuality and of sexual exploration, for instance, or the condemnation of traditional mores. In others cases, the attack takes an almost Puritanical form—such as the manufactured rape crisis movement or Ann Simonton's rebuke of women in advertisements. Occasionally the new Puritanism and the sexual revolution can be combined—such as in the decisions by RAs to ban parties where roommates found one another dates (in order not to hurt the feelings of closeted homosexuals). The only common denominator that remains, when all is said and done, is the attack itself.

Just because the multicultural agenda is at times inconsistent does not mean that it is random. It follows a rigorous logic of its own. Earlier, we approximated the multicultural agenda by saying it was simply the agenda of 1960s radicals. But this is not quite right, for over the last three decades the 1960s agenda has evolved. Its evolution into the multicultural agenda of the 1990s has involved a broadening of scope. No longer is multiculturalism merely political, taught in classrooms and through books. If that were still the case, multiculturalists would promote a single ideology, be it either liberation theology or the new Puritanism (but not both). Something altogether different is at stake when multicultural leaders passionately advocate totally contradictory views in relatively similar contexts. Were multiculturalism simply ideological, moreover, the debate would have been over long ago. Numerous critics have revealed the multicultural agenda's logical leaps and internal contradictions—only to be nonplussed by its endurance. The dragon cannot be slain so easily, because multiculturalism is much more than a political philosophy, an intellectual system, or even a blueprint for the new academy.

The transformation of students in settings like bedrooms, chapels, and dining halls suggests that multiculturalism involves a significant social component. Or rather, multiculturalism is no longer a 1960s-style political agenda at all, but a cultural phenomenon. Multiculturalism has become coeval with an all-out assault on the West, whereby historical landmarks, social responsibilities, religious values, interpersonal relations, and even artistic merit as understood by a new culture seek to displace the same as understood by the old. The new culture of multiculturalism (or "multiculture") defines its own taboos, creates its own mythos, initiates its own rites of passage, and distributes its own social roles. It is in many ways a self-contradictory culture—one that advocates liberation from moral certitude and all other forms of authority, but maintains itself with maximum authority and certainty of belief. This contradiction runs through the heart of the multiculture, and so runs through its denizens, whose daily choices ultimately must sustain it. Like all cultural systems, it has a sacred core—a bundle of values, superstitions, and beliefs never articulated by its citizens but fiercely guarded nonetheless. To pierce this sacred veil is to occasion sacrilege. As we explore the core of multiculturalism in the second half of this book, we will take our chances.

Notes

1. Allan Bloom, "Educational Trendiness," *The Wall Street Journal*, January 26, 1989.

2. Brooke Hart, "SCAAN 'abducts' English professor, senior," *The Stanford Daily*, May 1, 1990.

3. *Ibid.*

4. Maria Saldana and Marcia Klotz, "Mock kidnappings dramatized fear felt by Salvadorans," *The Stanford Daily*, May 3, 1989.

5. Susan Mizner, "SCAAN accurately portrayed terror of Salvadoran life," *The Stanford Daily*, May 10, 1989. *See also* "Poor performance," *The Stanford Daily*, May 5, 1989. Not surprisingly, the "educational" efforts of Project Awareness, which was sponsored by the Stanford Central America Action Network (SCAAN), backfired. According to Otero House residents interviewed by the *Daily*, "For the past two days El Salvador has not been the subject of interest; SCAAN's tactics have."

6. Rick St. John, "First Amendment Controversy Shakes Donner," *The Stanford Review*, April 15, 1991.

7. *Ibid. See also* Kim McCreery, "Sexist, violent graffiti in dorm disturbs Donner residents," *The Stanford Daily*, April 5, 1991; and David Sacks, "Political Correctness Pervades Donner Incident," *The Stanford Review*, April 15, 1991.

8. *Ibid.*

9. McCreery, *supra* note 7.

10. *Ibid.*

11. *Ibid.*

12. *Ibid.*

13. St. John, *supra* note 6.

14. Mary Ann Seawell, "The Politics of Art," *The Stanford Observer*, May–June 1992.

15. "Be a Resident Fellow," *The Stanford Review*, February 3, 1992.

16 . Evan Porteus and Ann Porteus, "Roble Resident Fellows urge rethinking budget," *Campus Report*, April 18, 1990.

17 . Brian Gerber, "Staff position added to Row: Program assistants will help RAs, plan programs," *The Stanford Daily*, April 2, 1991.

18 . Kathleen O'Toole, "Residential Education at Stanford: Does It Have a Hidden Agenda?" *Stanford University News Service*, October 12, 1988.

19. *See* "An overused theme: The increasing number of theme houses seems to defeat their purpose," *The Stanford Daily*, April 5, 1993.

20. Theresa Johnston, "In 'focus houses,' students explore arts, gender, the '60s," *Campus Report*, January 6, 1993.

21. Nehrad Lal, "Robinson, Lantana and Castano each gain a

focus," *The Stanford Daily*, April 2, 1993.

22. *See* Angie Kim, "Ex-model decries gender stereotypes," *The Stanford Daily*, January 28, 1988.

23. *Ibid.*

24. Gerald Davis, "Minority Residential Assistants Share Experiences With Applicants," *Stanford University News Service*, March 20, 1990.

25. *Ibid.*

26. O'Toole, *supra* note 18.

27. Marcus Mabry, "A View From the Front," *Newsweek*, December 24, 1990.

28. *Ibid.*

29. O'Toole, *supra* note 18.

30. History professor Mark Mancall, an RF, admitted exactly this point: "Eventually, I think what happened is that Res Ed became a vested interest in itself. Although the University said it eschewed it, Res Ed itself became *in loco parentis*. Educating people about racism, sexism...became the *raison d'etre* of Res Ed." *See* Julie Makinen, "Res Ed at a crucial crossroads; Program tries to look ahead despite budget cuts, staff loss," *The Stanford Daily*, March 9, 1994.

31. Porteus and Porteus, *supra* note 16.

32. Angie Chuang, "A first for Mem Chu," *The Stanford Daily*, October 18, 1993.

33. *Ibid.*

34. *Ibid.*

35. *Ibid.*

36. Ed Malone, "Out of the closet, into the Church," *The Stanford Review*, May 9, 1994.

37. *See* Angel R. Puerta, "Gay commitment ceremony was insensitive to Catholics," *The Stanford Daily*, October 21, 1993.

38. Chuang, *supra* note 32.

39. An advertisement in the spring of 1987, for example, stated: "Gay and lesbian students are encouraged to apply for RA positions, as are all students who can foster constructive discussion about sexual preference." *The Stanford Daily*, April 2, 1987.

40. Davis, *supra* note 24.

41. "Increasing awareness," *The Stanford Daily*, April 22, 1993. Anoop Prakash, "BGLAD should include speakers representing contrasting viewpoints," *The Stanford Daily*, April 20, 1993.

42. Marie Bui and Cecilia Tom, "Queerland aims to add visibility to homosexuals," *The Stanford Daily*, February 1, 1991.

43. "For the Record," *The Stanford Review*, April 1989.

44. S.L. Wykes, "Statue of Stanford's first family waits in limbo,"

The San Jose Mercury News, May 1, 1994.

45. In addition to these benefits, the LGBCC receives about $7,000 per year from the Office of Student Activities. *The Daily* observed that "GLAS competed for limited funding with the myriad of other clubs and groups on campus." *See* Chris Shuttlesworth, "University funds combined center," *The Stanford Daily*, September 27, 1988; and Miranda Doyle, "LGBCC also wary of budget cutbacks," *The Stanford Daily*, January 10, 1994.

46. David Sacks, "Apologizing for Deviance," *The Stanford Review*, January 25, 1993.

47. David Bianco, "Taking the next step: being openly gay in a non-gay world," *The Stanford Daily*, October 11, 1990.

48. David Cuff, "Restroom Sex Complaints Prompt Meeting Between Gays, Police," *Gay and Lesbian Alliance at Stanford: GLAS*, April 7, 1985. According to a press release by the Gay and Lesbian Alliance, "Representatives of the University's gay and lesbian community met with Stanford police chief Marvin Herrington on Friday, April 5 [1985]; the gay leaders argued strongly against police intervention." According to gay activist David Cuff, arrests would be inappropriate because the publicity surrounding them would compromise the identities of homosexuals who are not out of the closet.

49. Hanna Rosin, "Rubber Ducky," *The Stanford Daily*, December 18, 1990. Kenneth Wang, "Free Speech and the X-Rating: *Salo* to Be Screened Tuesday," *The Stanford Review*, May 6, 1991.

50. *See*, for instance, Rajiv Chandrasekeran, "Basic Training," *The Stanford Daily*, December 5, 1990.

51. Ken Ruebush, "Stanford Students Plan Workshops on Safer Sex," *Stanford University News Service*, March 31, 1987.

52. Chandrasekaran, *supra* note 50.

53. One suspects that students who could not afford to pay 50¢ for a condom would have more important worries than obtaining cheaper condoms.

54. University Housing Operations Advisory Committee Chairperson Marni Lum explained: "We decided that condom dispensers are a good idea...and therefore should be made readily available to students in the residences, and equally available to both men and women." Those residences that did not install machines would be "dealt with," she said. Ken Yew, "Residences to get condoms in bathrooms," *The Stanford Daily*, January 12, 1988.

55. Lara Filson, "Condom sales are sluggish," *The Stanford Daily*, November 30, 1988. In a five-week period, 82 condom machines had sold a total of 432 condoms. Student Housing Operations manager Suzanne Tamiesie explained that despite the slow sales, the machines

would not be removed. The machines were proposed not to make money, but to "make a loud and direct message" to students, Tamiesie admitted.

56. Tom Bethell, "Festive Foolery," *The Stanford Review*, June 9, 1987.

57. Mike Newman, "Condoms Spread Controversy," *The Stanford Review*, February 1989.

58. *Ibid.*

59. *Ibid.*

60. Jordan Seng, "Stanford Abortions Exceed National Rate: Unwanted pregnancies continue despite educational efforts," *The Stanford Review*, April 1989.

61. Precise data on AIDS deaths are not provided by the Stanford administration, but the indirect evidence suggests that the numbers are relatively high. At an exposition of the Names Project (commemorating AIDS victims) in Stanford's Memorial Auditorium in February 1988, 25 people with a Stanford connection were listed. The list included English professor Donald Howard, librarian David Thompson, and alumni Steven Block, Gerald Martin, Jay Spears, John Trowbridge, and Mark Zambrano. According to Daniel Bao, it was difficult to find the names of campus AIDS victims, but "it's safe to say that the number of people being honored were less than half of the people at Stanford who have died of AIDS." If, as Bao claims, over 50 members of the Stanford community had died of AIDS by early 1988, the proportion would be truly astronomical: With 13,000 students and faculty and staff of about 7,000, over 1 person in 400 would have died of AIDS. By comparison, in early 1988, the nationwide death toll was about 60,000—less than 1 person in 4,000. *See* Burke Smith, "University remembers AIDS victims," *The Stanford Daily*, February 19, 1988. A more recent indicator occurred in October 1993, when the Cowell Student Health Center considered ending HIV counseling by doctors because of the drain on resources. During 1992, Cowell had counseled 600 people on HIV. *See* Cathy Siciliano and Julie Tsai, "New director of Cowell to face budget, staff ills," *The Stanford Daily*, October 18, 1993.

62. Cynthia Benton, "It's a trip: Conference probes history, culture of drug use," *The Stanford Daily*, February 4, 1991.

63. *Ibid.*

64. *Ibid.*

65. *Ibid.*

66. *Ibid.*

67. Mike Langford, "A multicultural church," *The Stanford Daily*, February 10, 1993.

68. Monique VanderMarck, "Mem Chu should be a place where

everyone can worship," *The Stanford Daily*, February 24, 1993.

69. Perhaps one reason why Memorial Church has not yet experienced this fate is its importance to alumni fundraising. In 1993, the *Stanford Observer*, an alumni magazine, featured the church on its cover. The story gave alumni, many of whom remember the ornate institution fondly, a grossly exaggerated impression of its importance to campus life.

70. Cecilia Tom, "Student seeks 'sanctuary' designation for Stanford," *The Stanford Daily*, January 25, 1991.

71. Joseph Green, "El Salvador trip controversial," *The Stanford Review*, June 9, 1987.

72. *Ibid.*

73. *Ibid.*

74. Ashley Ryan, "Religious intolerance," *The Stanford Daily*, December 7, 1988.

75. *See*, for instance, Jeff Brock, "Say What? Dating at Stanford? Not!" *The Stanford Daily*, September 19, 1991.

76. Michael Ehrman, "The Sudden Tumbling of Our Greek System," *The Stanford Review*, October 11, 1993.

77. Eric Young, "Frat crackdown in works," *The Stanford Daily*, October 10, 1988.

78. Leigh Burnside, "Dekes get a sharp warning on house: They'll lose it if danger continues," *The Stanford Daily*, March 11, 1992.

79. Kimberly Chrisman, "Sigma Chis placed on social probation," *The Stanford Daily*, January 14, 1992.

80. Theresa Johnston, "Task Force Recommendation May Change the Way Housed Fraternities Choose Their Members," *Stanford University News Service*, February 16, 1988.

81. Sally Shuper, "Unhoused frat makes third plea for housing: AEPi's ask to take over existing house," *The Stanford Daily*, April 15, 1992.

82. Adam Ross, "Beta, Delta Upsilon ready to return: University's commitment to Greek system challenged," *The Stanford Review*, May 17, 1993.

83. Jessica Bar, "Women urged to make their own voices heard," *The Stanford Daily*, March 11, 1992.

84. Matthew Moran, "Stereotyping of Greeks as racist, sexist unfair." *The Stanford Daily*, March 2, 1992.

85. Arturo Armenta, "Individuals in MEChA do harbor anti-Greek sentiment," *The Stanford Daily*, March 31, 1992.

86. Suzanne Corkins, "Greeks to attend diversity discussion," *The Stanford Daily*, May 23, 1989.

87. Davis, *supra* note 24.

88. Carl Irving, "Date rape common on Stanford campus," *The San Francisco Examiner*, February 7, 1991.

89. *See* Rick St. John, "Cal professor calls rape stats inflated," *The Stanford Review*, January 21, 1992.

90. Peter Robison, "Student reports sexual assault in Stern Hall room," *The Stanford Daily*, September 25, 1991. Miranda Doyle and Andy Dworkin, "Reported rape stuns Stern Hall residents," *The Stanford Daily*, September 27, 1991. *See also* Louis Freedberg, "'Acquaintance Rape' Charged at Stanford," *The San Francisco Chronicle*, November 3, 1991.

91. Minal Hajratwala, "Coercion or consent? Alleged assault blurs definition of rape," *The Stanford Daily*, October 7, 1991.

92. Each year, for example, Stanford distributes to new female students *A Woman's Guide To Stanford*, which urges: "As women, we should feel comfortable about initiating sex, stating clearly and confidently what we want and don't want in sexual relationships with men, asking men to assume equal responsibility for communication in a relationship and exploring the meaning of our sexuality with the men in our lives." *A Woman's Guide to Stanford*, 1993–94

93. Hajratwala, *supra* note 91.

94. *Stanford Daily* columnist Jane Lin, for example, wrote: "Sexual coercion can be subtle or unconscious, and its impact long-lasting." See Jane Lin, "Of coercion and consent," *The Stanford Daily*, April 14, 1992.

95. Lisa Koven and David Sacks, "Rape at Stanford," *The Stanford Review*, January 21, 1992.

96. *Ibid.*

97. Mary Ann Seawell, "Men, Women Interpret Sexual Behavior Differently, Survey Finds," *Stanford University News Service*, February 5, 1991.

98. *Ibid.*

99. Koven and Sacks, *supra* note 95.

100. *Ibid.*

101. Jonathan Eisenberg, "Kennedy makes statement on rape," *The Stanford Daily*, May 15, 1990.

102. Neil Gilbert, "The Phantom Epidemic of Sexual Assault," *The Public Interest*, Spring 1991.

103. Jeanne Im, "Frosh confront date-rape in 'Sex in the 90s,'" *The Stanford Review*, October 5, 1992.

104. *Ibid.*

105. *Ibid.*

106. Holly Hacker, "Guilt standards perplex many," *The Stanford Daily*, November 8, 1991. *See also* Holly Hacker, "Some profs support lowered proof level," *The Stanford Daily*, December 12, 1991.

107. *See* Koven and Sacks, *supra* note 95.

108. Adrienne Rich, *Compulsory Heterosexuality and Lesbian Experience* (London, England: Onlywomen Press, 1981).

109. Lisa Lapin, "Was death a suicide born of sex probe?" *The San Jose Mercury News*, January 30, 1987.

110. Bob Beyers, "1,000 Attend Memorial Services for Cox," *Stanford University News Service*, February 4, 1987.

111. *Ibid.*

112. *Ibid.*

113. Lapin, *supra* note 109.

114. "Cox Medal will honor faculty who foster undergrad research," *Campus Report*, April 15, 1992.

Part II:

The New Culture

5

Stages of Oppression

In the 1960s, they told us coercion was a terrible thing and that you shouldn't coerce people, but now you will be coerced if you go to Stanford if you use language inappropriate to the American left.[1]

—Speaker of the House Newt Gingrich

As we turn to consider what the multiculture is, it is worth recalling what multiculturalism is not. Multiculturalism is neither relativist nor particularly diverse, even if the rhetoric about relativism and diversity occasionally leads to bizarre behavior on the part of the various actors. Nor is it especially helpful to describe multiculturalism as 1960s-style leftism, for this does not tell us what leftism has become since the 1960s or why leftism is good or bad. More generally, perhaps, a focus on intellectual issues can be misleading because multiculturalism is a cultural phenomenon. If multiculturalism were merely (or even primarily) an esoteric branch of academia, then it could be contained in elite universities and would not pose much of a threat to America.

A good place to begin trying to understand this new culture is with its obsession, apparent even to a very superficial observer, with victimization. Played out in myriad variations, the recurrent theme is the need to rehabilitate and make whole perceived victims, to undo present and historical injustices. The multicultural movement perceives itself as a radical improvement upon the cultures of the past, and Western culture in particular. Like Hegel's owl of Minerva, multiculturalism promises to bring forth a new consciousness, so as to transcend and overcome history: In the new society, there will no longer be victims and victimizers, only persons.

The multiculture is the means towards that new society. It

determines what kinds of distinctions are important, defines groups according to these criteria, and then divides people into groups, each according to his victimization. Once people have been so identified, it is hoped, concrete remedies may be offered to ensure the equal treatment of the members of each group in relation to those of all other groups. This diverse collection of groups and the ways in which they understand themselves and interact with one another constitute the new multiculture. Beneath the superficial diversity of the multiculture, therefore, also lurks a deep conformity: The divisions between all of these different groups are predicated upon a consensus regarding the propriety of these divisions. For the multiculture to work, everybody (or at least a large majority) must agree on what kinds of diversity should count for how much.

Perhaps all cultures require this type of consensus. In the Middle Ages, for instance, Western societies took as their reference the Great Chain of Being—a hierarchical ordering of Nature, with God and the angels at the apex. Just as the multiculture seeks to identify people's stations in relation to their victimization, medieval culture sought to identify people's stations in relation to the divine order. The king served as the living equivalent of God, and presided over a descending hierarchy of nobles, knights, clerics, townspeople (ordered into guilds of butchers, shoemakers, tailors, smiths, bakers, and so forth), peasants, and serfs. There were further subdivisions: Within each guild, for example, there would be a master craftsman, more junior craftsmen, and various apprentices. In this respect, medieval culture was more diverse than modern society, because no two persons ever could occupy the exact same position. Under the medieval regime (and its successor, mercantilism), these divisions guaranteed each person a unique niche; peace could be maintained by preventing people from competing against one another directly.

The diversity of medieval culture did not result in any genuine individuality, however. Even though each person's role was different from every other's, the set of differences (which added up to the medieval society) was itself closely circumscribed. As with multicultural diversity, medieval diversity depended on a deep conformity. People had to agree that the human world was divided into different groups (shoemakers, bakers, etc.) and that each of these groups performed its proper function only so long as it stayed in its proper place. The differences between groups could be maintained only if the members understood themselves to be truly different from the members of other groups. A shoemaker could not become a baker, and a baker could not become a shoemaker. For the most part, these stations were determined at birth: One could not choose to become a shoemaker, and one certainly could not choose to become the king. In practice, of course, the medieval order and the divine right of kings were not guaranteed by God, but depended on the unquestioning agreement of many (if not all) of each kingdom's subjects. When sufficient numbers of people started to challenge the Great Chain of Being and the related notion that each person occupied some well-defined place in the human world (and, indeed, that such well-defined places even existed), the social fabric of medieval society inevitably disintegrated.

The predominant line of thinking about contemporary cultural debates and conflicts in America is radically incomplete because it focuses on the superficial diversity of the multicultural movement but ignores the deeper conformity. The tack of most conservatives, as well as some traditional liberals, has been to denounce multiculturalism for focusing excessively on difference—and thus for being inimical to the common ground on which the educational process and, for that matter, any community must stand. All of these critics have compared multiculturalism to a kind of tribalism, which dissolves the cultural understandings that cement our polyglot society and which therefore threatens us with the sort of perpetual strife faced by other societies torn by ethnic or nationalist hatreds. Multiculturalism, they say, increasingly emphasizes differences over commonality, deconstructs cultural icons one by one, and defines groups in ever narrower and more precise terms. These critics have suggested that the logical conclusion of multicultural identification is a sort of extreme individualism. In the limiting case, each individual becomes his (or her) own multicultural group, judged by his own standards and evaluated on his own terms. Social life becomes either impossible or unbearable.

According to the critics, then, a "multicultural community" (at least of the sort envisioned at Stanford) involves something of an oxymoron, because no common elements are left in a society where every person is given free rein to be as different as he or she desires. And for these critics, conservative and liberal alike, the response to multiculturalism will require individuals to sacrifice parts of their identities into a collectivist "melting pot"—so that the larger American society can return to a more homogeneous, functioning whole.

We have serious reservations about the prescriptive aspects of such a response and doubt whether it is desirable or even possible—a point to which we return in the final chapter. But for the moment, we merely observe that the descriptive premise—that multicultural identification may be equated with extreme individualism—is simply false.

At Stanford, multicultural diversity has simply not led to extreme individualism. While extremely destructive in many ways, multiculturalism has not had precisely that kind of corrosive or fragmenting effect. The transformation of the curriculum (as we saw in chapter 3) and of extracurricular life (chapter 4) has been sweeping and unified. There were certain debates and controversies, but these pitted multiculturalists against everyone else—the CIV protestors versus recalcitrant faculty, for instance, or feminists versus heterosexual males. The multicultural advocates, in spite of all their cherished differences, proved remarkably cohesive and capable of cooperating with one another. More generally, the multicultural community meets challenges in a united way that quickly restores a consensus for multicultural "diversity"; there is no epidemic of strife among the various multicultural tribes. But the paradox remains: If the critics are mistaken in their diagnosis, then what is it exactly that holds the "multiculture" together?

We have already hinted at the answer. The Great Chain of Being, while hostile to genuine individuality, both effectively defined each person as his own group and held medieval society together for centuries. A very similar sort of "unity in diversity" (to borrow from the OMD's declaration of purpose) animates the new multicultural society.

Like the medieval social hierarchy, the carefully calibrated differences multiculturalism devises are not a threat to the continued survival of a unitary culture; this system of differences *has become* the new culture. If this diversity actually had preexisted the multiculture, then it might pose some real challenges because there would be no guarantee that the new culture could accommodate all of those who are truly different. But multicultural diversity is not natural in origin. The multiculture does not wake people up to long-ignored "diversity" that already exists within themselves and is just waiting to be discovered; it generates that diversity itself. The forging of this diversity is coeval with the genesis of the multicultural community. (As we shall see in the final chapter, this dangerous new culture is gradually reshaping American life and is increasingly becoming the dominant culture.)

Ultimately, the conventional understanding of multiculturalism does not really come to terms with the problem of how something like the multiculture may exist or work, or even get off the ground in the first place. Although the multiculture appears to be organized around the fault lines of race, gender, and sexual orientation, its real problem lies not with excessive diversity or individuality, but with conformity. For the multiculture to operate, individuals must sacrifice the freedom to determine their own paths in life and become actors in a larger communal drama.

Creating Difference

In late September of each year, 1,500 eager freshmen descend upon Stanford for a five-day "Freshman Orientation," to be introduced to their classmates and to campus life more generally, and to find their place in the new community. Before the freshmen arrive, their respective RFs and RAs have already memorized their names and photographs. They are greeted with balloons and screams, promptly handed schedules with long lists of orientation activities, and instructed to participate in a series of icebreaker games. After dinner, the Leland Stanford Junior University Marching Band careens through the dorms, announcing itself with a boisterous cacophony of blasting trumpets and drumbeats. The freshmen do not hesitate to join the band's raucous rally, and begin what will be the first of many celebrations.

But "the Farm" (as Stanford is known to undergraduates) is not always the Norman Rockwell image of rustic beneficence. Orientation also is the first stage on which the multicultural dramas of oppression are acted out, and in this sense these first few days well prepare freshmen for some of the trials and tribulations of their next four years.[2] The tone grows particularly serious when orientation leaders turn to diversity "programming." A process of differentiation begins with special events for minority students, sponsored by the Asian American New Student Orientation Committee, the Black Recruitment and Orientation Committee, the Chicano/Latino Orientation Committee, and the Native American Orientation Committee. Minority freshmen are invited to attend a variety of receptions, banquets, organizational meetings, beach trips, and panel discussions on "minority issues."[3] These logistical differences in activities soon lead to real barriers, as students become friends with other students from their particular groups. Within several weeks, many dining hall tables become self-segregated, as students eat their meals with others they have come to know from the same race.

What begins as a number of receptions and programs to make minorities feel welcome at Stanford quickly separates the freshman class along racial lines. "Within my first ten minutes at Stanford, I began to see the University dividing itself into separate groups," remarked freshmen Benji Jenkins, upon observing in 1989 that exclusive signs such as "Welcome Black" helped to segregate minority students from other freshmen.[4] Orientation's emphasis on differences can sometimes be so overpowering as to *disorient* new students. Recalling one such experience, freshman Brady Mickelson described "Faces of the Community," an orientation program designed to introduce the 1993 freshman class to Stanford's "diverse" student population:

> Professor James Adams, head of the VTSS CIV track, led us on a literal safari. He prefaced his remarks with the comment that "orientation is designed to disorient you." Then the fun began. Dividing us into groups by last names, he asked that we assume the voice of an animal—G through L, an ape; M through S, a seal, etc. Then, on his cue, we made our animal's sound at the top of our lungs. The resulting cacophony was likened to our lives

> as members of the Stanford community: "By the time you leave Stanford, you should be completely disoriented," declared Adams.[5]

The claims of racial difference are broadcast to all students. Thus, orientation features as "a celebration of cultural heritage and political will" a theatrical production called *The Fire Within*, sponsored by the Asian American Student Association, the Black Student Union, MEChA, and the Stanford American Indian Organization.[6] For two hours, freshmen watch a series of dances and plays with ethnic themes—such as a Pueblo hoop dance, scenes from *Paper Angels* (a play about mistreatment of Chinese immigrants in the 1910s), Ballet Folklorico (a Chicano dance troup), and the Kuumba Dance Ensemble (Kuumba is Swahili for "creativity"). The dancers attempt to get students to "understand what being African is, or what being African-American is."[7] These performances are punctuated with the reminder that "the culture and politics of students of color cannot be separated."[8] At the end of one year's events, representatives from the United Stanford Workers' Union—whose members, the audience was reminded, are mostly Hispanic—asked for student help in upcoming contract negotiations with the university.[9]

Further differentiation along ethnic and gender lines is reinforced in subsequent years. On the academic front, there are separate departments and courses ("Black Hair," "Group Communications") and special events that celebrate and reinforce these differences, such as Stanford Law School's "Women of Color and the Law" conference. In extracurricular matters, separate deans and ethnic centers exist to meet the supposedly very specialized needs of "students of color." There are even separate commencement ceremonies for Chicanos, Asian Americans, Native Americans, and African Americans.[10] It is not inconceivable that a minority student, if so inclined, could spend all four years at Stanford without ever eating, living, speaking, or graduating with someone from a different race.

For those who may be of such a mind, Stanford provides separate racial residences (Ujamaa for blacks, Casa Zapata for Hispanics, Muhwekmataw-ruk for American Indians, and Okada for Asian Americans).[11] These racial theme dorms have the effect of removing a large number of minority students from the rest of the university. Much of the activity in these dorms revolves around "racial programming," in which special events are held to celebrate each race's unique differences. Invariably, members of racial minorities claim to gain a special appreciation (or *gnosis*) for what it means to be of that minority group. And, not surprisingly, such racial theme dorms often become rather uncomfortable places for the few students forced to live there who are not members of the preferred group—that is, those whose identities are not specially celebrated. "Some residents who are not members of a theme house's ethnicity," the *Stanford Daily* observed, "become more alienated and isolated as a result."[12] For multiculturalists, however, such discomfort is a sign of success. Because they believe themselves to be restoring real identities (rather than creating new ones), such discomfort becomes further evidence of the successful rediscovery of a real difference that more mainstream society had ignored for too long.

Naturally, claims of ethnic difference and special needs are translated into demands for minority-based services. Thus, at one demonstration against racism, Octavio Pedroza of MEChA repeated familiar demands:

> A multicultural education is an education that insures that students of color at Stanford feel comfortable and respected, not singled out or ostracized because of their differences....How can we make this happen? Our community centers and theme houses must be strong. They are integral in creating an atmosphere on this campus where we can come together, talk and organize ourselves. That's why we are demanding a full-time dean, and increased staffing and resources for El Centro Chicano. Our center, like all university departments, should receive the adequate care, maintenance and respect that it deserves. Yet, with a half-time dean and few resources, the university is clearly showing its lack of commitment to the diversity we so often hear about.[13]

Pedroza's talk does not bring to mind the 1960s civil rights efforts at racial integration or school desegregation. Instead, it suggests a different approach—only if racial groups separate themselves from the rest of the community, secure in the blanket of university largesse, will they be able to "feel comfortable and respected...because of their differences."

There are few specifics on what exactly is so "different" about these groups, or how society is suppressing these "differences." Perhaps these details are missing because, upon their arrival at the university, most minority students are not nearly as different as the multiculturalists like to pretend. As with nonminority Stanford students, most minority students come from intact homes (that is, fairly traditional two-parent families), are from middle- to upper-middle-class backgrounds, and have families that placed a considerable stress on the value of education—likely the reason they achieved the academic success in high school needed for admission. Most minority admits have led lives similar to those of other prospective Stanford students: relatively tough academic classes, sports, a range of school clubs, participation in student government. They watched the same movies and TV shows. "Studies were done...showing that something like two-thirds of the black students from Stanford went to predominantly white high schools," explains Senior Hoover Fellow Thomas Sowell, "and so the notion that you've now got to create an enclave in which you're dealing with people who came from the South Seas or almost from another planet is just fraudulent."[14]

Although some minority students had different kinds of precollege experiences—for instance, growing up in South Central Los Angeles or the slums of Mexico City—they are very few in number. An unusual admission of this fact was made by *Stanford Daily* columnist Delia Ibarra, who complained about the low number of inner-city Hispanic students at Stanford:

> The thing I found most startling when I came here was how few people were like me....My problem with Stanford diversity is that there really isn't much diversity at all. We have a wide assortment of students of color; the numbers are quite impressive. Eight percent are Chicanas and Chicanos. But there are almost no students of color from the inner city.[15]

Ibarra's observation raises some interesting questions: If most minority students share backgrounds similar to those of most white students, then why is there a need for separate racial theme dorms? Why does orientation exaggerate differences that were almost nonexistent upon students' arrival at Stanford? Along these lines, one begins to realize that Pedroza's causation is backwards: Multicultural minorities do not need to be separated because they are different, but can become different only after they have been separated.

Creating Identity

The accentuation of differences between groups has a counterpoint in the forging of identity within groups. Or, to frame the matter in Dr. Sowell's terms: If one is going to try to convince others that one is "dealing with people...from another planet," then it would be helpful for all of the people from that other planet to be different in exactly the same way.

Since not all minority members think or act the same, however, multiculturalists have found it necessary to redefine what it means to be a member of a minority group. This process can be quite Orwellian. The *Real News*, a student newspaper published intermittently by the Black Student Union, went so far as to declare that many people with black skin were not really "Black." The editors explained that racial identity is "not a biological actuality." Other criteria were also necessary to qualify for membership in the "Black" community (the newspaper used the uppercase "B" to distinguish from mere membership in the lowercase "black" community):

> *Black, we will define, as not a state of melanin but a state of mind.* The state of mind of one realizing that she or he is in a local culture that systematically negates the humanity of Blacks....We assert that by accepting the system on its own terms, and by aspiring to the goals of wealth and over-consumption (the white aesthetic), which are only possible at the expense of the American inner cities and the people of third world countries, is to be in a white consciousness (more descriptively, a western oppressive consciousness) and therefore by definition, *not* Black. If you believe in an ideology and think in a manner that benefits whites at the expense of Blacks, then you, by definition, cannot be Black....
>
> The factor of melanin is only significant in that it fosters the forming of the Black consciousness, that it is because of melanin that one will be persecuted and conceived of as the "conceptual other" to our western culture definition of the human; but melanin alone does not constitute Blackness, and is no free pass. The consciousness is all.[16] (emphasis in original)

The editors' key distinction is between uppercase "Blacks" (who also have the proper politics) and lowercase "blacks" (who meet only the biological qualifications). Lowercase "blacks" do not count because they are trapped within the "white aesthetic," have accepted "a western oppressive consciousness," and have thereby forsaken their racial identity. Conversely, uppercase "Blacks" possess the proper consciousness and may speak for the group. Because they are a far more homogeneous group than blacks as a whole, uppercase "Blacks" can purport to have a distinct racial identity.

The special identities of multicultural minorities, then, are not based solely on a birthright. They also entail a complex of social values and political views. The most important of these views is that racial minorities, women, and homosexuals face deep-seated discrimination. Spanish and Portuguese professor Sylvia Wynter, for example, is one who defines the "Black" identity in terms of oppression. Professor Wynter contends that American society is primarily ordered by race, with white and black at the extremes: "The real distinction is between black and white... .This basic difference...functions for our order as the difference between the celestial and the terrestrial functioned for the feudal order."[17] Whites, she says, derive their identity by discriminating against blacks: "Through the negation of black, they can imagine themselves as white, as a sacred body of people."[18]

Out of suffering, in turn, blacks supposedly developed their own race consciousness. Since every victim of racism must have a victimizer, the new identities necessarily are defined in terms of the relation between oppressor and oppressed. Along these lines, *Stanford Daily* columnist Omar Wasow defined the new racial identity "blackness" in relation to its opposite, "whiteness":

> Now that I am more attuned to blackness, I am beginning to see whiteness as well. Spotting blackness in this country is easy: it is focused, visible and different. Whiteness, in contrast, is like air: it's everywhere yet no one can see it....In order for white people in this country to grow beyond their contemporary strains of bias and bigotry they must also see whiteness. Not whiteness just as skin color, but whiteness as culture, history and politics. Whiteness as the experiences and privileges that fairer people have in this society."[19]

Thus, while whites derive their identity from racial privilege, the unique *gnosis* accompanying "blackness" is forged from discrimination. Neither identity can exist in a vacuum. Just as day cannot exist without night, "whiteness" cannot exist without "blackness," and vice versa. Wasow's comments indicate that Professor Wynter could equally well have framed her principle the other way around: Through the negation of white, individuals like Wasow (or the editors of the *Real News*) can imagine themselves as Black, as a sacred body of people.

Individuals like Wasow can discover their group identities (or achieve "consciousness") only when they start thinking of their lives as experienced in opposition to some form of oppression. Once identity is conceived in such a way, it tends to become self-reinforcing. Tension between individuals of different races can become evidence of pervasive discrimination, and even the most insignificant setbacks can be taken as confirmation of one's oppressed status—of deep structures within society that are conspiring against one's success. Multicultural Educator Greg Ricks explained to the *Stanford Daily* how it all worked: "I started looking for racism everywhere, and I found it everywhere."[20] Kwame Anku, a 21-year old junior, also saw racism in unlikely places: "There's been a systemic misdiagnosis" by economists, psychologists and others in the humanities of the significance of deep-seated racism in the shaping of

American culture, he told the *San Francisco Chronicle.* "We're saying, hey look, blacks are not responsible for destroying the planet or laying off 150,000 people at IBM. But the culture is trapped in a mythology that would lead people to come to those conclusions."[21] Anku did not give any examples of such people, likely because no one has ever blamed blacks (or Blacks) exclusively or even primarily for layoffs at IBM or for "destroying the planet." Perhaps it would be more accurate to say that Anku was trapped in a mythology that led *him* to believe that people reached those conclusions.

Casa Zapata RF Cecilia Burciaga even kept a diary of racist episodes. Like Greg Ricks, she looked for racism everywhere and claimed to have found it everywhere. She called her anecdotes "all very small daily daggers one feels in the environment."[22] Some of these "daily daggers" included:

> One student told to shut up by a parent who was in the audience because he was translating a speech that Don Kennedy was making, from English to Spanish to some parents so the parents could understand.
>
> One very senior administrator, more concerned about asking over and over again why a minority student was admitted, rather than how you were going to help that minority student.
>
> Stanford tour guide refusing to take a group by a theme house because he felt the group wouldn't in fact be interested in that theme house anyway.[23]

There are numerous possible explanations for why any of these minor incidents occurred. But when oppression is perceived as ubiquitous, the most unintentional slight towards someone who happens to be a member of a minority becomes a painful reminder of racism. To the extent that multiculturalists simply read too much into these episodes, the psychological wounds of these "daily daggers" are self-inflicted. But they also receive something in return: By turning each episode into testimony of the prevalence of oppression, they bolster their victim status. Since a belief in their own oppression is the cornerstone of the new racial identity, these self-created episodes thus serve the useful purpose of reaffirming their identities.

Race and "Institutional Racism"

Race has always been an American obsession. No doubt the greatest injustices perpetrated in the history of America were committed against racial minorities: the enslavement of blacks, the second-class status of Mexicans and Asians for many years, not to mention the outrageous mistreatment of American Indians during the 16th through the 19th centuries. The awkward notion that each black person counted for three-fifths of a white person, a compromise between slave and free states during the writing of the Constitution, suggests that the founding of the Republic was far from complete. The troubled racial past serves as a reminder that this nation has not always lived up to the lofty ideals expressed in the Declaration of Independence concerning the inalienable rights of each individual.

In the 1950s and 1960s, the civil rights movement sought to end racism once and for all. Jim Crow laws were abolished, and most forms of racial discrimination were made illegal; new opportunities opened for nonwhites. The dream of a color-blind society attributed to Martin Luther King appeared within reach. Even more significantly, perhaps, the vast majority of the population properly came to see racism as a great evil, or at the very least an unacceptable sin of blind ignorance. The awareness of history promised a genuine break with the past, as those who could learn from the racist legacy would not be doomed to repeat it.

In recent years, however, race relations have taken a turn for the worse. King's dream is rarely mentioned, and the races remain divided. The reasons for this division have changed drastically, however. As paradoxical as it may seem, the extreme focus on racism has become the source of much acrimony, as multiculturalists charge whites with more evanescent and intangible forms of racism, such as "institutional racism" or "unconscious racism." As a result, the awareness of racism, once the main hope for ending racial division, today has become a major cause of debate and friction.

Events at Stanford, ever on the cutting edge of the debate, indicate the bizarre new direction in which thinking about race and racism in this country may be headed. The Ujamaa incident (involving the dispute over Beethoven's skin color) was not the first of its kind. Several months earlier, an even stranger "racial incident" had shaken Otero House, another Stanford residence. What is most notable about the Otero episode is that it would appear to a casual observer to have had nothing whatsoever to do with race.

It all began when freshman Kenny Ehrman allegedly called his RA, who was openly homosexual, a "faggot." Ehrman claimed to have made the remark behind the closed door of his own dorm room in Otero, and not to the RA about whom he was complaining. But that did not matter. On Friday, May 20, 1988, he was kicked out of university housing for "homophobic actions."[24] The RA, Jeff Sloan, observed that the penalty "sends out a very clear signal. We respond harshly to racist comments and abuse to gay students."[25] (What racism had to do with calling a homosexual a "faggot" Sloan did not make clear.) On the dorm's calendar, Sloan announced Ehrman's departure without disguising his glee: "Kenny's leaving; let's have a PARTY!!!"[26]

Clearly this RA was no impartial administrator of justice. Ehrman explained that the dorm's counselors had been uncommunicative throughout the year toward him and his group of friends. "They never wanted to hear your side; they would never even talk to you." He added, "The selection of RAs was pretty bad; there was no one we could relate to."[27] Freshman Matt Rogers, also an Otero House resident that year, charged that there was "severe tension and antagonism, and the house seemed divided between residents and residential education."[28] And Otero resident Kevin Malloy explained that Ehrman was a rebel who did not fit Res Ed's mold of a "tolerant" atmosphere: "They were going to foster a certain environment at all costs, and would do what was necessary to preserve that environment."[29]

Unlike the case in Ujamaa, the expulsion itself could not restore conformity. Others were willing to defend Kenny Ehrman's rights. The following evening, seven members of the Phi Delta Theta fraternity staged a silent candlelight vigil defending Ehrman's right to free speech and protesting the university's extreme reaction. The protestors, fearing the worst, decided to remain anonymous by wearing motorcycle helmets, ski goggles, and goalie masks. When Otero's residents noticed the protest outside, they proceeded to call friends and various authorities. Two police officers arrived on the scene, but left immediately, because the seven protestors were breaking no laws.[30]

Trained (perhaps by Multicultural Educator Greg Ricks) to find racism everywhere, the multiculturalists were not so forgiving. About 30 students arrived, and some of them threatened to beat up the protestors. Steven Phillips, a future multicultural editor of the *Stanford Daily*, declared, "They are parading around here in junior Klan outfits."[31] With this characterization, a silent candlelight protest over the University's decision to punish a student's use of the word "faggot" became transformed into racial harassment reminiscent of the Ku Klux Klan. President Kennedy and the dean of student affairs denounced the seven students in the campus press and placed them on probation for "racial" insensitivity. In a strange twist, a protest in favor of First Amendment rights became an occasion for the evisceration of those very rights. President Kennedy applauded the BSU in terms approaching the surreal:

> Members of the Black Student Union and other students who encountered the masked vigilers...displayed extraordinary restraint in attempting to start conversations instead of hostilities....It is remarkable that they controlled that anger in an effort to do something constructive for this community and the community owes them its thanks.[32]

The candlelight vigil probably bore more resemblance to a sorority initiation than to a Ku Klux Klan rally. But in Stanford's racially charged atmosphere, the imputation of ill will was not exceptional, but rather, judging from President Kennedy's praise of the BSU's "restraint," the expected and only natural interpretation of events.

Once mythologized as an incident of racial harassment, the Otero incident further buttressed the claims of minorities advocating racial theme dorms and programming. Without more "awareness" efforts, they claimed, such racist events would be repeated. In truth, however, such awareness efforts only would help to forge the new racial identities. In the resulting atmosphere of increased racial sensitivity, more Otero and Ujamaa incidents would occur as minorities began "to find racism everywhere." In a self-fulfilling circle, the very episodes generated by multicultural race-consciousness would serve as the excuse for more race-conscious programming.

In the midst of this escalating process, the original meaning of "racism" becomes totally forgotten. As used by Phillips and other multiculturalists, "racism" does not really mean prejudice on the basis of somebody's skin color. Nor does it refer to a belief in false racial differences. If anything, "racism" has come to mean almost the exact opposite—namely, a failure to recognize racial differences and special racial identities. Precisely along these lines, a campus conference defined "racism" as the failure to celebrate the unique perspectives of racial minorities.[33] This redefinition would solve the problem of students who were not receptive to the new racial identities: They could be dismissed as bigots.

In a sense, the primary problem for multiculturalists is that there are almost no real racists at Stanford or, for that matter, in America's younger generation. The few exceptions, like the "skinheads," are highly visible (precisely because there are so few) and are not often spotted at elite schools like Stanford. Most college-age students consider themselves open-minded and tolerant—that is why multiculturalism was able to gain such wide support in the first place. Dr. John Bunzel, former president of San Jose State University, interviewed dozens of minority students at Stanford and found that few could enumerate concrete incidents of racism on campus:

> Most of the black students who said they had personally encountered racist behavior at the university were hard-pressed to describe what it was like or how it worked. As many of them said, the racism they confronted, although it pervaded the whole campus, was subtle and could not be explained to others.
>
> "I've felt like an outcast in classes," a black senior woman noted. "The class breaks up into study groups and people don't want you in theirs." A black freshman said, "There's nothing that's actually been done to me, but there are things that have been hurtful—like people who don't think black writers have anything to say." Others just talked of subtle changes in the behavior of whites in the presence of a black, and a certain tension they felt in social situations.
>
> White students have repeatedly heard these complaints of subtle racism and are largely bewildered by them. As one senior put it, "It's hard to know how to react to charges of racism when there are no specific incidents or examples. That's pretty damn subtle."[34]

Even under the ever-expanding definition of "racism," minority students are hard pressed to find it among their peers (likely because white students, in order to avoid the accusation, adjust their behavior accordingly). Nevertheless, in order for the new racial identities to thrive, campus minority groups had to produce evidence of cradle-to-grave oppression. Without such evidence, the new identities would prove merely skin-deep.

If racism was not evident on an individual level, then perhaps it could be attributed to disembodied collective entities, such as universities, corporations, and government agencies. In a special report to investigate institutional racism, Stanford's leading activists offered the following insights on this elusive phenomenon:

> Institutional racism is not blatant. It is not the fault of individuals. Institutional racism is simply when an institution finds itself affected by the racism that pervades our entire society—often members of the institution are not even *aware* of the effects....When we find ourselves unconsciously participating in institutional racism, we have to admit it. We have to admit it in order to change it.[35] (emphasis in original)

The question of where such institutional racism comes from in the first place, if not from the individuals who comprise those institutions, was finessed. Indeed, subjective suspicions alone could be enough for a finding of institutional racism; it existed in many places:

- Tresidder Union, the central campus hangout, suffered from it. David Porter, of the University Committee on Minority Issues, declared that "it seems like people don't really want (minority students) to be there."[36] Committee member Faye McNair-Knox added, "The perception (minorities get) is a difference in the quality of the service....'I don't have to do the same for black people as I do for someone else.'" The building's employees were urged to engage in a thorough self-criticism: Before any improvements could be made, Tresidder needed to "get a clarification of (its) own image," according to McNair-Knox.[37]
- Stanford Law School's Multicultural Council demanded a quota system, in which four of six open faculty positions would be filled with women or minorities. Second-year law student Laura Allan explained that "only a formula will guarantee that the composition of the Law School's faculty will no longer reflect institutional racism."[38]
- In the spring of 1988, several leading members of the student government (ASSU) accused the organization of institutional racism because of "behind-the-scenes and closed-door movements" blocking minority students from receiving more appointments. Even so, 22 out of 36 appointments went to minority students, and 20 out of 36 went to women.[39] Such numbers, however, did not convince everyone. Student Senator Lucky Gutierrez charged the ASSU with "institutional racism," and President Roechelle Smith added that racial incidents occur "time and time again" in the ASSU.[40] Not surprisingly, with all the accusations of "racism" flying around, junior Rachel Wiesen, who was denied a position, also became convinced there was a problem; she had heard "lots of rumors of racism."[41] The final report on ASSU staff hiring tied everything together: "Like most other institutions on this campus and in this society, we are troubled by the problem of institutional racism."[42] Because the problem was everywhere, the student government's own leaders decided, it must therefore also be in the ASSU.

In important respects, these portrayals of a society gripped by institutional racism, and the concessions they beget, generate the very differences that define multicultural "diversity." At the end of this circular process, many students actually become convinced that their races give them different perspectives and different needs. Consider the self-description of Leta Hong Fincher, a leader of HAPA, Stanford's Half-Asian People's Association (yes, there is such a thing):

> [There is much] discrimination against people of mixed heritage, which necessitates the existence of a group such as HAPA....As a half-Asian, I frequently feel denied legitimacy by society at large (imagine having your ethnic identity on official documents defined as "Other"). I am elated to discover that HAPA exists at Stanford, and that there are other people with backgrounds similar to mine....You should rejoice in the diversity of your fellow students and the organizations they create.[43]

Fincher's account suggests the opposite of what it explicitly states. Although she feels "denied legitimacy by society at large," how terrible can this denial really be, if the very worst example she can cite is a lack of specific recognition on official documents? Even more strangely, while others "should rejoice in the diversity" created by HAPA, Fincher's own elation stems from the fact "that there are other people with backgrounds similar" to hers. If diversity is an absolute good, then what benefit is there for Fincher to be in an organization of people just like her?

Indeed, an ironic requirement of the new group identities is self-segregation. There is often great pressure to socialize only with people from the same group. Informal sanctions are most immediate for offenders from minority groups, since congregation with whites might reveal the nonexistence of important group differences. Dr. Bunzel's interviews reflected these results:

> Almost 70 percent of blacks talked of the pressure they felt from other black students to subscribe to a set of "black" positions and attitudes. "Oh yeah, that's everywhere," said a black sophomore. "It involves certain standards you're supposed to adopt."....In the personal interviews with black students, over two-thirds of them indicated that social affiliation with whites reduces their acceptance by their peers. "If you hang around with just white people, you might get dropped in status."[44]

Simultaneously, Bunzel found, white students "learn right away that blacks want to be viewed as blacks, that there are important differences between the black and white communities on campus, and that they must be sensitive to those differences"—even if "specific differences remain ill-defined."[45] Because racism is so often attributed to the most benign words and actions, many white students do not go out of their way to make friendships with minority students. As one white student noted, "The motivation is often too little and the risk too great to spend the energy required to bridge a cultural gap in interpersonal relations."[46]

Whether this "cultural gap" is due to society at large, as multiculturalists maintain, or is the result of the multiculture itself is another question. But the comments of one senior, a Mexican American male, are highly suggestive of the latter. He conjoined ethnic separatism in Casa Zapata with the creation of Chicano identity:

> I can't compare any year with the one in Zapata....As a minority in the dorm I was expected to choose (the right friends) and take part in the separatism. I couldn't understand that. One person came up to me and said, "Why don't you stick to your own?" Before, we never looked at ourselves as Chicanos.[47]

There can be little doubt that Casa Zapata's race-conscious policies foster distrust and ultimately separatism. But blinded by dogmatism, multiculturalists typically blame the separatism they create on institutional racism. That specific cases of this pervasive affliction are practically undetectable is only taken as a sign that the "racism" is all the more intransigent and deep-seated.

These instances where individuals identify themselves as victimized minorities can have bizarre repercussions. In Spring 1994, for instance, Stanford's Chicano community launched a hunger strike to convince the campus of its oppressed status. The triggering events were the layoff of the Casa Zapata RF and the panning of a MEChA preview called *No Grapes* at student movies.[48] Typically, both were interpreted as racial incidents. In reality, the RF was laid off because of budget cuts, and moviegoers booed because they wanted to see a movie, not hear why they should boycott grapes. But MEChA members saw matters rather differently: "What we witnessed were callous creatures acting out of brazen hate and racism."[49] In response, four women—seniors Eva Silva and Julia Gonzalez Luna, junior Tamara Alvarado, and sophomore Elvira Prieta—began a hunger strike. They fasted for three days until the university agreed to provide more programming centered around themes of Chicano identity.[50]

Perhaps the most remarkable feature of these protests involved the disparity between demands and tactics. Grapes hardly seemed sufficient cause for a hunger strike. The ends simply did not justify the means. In any case, a grape boycott could not possibly help migrant grape pickers on California farms (the stated purpose of the sanction) because Stanford Dining Services imports its grapes from Chile.[51] Nevertheless, MEChA claimed, the grape ban was a fundamental matter of "respect" for its community, a complex issue involving "worker exploitation" and "environmental racism." Indeed, "out of respect" for the Chicano community, a number of dorms across campus started complying with the grape ban voluntarily.[52]

In practice, racial politics tends to become a negative-sum game, in which people's energies are directed into trendy but ultimately futile directions. The new racial programming, justified as a response to pervasive but simultaneously hidden societal racism, may give racial minorities a temporary feeling of self-esteem. These efforts may even enable certain ideological coalitions to be sustained and provide the multiculture with a governing majority. But the new racial consciousness does not promise peace.

These artificial racial identities and manufactured grievances have many serious consequences for the nation. As we shall see in the last chapter, America is gradually moving towards a culture of victimization and complaint, in which some people use their victim status to extract concessions and benefits from everyone else. Never are any time tables offered for success. It is never said whether racial theme houses or racial programming, to take but two examples, will be needed for the next 10 years, the next 20, the next 50, or the next 100. That racial barriers may have been overcome long before then scarcely matters to the advocates of these programs: Today, these programs are no longer designed to remedy past injustices, but, in the absence of a statute of limitations on grievances, have become a means to perpetuate the new racial identities indefinitely.

Homosexuality and "Homophobia"

In the last decade or so, no movement in America has gained quite as much attention as the gay rights movement. With parades, "coming out" days, and public awareness efforts, homosexual activists have loudly proclaimed their identities. Their goal has been to add to the multicultural rainbow a lavender stripe of victimization.

Many Americans are of two minds about all of this. Homosexuals have often been mistreated, and criminal assaults today against individuals, regardless of sexual preference, should receive the full force of the law, swiftly and forcefully. But while generally supportive of abstract principles like tolerance and open-mindedness, many Americans sense that something more is at stake in the case of "gay rights"—although most would be hard pressed to say exactly what. There is a vague uneasiness, a sense of foreboding, that "tolerance" and "acceptance" (conventionally understood as you leave me alone and I'll leave you alone) would not be quite enough to satisfy some of the more militant homosexual activists. Much of the gay rights movement seems to go beyond what would be needed for public education or awareness, and appears more designed to offend and to shock the general public. If homosexuals merely want to be tolerated like everyone else, many Americans wonder, then why do they have to go out of their way to define themselves not just as individuals seeking to live freely, but as a special class of victims demanding reparations.

As in the case of the new racial consciousness, the multicultural movement has pushed homosexual awareness furthest on America's college campuses. Stanford is in the forefront. In recent years, the campus has been convulsed by homosexual protests, awareness days, and AIDS die-ins. California Governor Pete Wilson was booed and whistled down by homosexual activists when he tried to give a campus speech in 1991.[53] In all these instances, the protestors directed their indignation at pervasive "homophobia" (defined as the irrational fear of homosexuals). But as with the elusive institutional racism, it is easier to complain about homophobia than to find it.

A case study of this evidentiary difficulty, and of how it could be creatively overcome, was provided in the fall of 1988. At the time, several of Stanford's homosexual activists were seeking to push the university administration to be more sympathetic to their agenda. These activists had determined that their best strategy would involve casting homosexuals as victims in the multicultural drama. The centerpiece of their effort would be to convince others that homophobia was a major problem on campus. In an open letter on Stanford's gay computer bulletin board, computer science lecturer Stuart Reges summarized the dilemma confronted by these activists and suggested a solution:

> If the only evidence [of homophobia] we have to give [President] Kennedy is the Otero incident [involving Kenny Ehrman] and the fact that our posters are constantly abused, I don't think we have a compelling case. If there are lots of other recent specifics, I'd love to hear about them. If not I think the best way to move forward on this front is to try to generate such evidence.[54]

To Reges, the lack of evidence did not imply the lack of a "compelling case." He would not so easily be deterred from his crusade. Comparing himself to Gandhi in his desire to "expose injustice," Reges suggested generating evidence by provoking homophobic incidents. Stanford's fraternities would be "a great place to start":

> Try leaving flyers announcing the upcoming dance on tables in their dining halls and see if some of them get

> angry and tell you to leave....If a lot of gay couples showed up [to fraternity parties] and started drinking their beer and dancing together, I bet we'd find out just how open they are.[55]

Should fraternities fail to display the requisite degree of homophobia, Reges urged gays to target Encina gym, "another hotbed of homophobia:"

> If the posters [for the gay, lesbian, and bisexual dance] are constantly ripped down, you'll have a perfect excuse to declare the area a disaster and have a kiss-in outside the gym some afternoon, and be sure to stay long enough that you force the football team to walk past you at the end of practice.[56]

Reges correctly noted that such incidents had been "the best way to get the University to act" in the past: "Three years ago the Steering Committee [comprised of leaders of the gay community] was composed of a group of students who were particularly good at this, and we managed to collect a lot of powerful anecdotes."[57] In other words, Reges encouraged protests against a homophobia these very demonstrations were designed to generate. Just as the new race-conscious programming resulted in "racial" episodes, Reges's plan would generate homophobic episodes.

In more than one sense, one suspects that the gentleman doth protest too much. At Stanford, attacks on homosexuals almost never occur. Even private disapproval of homosexuality is extremely infrequent and is dealt with in a harsh way—witness the reaction to Kenny Ehrman. For that matter, the specific provocations suggested by Reges were unlikely to lead to major incidents. One member of the Beta Theta Pi fraternity calmly explained, "Our parties are open to the whole student body. But nobody coming expressly to incite an incident is welcome."[58] And while students on the football team might stare at people staging a "kiss-in outside the gym," probably not much more than that would happen.

If homophobia did not exist in the Beta fraternity house or Encina gym, then maybe it could be found among those who thought Reges's proposal was a silly idea. And, in a final twist, that is exactly what happened: When the *Stanford Review* reprinted Reges's advice in a news story, he declared that this article itself provided the much-needed evidence of a pervasive "anti-gay" bias; the very existence of such students who wrote for the *Review*, according to Reges, suggested that things had gotten "even worse" for campus homosexuals.[59]

Obviously, Reges's strategy is self-falsifying, because the need to manufacture incidents indicates that there is not much of a problem.

Nevertheless, for purposes of galvanizing the homosexual community, Reges's proposals were not self-defeating. Quite the contrary, one student wrote back: "I thought [Reges's] suggestions about uncovering homophobia in order to spur the University into action were great!!"[60] Even though this student would play a role in Reges's homophobic production, he apparently did not perceive the fiction he (like Reges) was helping to create. The line between drama ("generating" homophobia) and reality ("uncovering" homophobia) had evaporated, as even the actors staging these spectacles had brought themselves to believe that their oppression was real. So long as no single actor stars in every scene, presumably, every actor could believe that not all of the multicultural world is just a stage.

These stages of oppression are not part of a grand theater in which some people cleverly deceive others in order to receive various kinds of benefits. The actors in these dramas simply do not realize that they are on stage. Unlike in *The Wizard Of Oz*, there is nobody behind the curtain pulling levers to create an illusion for the spectators. Rather, these spectacles are exercises in narcissism that depend on the passionate commitment of all participants, whose very being is defined by their supposed oppression. Just as the essence of the new racial identity is institutional racism, so also is homosexual identification linked to the hunt for nonexistent homophobia.

In spite of its chimerical nature, the homophobia desperately sought by Reges served its function well, because it drew attention to the supposedly special needs of homosexual faculty, students, and staff as a class of victims defined by their sexual preference. And his efforts opened the door for others to push homosexual identification in ever more aggressive ways. Freshman Brady Mickelson described one of these performances, staged during the "Faces of the Community" orientation program:

> [W]e frosh were greeted by a young woman who, as a freshman troubled by depression and anxiety, discovered that she was a lesbian (or, in her words, queer). She explained how "free and relieved" she felt after declaring her queerness to her dormmates. After relating her struggles as a queer in today's world, she counseled us to "overcome our fears of being queer" and to question our own sexuality, rather than to be influenced by the opinions of society. She closed her remarks by commenting on how she had overcome her fears about being queer to the point that she was able to declare her status to an audience of 1500 people. She retired to great applause.[61]

The favorable reaction directly contradicts the woman's claims about hostility towards homosexuals, but simultaneously the crowd's applause is an indispensable part of an identity that demands recognition.

These bizarre shows continue throughout the school year. As another telling example, consider the grandiose fears voiced by *Stanford Daily* columnist and RA Corey Davis:

> I'm still scared to be an RA. As a politically conscious and openly gay black man, my biggest worry is how I'm going to relate to a generally naive group of freshmen, some of whom have never met a black or openly gay person, let alone discussed issues of race or sexuality. Will someone scribble "nigger" on my door, or hold a KKK-like vigil outside the dorm? Will some macho stud threaten to kick my ass because I'm gay? *Or worse, will the residents ignore me and refuse to engage me about issues of race and sexuality, and about myself?* [62] (emphasis added)

Of course, nobody at Stanford would organize a "KKK-like vigil" outside Davis's dorm room (presumably a reference to the Otero episode—it had by now evolved into an elaborate myth), and it seems unlikely that "some macho stud" would attack Davis for being homosexual. But, so long as Davis could imagine there might be such people, that was all that mattered. His self-characterization unwittingly admitted the truth: It would be "worse" for him to be ignored than to be beaten, so determined was he to live out the drama of his oppression.

Over time, these shows convinced others as well. In the fall of 1988, the university began funding the Lesbian, Gay, and Bisexual Community Center (LGBCC) in order for the group to pay for "coming out" days, Gay and Lesbian Awareness Week, and other events to combat homophobia.[63] In 1991, married-student housing was made available to homosexual partners who wished to live together (the fact that the children of married couples would gain exposure to homosexual relationships was seen as an additional plus).[64] And in 1991, Stanford Law School hired its first openly homosexual faculty member under a new affirmative action policy that gave preferences to openly homosexual applicants.[65] The law school's hiring committee argued that those who had proclaimed their homosexuality would provide positive role models for students to emulate. The professor's arrival itself became the occasion for more awareness, as the entire law school was decorated with a display of lavender balloons to mark the festive day. The fact that performance in the bedroom could be viewed as a predictor for performance as a law professor speaks volumes about the homosexual movement's desire not merely for equal treatment, but for special treatment.

The major danger posed by this agenda has nothing to do with the rights of individuals to do as they please in private. It is irrelevant, in large part, whether homosexual behavior is in any sense right or wrong. What is instead relevant is that much of the behavior is being conducted *in public*, for the express purpose of shocking and offending others. This shock is then called "homophobia" and is used as evidence of the oppression and victimization of homosexuals. It is this victim status that is important, resulting in special privileges and concessions for homosexuals. Over time, as Americans become increasingly jaded and indifferent to all sorts of self-proclaimed victims, the dosage will have to be increased. More outrageous behavior will be needed to generate the same sort of response and the same level of privileges. Already, deeds and acts that would have led to shock and outrage only two decades ago hardly raise an eyebrow today. As the cycle escalates, the demands have less to do with tolerance or acceptance than with aggressive advocacy.

Even in purely economic terms, the costs are substantial. In early 1993, for instance, Stanford extended employee housing and health benefits to the "domestic partners" of homosexual faculty and staff. The university's explanation hardly drew notice when it declared, "We think that redefining 'family' for purposes of the benefits program to include longterm, committed domestic partnerships appropriately reflects the changing social reality and values of the Stanford community."[66] With this rhetoric, the university carried the irrational fear of homophobia to a logical conclusion. Even the absence of benefits had become interpreted as a "penalty" on gay and lesbian relationships—presumably, one that was not even noticed by the larger society, which had not defined cohabitant homosexuals as "families."

On its face, the argument proved too much. If "domestic partner" relationships should be subsidized by the larger community, then why not a whole range of others, like parent-child, grandparent-grandchild, sibling-sibling, friend-friend, etc.? Indeed, why should those who are fortunate enough to enjoy "committed" and "longterm relationships" receive an entitlement funded by those unhappy souls who are all alone? Why should the lonely be "penalized"? Why, alternately, should the policy be limited to monogamous relationships? If heterosexuality is no longer a standard, why should monogamy be? Is it not "intolerant" to deprive any alternative lifestyle of support including polygamy, polygyny, etc.? The end result is something of a random scrambling of people into "relationships," all claiming the right to live off everyone else.

In practice, only a small subset of all possible relationships can receive special rewards indirectly paid for by everyone else. Society may have an interest in helping parents raise children, and this was the traditional justification for benefits to married couples. No analogous justification was offered for the "domestic partners" policy. But none was needed, because once the debate had been framed in terms of ending an oppressive penalty for a new class of victims, the burden of proof had shifted to the "homophobic" status quo.

Gender and "Sexism"

Far more than racial issues or questions of sexual preference, gender relations stand at the foundation of the social order. In the case of angry racial minorities and militant homosexuals, hostile separatism is bad, but at least it may enable people on different sides to avoid outright conflict. In the case of men and women, however, such a systematic separatism can scarcely be conceived if society is to continue. If gender relations become dysfunctional, everyone will be impacted in an immediate and obvious way. Multiculturalists have spent a great deal of effort recruiting women (even though they are not a minority), because if they were ever able to enlist even one of the two genders, then the cultural war against the West would largely be won.

Although no unitary conception of sexual and gender identity has gained ascendancy in America, the multiculture offers its own well-defined framework. The multiculture's conception of "sexism" plays a role analogous to that of homophobia or institutional racism in other contexts, informing women of how they should view themselves and how they should view men. Junior Sarah Horsley, representing the Stanford Women's Center, hinted at the connection between all of these vectors of oppression: "We believe that race, class, gender and sexual orientation intersect. Disrespect for one community translates into disrespect for us all."[67]

In important respects, the multiculture has co-opted feminist attitudes about gender relations, although one must be very specific about just what that means. American feminists have changed since the 1920s, when they fought for women's suffrage, and since the 1960s, when they sought equal rights. As with the metamorphosis of the civil rights movement, the focus of the feminist movement gradually shifted from equality to differentialism. Modern feminism cares less about equality than about celebrating a distinct female identity. Feminists sometimes describe the new identity in terms that suggest there is some radical incommensurability between men and women. The implication is that men cannot understand women and women cannot understand men, they are so different from one another. "There is a particular ideology that people have because of their identity," explained OMD Director Sally Dickson. "You are a male. You think in a way that I will never be able to understand because I am a woman."[68]

There is nothing *a priori* wrong with the idea that there are some differences between men and women. Unlike in the case of racial groups, there are indeed some real differences between the two sexes. It was a major mistake of academic feminists to reject gender distinctions grounded in nature as the product of culture (see chapter 3). But the mere existence of some distinctions does not tell us exactly what those distinctions are—and it is in these details that cultural feminism becomes truly radical.

For cultural feminists, women are different from men primarily because women have a unique consciousness that gives them special insights into reality. As in so many other contexts, this new consciousness primarily involves the awareness of oppression, in this case along a gender vector—oppression against women, by men. Men will never be able to understand women because they are not the victims of sexism. In the formulation of Anita Hill's supporters, men "just don't get it," and perhaps never will. Like the new upper-case Black identity, the new gender identity has relatively little to do with biology. It is ideological in nature: Biological women can become real Women only when they recognize that they are being oppressed by men. The biology may be necessary, but it is not a sufficient condition.

To generate awareness of the special identity of women, each year Stanford distributes *A Woman's Guide to Stanford*.[69] The book focuses on the need to combat sexism, since that is what the new gender identity is all about. Incoming female students are warned that "Sexism is more than discrimination or exploitation; it is an attitude. As such it can be manifested in numerous ways—words as well as actions, explicit or implicit. Sexism can be conscious or unconscious, but either way it is offensive and uncomfortable and should be exposed."[70] As in the case of institutional racism and homophobia, the most common forms of sexism are not readily apparent. Because most men in America no longer believe (if they ever did) that women should be pregnant, barefoot, and in the kitchen, exposing the remaining vestiges of sexism becomes much more complicated. Professor Dolores Huerta went so far as to declare that the lack of evidence might be evidence: Women "are so oppressed that we don't even know how oppressed we are—there are layers and layers of institutionalized oppression."[71] Paradoxically, oppression was both pervasive and undetectable. Once again, sexism (like homophobia and institutional racism) had been defined so subtly as to be nonfalsifiable.

If sexism has prevented women from recognizing their own identities, or even the fact of oppression itself, then perhaps special education efforts could make them aware of their submerged gender identity. That was the rationale for the two-week annual women's "herstory" conference.[72] The name of the event, which includes lectures on birth control, speeches on feminism, and an open-mike dance, contrasts explicitly with regular history (the study, presumably, of "his story"). "It's important to acknowledge that women's history is not taught in mainstream education," explained Elizabeth Osgood, a junior involved with the Stanford Women's Center.[73] "His story" was not telling women about male oppression. "Just the use of the word 'herstory' draws attention to the gender bias built into our society—a problem that extends even to the structure of our language," organizers proclaimed.[74] As in the case of institutional racism, the failure to acknowledge a distinct female "perspective" was itself indicative of oppression. The coincidence that a single word ("history") contained a male pronoun ("his") was the one remaining trace that gave everything away, as the all-consuming hunt for sexism had reached the recesses of the English language itself.

Invoking the fears of women *vis-à-vis* men is perhaps the most common means to reinforce the new gender identity. In 1993, for instance, a large contingent of female students participated in Stanford's annual "Take Back the Night" march, demonstrating against the fear women have of being attacked while walking home alone at night.[75] The demonstration provided the chance for women to march through campus at night (which at Stanford was decidedly safe)—something they supposedly were unable to do on other occasions. Of course, the fear of criminal attack is not exclusive to women (especially given the activities in library bathrooms and the Rape Education Project's findings that one in eight males had been "coerced" into sex), but organizers used the event as an excuse to remind the audience of the pervasive oppression women supposedly face in society at large. "It's such an oppression to feel boxed in and closed up all the time," pronounced organizer Amy Solomon, implying that the oppression of women was so vast that the march should perhaps have been entitled "Take Back the Entire Day." Added graduate student Sara Duckler, "We want women to know that they have a right to exist and to make choices about where they are going and who they are going with." But what woman, let alone what Stanford woman, would not know that she had "a right to exist"? Again, the purpose of these events was not to tell women the obvious, but to create a new identity for (oppressed) women, in relation to (oppressive) men, who supposedly sought to deny women's "right to exist."[76] These systematic exaggerations about the dangers to women, much like Reges's homophobic theater and Casa Zapata's race-conscious programming, have something of a circular character, in that they often generate the very fears these demonstrations protest against.

Because the new gender identity constitutes little more than the passionate conviction that women are oppressed, even devoted campus feminists, like Women's Center Director Rebecca Bliss, can rarely describe anything more about what the identity entails. Bliss was asked what a society without sexism would look like:

> I can't even begin to imagine it. I can't imagine that it (sexism) would not be there on some level, any more than I can imagine that racism or any of the other "isms" wouldn't be there. So, what would it look like? It would look a lot different than society does today. But I can't imagine what it would look like.[77]

One feminist studies class offered a little more direction. The aptly named "Going Out of Our Minds: From Women's Movement to Women's World" sought to provide a sketch of what the new social order might look like.[78] Feminist writer Sonia Johnson spoke in Robinson House (Stanford's "feminist studies" dorm) on her hopes for a utopian women's revolution in America:

> The pie is rotten. We have got to bake a new pie. We need to start from scratch. Have you ever wondered why things are the way they are? I mean, think of the legislature. It is just so bizarre. The economy. Why do we need an economy? All they have brought are war and destruction and were they not the work of men?[79]

In a sense, Johnson had carried the ideas about sexism just one step further than everyone else. For her, it was unthinkable that men and women could ever become friends; they could relate to one another only as enemies.

"The work of men" in Johnson's new feminist order plays a role analogous to "the work of the devil" in the medieval order. It is evil incarnate and must be condemned utterly, even if this requires us "to bake a new pie" and "to start from scratch." The oppression is so ubiquitous that many cannot even recognize it, but Johnson offered a sketch on how one might achieve the new gender consciousness. Through indirection one would find direction:

> Think about it. Everything that you have ever been taught. You think they are true? I'll tell you what. If you want to know the real truth, take the exact opposite of what you hear should be or is correct; that will be the truth in its purest form. At a crucial point in my life, I realized that I had been programmed to believe everything that I believe. Then I decided that I would forget everything and resort instead to my inner voice. I was determined to

> believe nothing until I had actually tried it out. Literally, I started to go out of my mind. To everyone else, I appeared insane. But you know, I believe the exact opposite: I am very sane and everyone else is insane.[80]

Johnson's "inner voice" speaks to her about the oppression of women and gives her a new identity as a woman—the two are the same. Whereas before multiculturalism the women's movement was limited to eliminating false differences between men and women, the proponents of the new gender identity seek to achieve precisely the opposite goal—to create additional distinctions between men and women. Indeed, Johnson concluded her presentation with an apocalyptic prophecy regarding the dawn of a "woman's world":

> Yes, women are starting to listen to their own inner voices. They are starting to remember a time before patriarchy, before this mad, destructive world was brought about. It was a different world. This world will come again. The men's world is dying. It may kill us with it but it is dying. Prepare for the dawn of a new world of women. One without control.[81]

Johnson, incidentally, has thrice been a candidate for president of the United States.[82]

The Double Bind

The treatment of race, gender, and sexual preference in relation to crimes like institutional racism, sexism, and homophobia suggests a more refined answer to our original question: What holds the multiculture together?

Multicultural identification does not lead to extreme individualism, but rather promotes its exact opposite. Multicultural identities are *interdividual*—that is, multicultural distinctions and differences do not stand on their own, but exist only in relation to one another. Multiculturalists act as if each "victim" is endowed with some sort of independent essence, requiring special needs (hence, specialized deans) and separate space (hence, ethnic dormitories). But to describe this position is to refute it: "Victims" can exist only if there exist oppressors, in relation to whom victim status may be defined. One should not take the multiculturalists at face value when they claim to be recognizing individual identities that, like some sort of Platonic forms, preexist the multiculture—and that have been submerged (often for centuries) by oppressive Western society. The opposite is the case: Multicultural identities are constructed by the multiculture itself, which determines precisely what role each actor may play in the larger theatrical production. Without the Kennys, Bens, and Guses to play the role of Prospero, there can be no Calibans.

Because the new identities are defined as a counterpoint to pervasive oppression, grievances and complaints must be recycled continuously. Without institutional racism or widespread homophobia, the new identities would cease to exist. "Disrespect for one community" must translate into "disrespect for us all" to ensure that there are enough examples of oppression to go around and, thereby, to magnify the claims of each. If necessary, episodes must even be manufactured. The most elaborate of productions are acted upon these stages of oppression. Perhaps the only difference from Broadway is the lack of a clear line between actors and spectators.

Multicultural victimology is so powerful because it taps into two base emotions that are not often found together—self-pity and self-importance. The self-pity comes from believing oneself a victim, the self-importance from casting oneself in a fantastical historical melodrama. But, however psychologically gratifying in the short term, the focus on victimization creates a double bind for multiculturalists in the long run: If they ever succeeded in their struggle to end oppression, then they would lose their identities. At the same time, to give up the struggle to end oppression would also force them to lose their identities—since the oppression (and, hence, their identity) is evidenced, in large measure, by the intensity of the struggle. "I can't see [sexism] ever being 100 percent eliminated from society," remarked Women's Center Director Rebecca Bliss. "I think if sexism isn't there, there will be a new 'ism' to take its place, there will be a new something."[83] The "struggle continues unabated" (to borrow Dean Jackson's words) because it must never end. A successful outcome is absolutely precluded. It would be difficult to imagine a pursuit more sterile.

In a sense, multiculturalists like thinking of themselves as victims far too much to want to end their victimization. They need their imaginary oppressors to give their lives meaning. Consider, in this context, the response of MEChA member Gloria Sanchez to students' booing the film *No Grapes* at Sunday Night Flicks: "I'm glad it happened. Thank God it finally happened and hundreds and hundreds of people woke up to what the climate is on this campus."[84] Of course, if the episode really had been as racist as MEChA members maintained, one would hardly expect them to thank the Deity for it. But the episode served the useful purpose of reinforcing their victim status (if only in their own minds) and, in turn, their interdividual racial identity. One is reminded of Mike Newman's satirical description of the Algerian peasantry: "The Algerian peasants...and by extension all oppressed peoples, can achieve revolutionary consciousness and fight back, even though....the peasants often depend on their oppressors even as they curse them." With a few word changes, this would provide a fairly accurate sketch of the multiculture: "Oppressed peoples can achieve revolutionary consciousness and fight back, even though they often depend on their oppressors, because they *need* to curse them."

This double bind fuels a vicious cycle of what may be called multicultural *ressentiment*. *Ressentiment* is not merely resentment; it is resentment compounded by a frustration over not being able to relieve the source of that resentment. In a destructive circle, frustration breeds more resentment, which in turn exacerbates the frustration. For multiculturalists who have adopted fake racial and gender identities, the resentment of their oppression is compounded by a frustration over not being able to relieve its source. They cannot relieve their oppression both because it is largely imaginary (as in the Phi Delt protest mistaken for a KKK rally) and because this fantasy provides the backbone of their identity. Feminist Sally Kempton unwittingly summed up the dilemma: "It is hard to fight an enemy who has outposts in your head."[85] Like Cervantes's Don Quixote, who transfigured windmills into monsters so that he could play the role of knight in a postmedieval world, Stanford's multiculturalists struggle to break down racial and sexual doors that have been wide open for some time. At the end of each day's unabated struggle, multiculturalists have only succeeded in making themselves look rather silly.

Ressentiment is the interdividual force that bonds the disparate elements of the multiculture. The multiculturalists' many protests, from the march against Western Culture to MEChA's hunger strike against grapes, focus this *ressentiment*, concentrating the anger of the community against its designated enemies. Day-to-day accusations also manifest the same resentments and collective anger. This collective unanimity is the fundamental component of the multiculture: Even though the victim groups differ from one another in many respects, they are generally able to agree on who their oppressors are. The multicultural actors misperceive these collective efforts as the recognition of a diversity that preexisted the founding of the new state. The reality is the reverse: The new multicultural "cultures" (or, more precisely, the multiculture) did not have an existence anterior to the protests themselves. The protests created the new multiculture, just as the collective attacks on racism or sexism or homophobia provide the prism through which the multicultural rainbow is refracted.

Notes

1. Newt Gingrich, "An America That Works," GOPAC Audiocassette, December 18, 1990.

2. Linda Friedlieb, "Orientation continues usual focus on multiculturalism," *The Stanford Daily*, September 24, 1992. Colleen Krueger and Cathy Siciliano, "Diversity a source of campus vitality; Stanford students enhance their education with multiculturalism," *The Stanford Daily*, September 23, 1993. According to Krueger and Siciliano, "New students get their first taste of multiculturalism at Stanford during Orientation." Incidentally, the head orientation coordinator was Victor Madrigal, a leader of the MEChA hunger strike.

3. *See*, for instance, "Orientation Calendar," *The Stanford Daily*, September 19, 1991; and "Orientation Calendar," *The Stanford Daily*, September 23, 1993.

4. Benji Jenkins, "Frosh Relate Their Impressions of the Farm," *The Stanford Review*, October 8, 1989.

5. Brady Mickelson, "Welcome to Freshmen 'Disorientation,'" *The Stanford Review*, October 5, 1992.

6. Mark Robinson, "Cultural heritage and diversity celebrated during Orientation," *The Stanford Daily*, September 28, 1988.

7. *Ibid.*

8. *Ibid.*

9. *Ibid.*

10. Stanford University, *Program, 103rd Commencement Weekend*, June 10–12, 1994.

11. Bob Beyers, "Committee Recommends Guidelines for Theme Houses at Stanford," *Stanford University News Service*, December 2, 1986.

12. "Theme house life: Freshmen should not be randomly assigned to theme houses," *The Stanford Daily*, October 25, 1990.

13. Octavio Pedroza, speech at "Rally Against Racism," October 26, 1988. His remarks were reprinted in "A Mandate for Change," October 26, 1988, a press statement printed and distributed by the Black Student Union, MEChA, Stanford American Indian Organization, and Asian American Students Association.

14. Tony Mecia, "Sowell Blasts Affirmative Action's Harmful Effects," *Campus: America's Student Newspaper*, Fall 1991.

15. Delia Ibarra, "Feeling out of place here," *The Stanford Daily*, February 17, 1991.

16. "What is Blackness?" *The Real News*, Spring 1994.

17. Raoul Mowatt, "Wynter: University must explore intellectual wonderland," *The Stanford Daily*, February 23, 1990.

18. Cametra Thompson, "Wynter speaks on inner city, race relations,"

The Stanford Daily, November 12, 1993.

19. Omar Wasow, "Learning to see whiteness," *The Stanford Daily*, March 5, 1992.

20. Jeff Brock, "Greg Ricks provides new spark for Res Ed," *The Stanford Daily*, March 1, 1990.

21 . Bill Workman, "Anti-Black 'Hysteria' Protested," *The San Francisco Chronicle*, March 4, 1994.

22. Cecilia Burciaga, "'Small daily daggers that one feels in the environment,'" *Stanford University News Service*, June 3, 1987. The article reprinted her speech from a Forum on Racism.

23. *Ibid.*

24. David Dirks, "Freshman loses housing for insensitive conduct," *The Stanford Daily*, May 23, 1988.

25. *Ibid.*

26. Interview with Kenny Ehrman (class of 1991).

27. Dirks, *supra* note 24.

28. *Ibid.*

29. *Ibid.*

30 . Bob Michitarian and Glen Tripp, "Night vigil causes racial scare," *The Stanford Daily*, May 25, 1988.

31. *Ibid.*

32. "Faculty cautioned about stereotypes in the classroom," *Campus Report*, June 1, 1988.

33. "Two prongs of racism," *The Stanford Daily*, November 12, 1987.

34. John H. Bunzel, "Black and White at Stanford," *Hoover Institution Reprint Series*, No. 139. *See also* John Bunzel, *Race Relations on Campus: Stanford Students Speak* (Stanford, CA: The Portable Stanford Book Series, 1992).

35. David Smolen, "Final Report: Senate Chair's Task Force on ASSU Staff Hiring," May 16, 1988.

36. Matthew Poppe, "Panel accuses Tresidder of racism," *The Stanford Daily*, February 19, 1988.

37. *Ibid.*

38. Nick Anderson, "Law dean apologizes to ex-visiting prof.," *The Stanford Daily*, November 23, 1987.

39. Tim Marklein, "BSU charges ASSU with racism," *The Stanford Daily*, April 6, 1988.

40. *Ibid.*

41. *Ibid.*

42. Smolen, *supra* note 35.

43. Leta Hong Fincher, "Learn from HAPA," *The Stanford Review*, November 11, 1991.

44. Bunzel, *supra* note 34.

45. *Ibid.*

46. *Ibid.*

47. *Ibid.*

48. Rajiv Chandrasekaran, "Budget cuts force Burciaga from job," *The Stanford Daily*, April 1, 1994.

49. Ann-Marie Gallegos, Lisa Gallegos, Yvette Espinoza, Amanda Navar, Ben Olguin, Lubia Sanchez, and Nicole Sanchez, "Responses to video on grape boycott showed intolerance of campus," *The Stanford Daily*, May 3, 1994.

50. A poignant reminder of Sowell's insight was provided during MEChA's hunger strike. When asked whether they would like anything to read or do, according to Gonzalez Luna, fasters requested copies of *Esquire* or *Glamour* and some cards—nothing in Spanish, much less in Aztec hieroglyphics. Even during a demonstration for cultural difference, the protestors engaged in activities not foreign to any other student. They were not occupying their time shaping clay pots or memorizing unique oral traditions. *See* Sarah Katz, "Strike ends after three days, agreement reached: Committees to look into possible grape boycott, Chicano Studies and EPA community center," *The Stanford Daily*, May 9, 1994.

51. Jim Luh, "Few eateries serve grapes," *The Stanford Daily*, May 6, 1994.

52. *Ibid.*

53. Brad Hayward, "Loud protest disrupts governor's speech: Gay-rights demonstrators face off with police at convocation," *The Stanford Daily*, October 2, 1991.

54. John Abbott, "Open Letter Urges Gays To Incite Homophobic Incidents," *The Stanford Review*, December 1988.

55. *Ibid.*

56. *Ibid.*

57. *Ibid.*

58. *Ibid.*

59. Stuart Reges, "Feigned acceptance of gays is toughest barrier to break," *The Stanford Daily*, January 11, 1989.

60. Abbott, *supra* note 54.

61. Mickelson, *supra* note 5.

62. Corey Davis, "Facing fear has rewards," *The Stanford Daily*, May 23, 1990.

63. Daniel Bao of the Gay and Lesbian Alliance at Stanford offered some perspective: "Only a few schools have taken this positive, groundbreaking step of officially sponsoring a gay, lesbian and bisexual organization. The move is a bold action by the University—GLAS had not even asked for total sponsorship until early last year." Chris Shuttlesworth, "University funds combined center," *The Stanford Daily*, September 27, 1988.

64. Bart Romney, "Married Students Oppose 'Domestic Partners,'" *The Stanford Review*, October 22, 1990.

65. Marci Shore, "Stanford coalition demands University diversify faculty," *The Stanford Daily*, April 5, 1991.

66. Somewhat more aggressively, the Stanford policy directly privileged homosexuals over unmarried heterosexuals, limiting the new benefits to the partners of homosexual employees only: "The subcommittee is unanimous in the view that the case for extending benefits to heterosexual partners is weaker than for gay and lesbian partners. As a result, the subcommittee recommends that if current cost considerations militate against extending coverage to both groups, coverage be extended now to gays and lesbians, and the question of coverage for heterosexual partners be reconsidered at a later date." *See* Anoop Prakash, "Domestic partners proposal would give preference to same-sex partners," *The Stanford Review*, October 5, 1992 (citing "The Report of the University Subcommittee on Domestic Partners' Benefits," June 1992).

67. Miranda Doyle, "Talks reach stalemate; hunger strike continues," *The Stanford Daily*, May 6, 1994.

68. Interview with Sally Dickson, May 1994.

69. *A Woman's Guide to Stanford*, Stanford, CA 1993–94.

70. *Ibid.*

71. Debby Lu, "Women struggling for 'Herstory,'" *The Stanford Daily*, March 3, 1989.

72. June Cohen, "Month to celebrate women's herstory," *The Stanford Daily*, March 1, 1991.

73. *Ibid.*

74. *Ibid.*

75. Lesley Edwards, "Taking Back the Night: 75 march for women's right to walk alone, without fear," *The Stanford Daily*, March 1, 1993.

76. In his address, for instance, UC Berkeley sociology professor Michael Kimmel emphasized the deep psychological differences between men and women, arguing that men had a "predatory" and "sexual entitlement" mind set. *See* Johnathon Briggs, "Kimmel attacks apathy about rape: Speaker says male drive to be macho helps cause crime," *The Stanford Daily*, April 22, 1993. *See also* Johnathon Briggs, "Events to raise rape awareness," *The Stanford Daily*, April 19, 1993.

77. Interview with Rebecca Bliss, May 2, 1994.

78. Edmund Yeh, "SWOPSI class 'goes out of its mind,'" *The Stanford Review*, January 27, 1992. *See also* Grace Lee, "Carrying the world on her shoulders: Feminist leader teaches course on stereotypes," *The Stanford Daily*, January 21, 1992. According to *The Daily*, "After the defeat of the ERA in Illinois, Johnson said she decided that women must not merely reform the existing society, but actually create a new one, resolving that

women were 'essentially different' from men."

79. *Ibid.*

80. *Ibid.*

81. *Ibid.*

82. *Ibid.*

83. Bliss, *supra* note 77.

84. Miranda Doyle, "Talks reach stalemate; hunger strike continues," *The Stanford Daily*, May 6, 1994.

85. *A Woman's Guide to Stanford*, *supra* note 69.

6

"Welcome to Salem"

If you cannot freely express your opinion...then you have lost what makes universities important....I studied a country that thought that everyone would be better off if it controlled what people said and thought, and that nation just committed suicide.[1]

—Sovietologist and Stanford Provost Condoleezza Rice

Multicultural identities require the proclamation of victimization. Or, more precisely: Multicultural identification *is* the proclamation of victimization. Absent such a proclamation (whether in terms of race, gender, sexual preference, or some other vector of oppression), the new-found identities would lack substance. The multiculture, which is nothing more than the set of these myriad new identities, would dissolve into nothingness—like a rainbow under a clear sky.

Few of the multicultural claims withstand close scrutiny. Even when particular groups have experienced real oppression in the past, the present-day picture tends to be more hazy and confused. The very recognition of historical injustices distinguishes the present from the past and indicates that progress has been made in the interval. Those persons complaining about oppression are generally not the ones to have experienced it first-hand. To the outside observer, the resulting multicultural theater appears contrived and fictional, sometimes even bordering on the surreal or the absurd.

From the inside, however, these roles are assumed with great seriousness of purpose. To question the validity of these grievances is to violate the most fundamental of taboos. Multicultural identification, depending on a never-ending cycle of oppression and resistance, entraps the very people it seeks to liberate within a narrowly constructed set of victimized identities. If there is any sense in which these people are "victims," then perhaps they are largely their own.

But there exists a more troublesome dimension to multicultural identification. As stressed in the last chapter, the new-found identities are *interdividual*, not individual. Oppression is relational. For every victim of racism, there must be a racist; for every victim of sexism, a sexist; for every victim of homophobia, a homophobe; for every Caliban, a Prospero. The multiculture cannot simply celebrate its new-found identities: They do not stand on their own. To affirm their victimization, multiculturalists must hunt down and eliminate their supposed oppressors. This expulsion of oppression does not occur once and for all, but must be periodically reenacted, to reconstruct victimized identities threatened with dissipation over time.

Of course, because the multicultural victims are largely mythical, the "victimizers" identified by the multiculture are similarly fictitious. By and large, these "victimizers" are innocent of the crimes of which they stand accused. And so, in a final paradox, the multicultural liberation of mythological victims necessarily will culminate with the generation of real victims, singled out for reprisal due to no fault of their own. The unfortunate reality is that Stanford's multiculturalists have become expert in generating enemies and dealing with them, and these same graduates will likely use similar strategies to punish the enemies they create in the outside world.

Enforcing Orthodoxy: The Speech Code

We have already met some of the multiculture's victims—the Donner Four (with their "conservative" graffiti art), the seven Phi Delts at Otero (whose candlelight vigil reminded observers of the KKK), the two freshmen thrown out of Ujamaa (for making fun of the notion that Beethoven was black). On their face, none of these "oppressors" engaged in threatening behavior. Indeed, if one imagined a silent tableau—depicting, for instance, the seven Phi Delts surrounded by a mob threatening to beat them up—one could not help but reach the opposite conclusion. The only immediate threats were coming from multiculturalists themselves.

But none of this should detract from the fact that multiculturalists experienced these behaviors as dangerous attacks. And, indeed, these challenges did threaten multicultural identification—by rendering hollow the mythological claims upon which it is based. And so, it should hardly be surprising that such challenges became reinterpreted as *prima facie* evidence of widespread oppression against multiculturalists. Thus, in a double elimination, multiculturalists would remove as "oppressors" precisely those individuals who were, in some measure, pointing to multicultural intolerance and oppression.

Of course, the fact that challenges to multiculturalism occurred in the first place was a big problem. With respect to the Ujamaa incident, for example, even if nobody defended Ben and Gus in public, people would think for themselves in the privacy of their own dorm rooms and realize that Beethoven was not black, that the two freshmen had been mistreated, and that there was something wrong with a regime that punished people for speaking the truth. There would always be an interval between the subversive incident and the multicultural reaction. No matter how fierce that reaction, not all traces of the unorthodox ideas could be removed. In the hope of preventing dissent such as that at Ujamaa or at Otero from occurring in the first place, Stanford's multiculturalists sought to enact a set of formal rules specifying who could say what to whom. "You have to set up something that tells students what the limits are, what they can do and what they can't," explained student leader Canetta Ivy to the *New York Times*. "What we are proposing is not completely in line with the First Amendment," she added. "We don't put as many restrictions on freedom of speech as we should."[2]

In the two years following the Otero and Ujamaa incidents, law professor Thomas Grey, with the help of other faculty, students and administrators, drafted a revision of Stanford's student conduct code, the Fundamental Standard. Like the regulations implemented at many other college campuses, Stanford's new speech code, adopted in May 1990, prohibited so-called "fighting words" directed at other students. Outlawed speech included words "intended to insult or stigmatize an individual or a small number of individuals on the basis of their sex, race, color, handicap, religion, sexual orientation, or national and ethnic origin."[3]

Although Stanford's code seemed to prohibit all vilification on the basis of sex, race, and these other characteristics, there was a catch. Only epithets targeted at so-called "subordinated" groups were considered "fighting words." Those with a "superordinate" role in society were not protected. For these individuals, explained law professor Charles Lawrence, a supporter of the speech code, there were no "fighting words" in the English language that would "inflict injury."[4] In other words, those who were superordinate were so dominant that, by definition, they could never be hurt by others, and those who were subordinate were so powerless that they could never hurt others.

Because multiculturalists view whites, men, heterosexuals, and Christians as "superordinate," the speech code did not protect most Americans from abuse. Indeed, Judicial Affairs Officer Sally Cole, who enforced the code, said that it would not constitute a violation for an African American to call a Caucasian a "honkey." "Anything that comes to me as a possible violation is going to be looked at in the context of who does what to whom," Cole explained.[5] Clearly, much turns on the definition of what counts as a "subordinate" and what counts as a "superordinate" group—and, predictably, these groups turn out to be the ones that fit the standard multicultural victimology. Of course, it goes without saying that the groups protected by the speech code were sufficiently dominant (or "superordinate") to insure their inclusion in the list of protected groups. In this respect, the fact of the code's enactment suggests that it identified precisely the wrong groups for special protection.

Taken at face value, the code was inconsistent with the reasoning used to rationalize it. One basic problem had to do with the strange notion, argued by Professor Lawrence, that fighting words aimed at subordinated individuals "produce physical symptoms that temporarily disable the victim."[6] With this far-fetched claim, the speech code created an especially invidious distinction of its own. White people presumably could respond to insults, but for racial minorities "there is little (if anything) that can be said to redress either the emotional or reputational injury," according to Professor Lawrence.[7] Because of some (genetic?!) differences between racial groups, speech code advocates seemed to maintain, a code was needed to specially "protect" those people who, by nature, were incapable of doing so for themselves. Even if Professors Lawrence and Grey were right about their psychological speculations, they should have reached very different conclusions. For if Professor Lawrence's claims about "temporarily disabling" the victims were true, then it would follow that there could be *no* "fighting words" aimed at "subordinated" peoples, because such peoples were literally incapable of fighting back. This line of reasoning suggests that if the purpose really had been to maintain peace on campus, the speech code got it exactly backwards, since the only kind of speech that could possibly involve "fighting words" would be that aimed at "superordinated" peoples.

Serious as these theoretical problems may have been, the speech code also suffered from impossible practical hurdles. One of its absurd consequences was that many words were deemed bad only if spoken by certain types of people to other types of people. For example, calling somebody a "faggot" would be a problem only if the person targeted really were homosexual. The finding of a speech code violation would require a determination regarding the sexual practices of the person to whom the word was targeted. And even if the person targeted were shown to be homosexual, one would still have to demonstrate that the speaker was heterosexual—since such epithets presumably would only rise to the level of a violation if made by a "superordinate" person against a "subordinate" person. Thus, two homosexuals could call one another "faggot" with impunity. So could two heterosexuals. A homosexual could use the epithet against a heterosexual. The code only prohibited a heterosexual from hurling the charge at a homosexual. As this example suggests, the complexity of the requisite fact-finding would have made the code unworkable in any proper judicial proceedings.

The speech code's advocates never confronted these serious difficulties with enforcement because they never had to. The fact is that documented incidents involving direct verbal abuse are virtually nonexistent at Stanford. The overwhelming majority of Stanford students, whatever their other shortcomings may be, do not insult one another personally. The code never had to be enforced because it had not really been needed, at least not for the stated reason of combating an epidemic of fighting words and similar abuse. Thus, in January 1993, Judicial Affairs Officer Sally Cole admitted that the speech code had "not been invoked in the more than two years that it's been on the books."[8]

The same, one might add, would have been true in the years preceding the enactment of the speech code. Even the two best documented cases of offensive speech—those at Ujamaa and Otero, which provided much of the impetus for the code's enactment— would not have involved a violation of the actual speech code. At Ujamaa, the challenge came in the form of a picture, not any verbal "fighting words." Even Kenny Ehrman's epithet "faggot" would not have fallen within the ambit of the speech code, because Kenny made this comment behind the closed doors of his dorm room, and not directly to the RA about whom he was complaining.

If there was no epidemic of offensive speech on campus, then why was there a need for a speech code? Its real purpose was not to protect students from racial fights, but rather to seal the door, once and for all, on any disruptive voices. The ambiguities in the code reflected this goal. A comprehensive list of disruptive speech could not simply be banned, because to the extent such a list is explicit (and enumerates the forbidden words and ideas) the list itself would be subversive. The code would actually be more effective in discouraging speech if it were not precise about exactly what words were forbidden. And so, the speech code ignored the precise definitions so essential to a legal framework and only hinted and suggested that there were forbidden ideas and suspect people. Students wishing to avoid the fate of the Otero seven would do best to err on the side of silence. Thus, although Stanford's speech code (along with others like it) would not be comprehensive enough to stifle dissent within the letter of the law, it nonetheless had a chilling effect on student speech—an effect far too comprehensive to avoid suggesting that such a result was not desired.

Over the long term, a speech code that is never applied may be more useful than one that is applied vigorously. Every time a code is officially invoked, after all, there would be a new controversy concerning the invocation itself—over whether the speech at issue really was so terrible, whether the punishment was appropriate, and whether the ideas were clearly mistaken. A vigorous application of a speech code would have the important side effect of drawing further attention to particular instances of the speech that the code was designed to prohibit. By contrast, a code that is never applied may still discourage speech, but will never draw additional attention to subversive ideas. In the case of speech codes, the threat is greater than the execution.

Consider, once more, the Beethoven incident in Ujamaa. Even if the speech code had explicitly prohibited such speech and had been applied against Ben Dugan and Gus Heldt, the net effect would not have been favorable to the multicultural movement. There would have been a judicial investigation and a thorough fact-finding process, including a full review of the surreal discussion about classical music. The two freshmen would have been able to defend themselves and present the other side of events. Indeed, if truth were a complete defense, such a judicial inquiry might even have had to make a factual finding regarding the question of whether Beethoven was black—which, after all, had been the original claim advanced by B. J. Kerr. The national media would have had a field day with the incident, and many unpleasant questions would have been raised about the true meaning of "diversity."

The actual unfolding of events in the Ujamaa episode was much to be preferred. Nobody could say exactly what the two freshmen had done wrong, but everyone was left with the ineffable feeling that the two were guilty of some (literally) unspeakable crime. The lack of a formal judicial process ensured that people would be slow to ask difficult questions about the precise context of these events. Some nagging doubts would remain, but that might not be enough to shatter the multicultural consensus.

Although relentlessly pushed by Stanford's most militant multiculturalists, the campus speech code nevertheless may have represented a miscalculation on their part. The speech code probably added little to the various informal efforts already in place; the prospect of being thrown out of campus housing, after all, already represented quite a powerful deterrent to would-be dissenters. And although the code was symptomatic of the widespread desire to tell students "what they can and cannot say," it was more counterproductive than helpful in this regard. The code drew considerable and unwanted attention to the phenomenon of "political correctness" on campus, and these revelations of multicultural repression helped to discredit the multicultural state. Finally, in May 1994, several Stanford students brought a suit against the university, on the grounds that Stanford's speech code violated the U.S. Constitution and California law. In March 1995, the Santa Clara County Superior Court agreed with the students and found Stanford's speech code unconstitutional.[9] Because of the ruling, Stanford students are no longer prohibited from speaking as freely as the residents of neighboring Palo Alto.

Otero II: The Empire Strikes Back

Because the freedom of speech has been enshrined in the First Amendment of the U.S. Constitution, any direct attempt to limit speech draws criticism from across the ideological spectrum. No matter how narrowly drawn, campus speech codes are a red flag, indicating that something has gone very badly askew in the nation's colleges and universities. But campus speech codes are merely a symptom of the underlying problem—of the multicultural regime's need to prevent people from challenging its fundamental premises. Speech codes may be the most obvious way to approach this issue, but they are not the only way, and they are only the tip of the iceberg. The formal code points to the existence of a whole set of informal, but far more powerful, prohibitions and taboos.

Some of these informal efforts include the incidents in Donner, Ujamaa, and Otero. In these cases, no code of rules served as a restraint on multicultural *ressentiment*. Nevertheless, the lack of a regulatory code does not imply that these violent attacks and accusations are completely at random. On the contrary, they are systematic and follow a rigorous logic of their own—albeit one that the multicultural framework cannot make explicit or encode.

These episodes seem to come from nowhere, periodically interrupting the day-to-day calm of the multicultural regime. Although nobody at the time realized it, Kenny Ehrman's expulsion from Otero in May 1988 proved to be only the prelude to a much greater spectacle that would take place a few years later. After a party on the evening of January 19, 1992, three students were walking through Otero, with the intent of visiting some friends in a neighboring dorm. Two of the students, Keith Rabois and Bret Scher, were friends of Kenny; the third, Michael Ehrman, was Kenny's younger brother.[10] The three were not particularly fond of Otero's RF Dennis Matthies, both for what he had done to Kenny and for the ideological fervor with which he indoctrinated a new group of freshmen each year. One of Dennis's favorite targets is Stanford's fraternities, which he considers bastions of racism and sexism.[11] Keith, Bret, and Michael were all members of the Alpha Epsilon Pi fraternity.

The three complained about RF Matthies to several of the residents they encountered in Otero. Keith, a first-year law student, decided to show his listeners that one could get away with a great deal at Stanford and that the speech code was really quite narrow in scope. As he was leaving Otero and walking past RF Matthies's cottage, Keith shouted,

"Faggot! Faggot! Hope you die of AIDS!" And then, in a pointed reference to the episode involving Kenny, Keith added, "See if you can kick me out of housing!"[12] In a more sober moment, Keith would concede that "the comments made were not very articulate, not very intellectual, nor profound." But that had not been the point: "The intention was for the speech to be outrageous enough to provoke a thought of 'Wow, if he can say that, I guess I can say a little more than I thought.'"[13]

As a matter of law, Keith was correct. His words did not violate the speech code. The code was limited to epithets directed towards students. For that matter, Matthies was not even in his residence at the time Keith gave his demonstration. But Keith was dead wrong to think that he could get away with saying what he said, even if he had violated no written policy. For starters, his demonstration directly challenged one of the most fundamental taboos: To suggest a correlation between homosexual acts and AIDS implies that one of the multiculturalists' favorite lifestyles is more prone to contracting the disease and that not all lifestyles are equally desirable. But by far the most troublesome aspect, to many of the multicultural observers, was Keith's encouragement to other students to see what they could get away with: If others would follow his lead in saying what they thought, then the multicultural regime would be in serious trouble. And so, if for no reason other than deterrence, Keith would have to be punished, albeit necessarily outside the letter of law.

Over the preceding four years (he also had attended Stanford as an undergraduate), Keith had acquired quite a reputation on campus—as an outspoken College Republican, an advocate for his fraternity, and a leading critic of Stanford's administrators. None of these causes were popular with Stanford's multiculturalists, and they could not pass up the perfect opportunity to exact some kind of revenge for the headaches Keith had caused them over the years, while simultaneously reconstituting the multicultural polity.

The charge was led by Dean of Student Affairs Michael Jackson, who in a letter "leaked" the story to the *Stanford Daily*:

> I want to put a big spotlight on the actions of these individuals. I invite others to join me in condemning their behavior, the meanness and viciousness behind it, and in expressing our shock that Stanford students would deliberately behave in so disgusting and hurtful a manner....The speech...presents an invitation, even an obligation, for the good citizens of our community to speak out against the few who care more for their constitutional rights than for their campus community's need for respect and decency.[14]

With this letter, Dean Jackson outlined the general strategy: All of the "good citizens" of the multicultural state had an "obligation" to punish Keith through a public outpouring of anger and outrage. Those who did not publicly condemn Keith would be suspected of sharing his views and of not being "good citizens." Jackson knew that he would be able to trigger a massive response, especially after the *Stanford Daily* proceeded to vilify Keith: For the next two weeks, front-page articles repeated an exaggerated account of events that failed to present Keith's explanation for what had happened and why.[15] Even Stanford President Donald Kennedy issued a statement condemning him.[16]

The pressure was particularly strong on those who knew Keith. Even his fraternity felt compelled to oblige. It joined Dean Jackson "in publicly condemning his actions," while emphasizing that "his actions were undertaken independently of our organization and should in no way be construed as indicative of our membership."[17]

The excitement surrounding Keith's exorcism was infectious. Stanford lawyer Robin Kennedy (second wife of President Kennedy), in the name of "human dignity," expressed her hopes that Keith would be punished for the rest of his life:

> I am deeply disturbed that a person of Rabois' character—and with his obvious disrespect for human dignity—may someday become qualified as a member of my profession, displaying two Stanford degrees on his wall. I hope the Bar Association of whatever state in which Rabois elects to practice is informed of his behavior in this incident and aware that such behavior represents a violation of this community's values.[18]

Senior Gina Durante added her voice to the chorus, suggesting that Keith should be treated like a "hardened criminal":

> Keith Rabois went out of his way to prove that he is capable of spewing the kind of ignorant filth common among hardened criminals....If nothing else, the majority of people in the Stanford Community can hope that Rabois has learned a thing or two about decorum and public relations from this incident and its resulting publicity. If not, perhaps then the community will subject him to the sort of loathing that his kind has always directed toward whatever group happens to be the scapegoat of the day.[19]

The repetitive nature of these accusations did not make them any more true. But they reinforced the sense among the Stanford community that Keith was guilty of a truly heinous crime. And the more the community focused on Keith's terrible deed, the more convinced it became of how hideously oppressed the everyday lives of homosexuals must be. It was important for all the "good citizens" to attack Keith so as to reinforce the victimized identities of gays and lesbians.

Graduate student Mario Huerta got even more carried away in the enthusiasm of the moment:

> When I read in *The Daily* about the incident at Otero Jan. 19, I was relieved to find out that there had been another homophobic attack. One, that is, which hadn't culminated in murder....So what is the lesson? Put simply, it is that education is not enough....If it weren't for the privileges, sanctioned by law, favoring heterosexually-oriented people, nobody—whether educated or uneducated—would be able to get away with his or her homophobic neuroses-turned mad attacks....The time is ripe for going out to the streets, linking up internationally and demanding the rights that will ensure the liberation of all sexually oppressed sectors. These demands, to be effectuated worldwide, must include:
> — The abolition of marriage;
> — The abolition of all privileges (such as tax breaks, government subsidies, reduced rates for memberships, etc.) granted to families;
> — The complete legalization of abortion, contraceptives, sexual education, prostitution, surrogate motherhood and pornography;
> — The recognition of all relationships consented to by people...
> — The formation of reproduction (including physical and sexual) and sexual workers' unions on a transnational level;
> — The formation of household inspection committees to put an end to domestic violence and to all undemocratic, sexist, chauvinist and other types of oppressive practices.[20]

For Huerta, as for many others, the "Otero II" incident provided excellent cover for all forms of multicultural *ressentiment,* even if some of his demands were inconsistent (simultaneously abolishing marriage and allowing "all relationships consented to by people").

Stanford Law School was the epicenter of the fury. All notions of due process were thrown out. The reaction was even more personally nasty than elsewhere in the University:

- Several law students called a meeting (advertised as "Free Speech, Hate Speech") for the express purpose of letting other students and faculty vent their anger at Keith. The 100 participants soon found something else to be angry about: Keith had chosen not to attend.[21]
- 443 law students, faculty (including those who taught Keith), and administrators signed a quarter-page "Open Letter" in the *Stanford Daily* denouncing Keith as a bigot.[22]
- Several law students organized a letter-writing campaign to prevent Keith from getting a summer job. The organizers knew that Keith hoped to work in California in 1992, but did not know where—and so they proceeded to write to several hundred California law firms, urging all of them not to hire Keith as a summer associate. Second-year law student Jamie Kershaw described the campaign as "retributive justice or vengeance or whatever."[23]
- One law student placed two large bulletin boards, adorned with a picture of Keith's face, at the law library entrance. She encouraged other students and faculty to use these boards to sign their own personalized attacks on Keith. These denunciations eventually numbered in the hundreds. Keith was urged to behave more responsibly, encouraged to grow up, and scolded for his "insensitivity." Others said that they were ashamed to be associated with him by virtue of their common attendance at Stanford Law School, and expressed their shock and anger in a variety of other ways. Another person even questioned Keith's sanity. By chance or design, however, one writer managed to say something profound: "Keith, you witch. Welcome to Salem."[24]

Indeed, the group attack eerily recalled the scapegoating of witches in Salem or the collective catharsis achieved during George Orwell's "Minute of Hate" in *1984*. Consider cultural critic Jean-Michel Oughourlian's account of a witch-hunt:

> When everyone gathers in the village square of the city to burn a sorcerer or a witch, it is a great feast, a very special day. Gathered to take part in the sacrifice, the whole population participates in it and is purified by the fire, united by its belief in the victim's guilt and comforted to be rid of the source of all its troubles. The execution is ritualized, public, and surrounded with civil, military,

> and religious trappings. Everything is set in motion to make of this punishment a "founding lynching," to make of this assassination a myth of foundation, so that from this death may come peace, security, and well-being for all the citizens.[25]

Under the pretense of reacting to some violation or other, Stanford's leaders generated a massive outpouring of popular anger and retribution—focused on Keith, but also encompassing conservatives, fraternities, and the other usual targets. When all was said and done, the particulars of the original incident that led to this chain of events mattered very little. That incident (real or imaginary) had become transformed into a myth which served to reconstitute and rejuvenate the multicultural community. This myth would continue to reassure all those who had participated in Keith's *auto-da-fé* that they were "good citizens."

By year's end, Keith had transferred to another law school. For all practical purposes he had been expelled. But before he left, Keith offered some reflections of his own:

> When all the resources of the multicultural agenda are directed against you, you quickly find out who your real friends are. In this way, this has been one of the most valuable experiences of my life....It has certainly not been fun. But if my serving as the personification of "evil" allows the rest of campus to reassure itself that it is "good," so be it. Others know better.[26]

Most of the multiculturalists did not know better. They believed their own exaggerations regarding the incident, and concluded that their response had been perfectly even-handed; the punishment had fit the crime.

The storm over Keith's action convulsed the campus for several months. By the end of the process, nobody dared to challenge the claim that homosexuals truly were oppressed. Their fragile identities had been thoroughly reaffirmed. At the same time, the denizens of the multicultural community could be reassured that they were "good citizens" because they were helping victimized homosexuals to confront and overcome their "oppressor." The crisis was largely self-created, even if its eventual resolution required Keith's physical removal from the multicultural polis. But by that point in time, this removal did not seem like a high price to pay: From the midst of the crisis, calm had been restored.

"Retributive Justice or Vengeance or Whatever"

Keith's condemnation was not the first such hysteria at Stanford, or even at Stanford Law School. Several years earlier, the men's bathroom in the law school had contained chalkboards for people to write messages. On one such board, someone anonymously enumerated a (relatively short) list of attractive women at Stanford Law School. A brigade of activists removed the chalkboard from the bathroom, and deposited it in the student lounge. For the next several months, life at the law school revolved around the chalkboard list, just as several years later it would revolve around Keith Rabois. The law school community generally (and the women not listed, in particular) condemned the chalkboard list—it was taken as evidence of widespread sexism and other forms of oppression. Once again, an "oppressor" served the important role of reinforcing multicultural identities. Law school activists exhorted, implored, and begged the person who had written these things to come forward; they promised that nothing would happen to him—they would just seek to reeducate him. Having some premonition of what might befall him, however, this particular culprit wisely chose to remain silent.

It should be noted that neither Keith Rabois nor the unknown law student was completely innocent. Keith had said something rude, and the enumeration of good-looking women was hurtful to the others. But it must also be said that in the larger scheme of things, these actions injured nobody physically, and any psychological wounds were largely self-created. In every case, the multiculturalists behaved far more inappropriately. Their convulsive reaction bore no relation to the offending action. Keith did not deserve months of public condemnation and ostracism, and the unknown law student's list should not have become the focus of law school life.

Consider the analogy to Salem suggested on the law school bulletin board. In the case of the witchcraft trials, the accused women likely were not angelic people. Quite the contrary, many of the accused were probably rather unpleasant people who had behaved imperfectly in the past and were partially to blame for the negative attention they received. Nevertheless, the overreaction of the Salem community was as wrong as that of Stanford's multiculturalists. For none of the accused women were witches, just as neither Keith nor the admirer of pretty women were "hardened criminals."

Scarcely a week would pass at Stanford without exaggerated denunciations and attacks on some individual or other who was saying or doing things the multiculturalists did not like. Over the course of several years, numerous individuals were singled out for being "racist," "sexist," "homophobic," or just plain "insensitive," often in contexts that had seemingly little to do with any of these matters. For example:

- In November 1988, the organizers of the traditional football rally before the annual Big Game against UC Berkeley were accused of racism for naming the event "Cardinal and White Night" (Stanford's school colors are cardinal and white).[27]
- In May 1989, Stanford's College Republicans organized a "Republican Appreciation Day," in which students were encouraged to ride their bikes to show support for Republican causes. Perhaps because of the parallel to the Gay and Lesbian Alliance's "Shorts Day," a warm day each spring in which people are exhorted to wear shorts, the Republicans were criticized for being "insulting and disrespectful to truly oppressed minority groups."[28]
- In an October 1990 football game against Oregon, Stanford's irreverent band poked fun at the spotted owl controversy. The most offensive part of the script included the following lines: "Trees and spotted owls are disappearing like crazy and everybody wants to know why....Mr. Spotted Owl! Mr. Spotted Owl! Your environment has been destroyed, your home is now a roll of Brawny, and your family has flown the coop."[29] Alan Cummings, Stanford's acting director of athletics, suspended the Stanford Band for displaying "an insensitivity and disrespect to the Oregon community."[30] More precisely, of course, the Stanford Band had been "insensitive" to Oregon's humorless *environmental* community (none of the people employed in that state's logging industry had complained, but for multicultural purposes the loggers apparently were not part of the "Oregon community").
- In the summer of 1991, several Stanford students had the opportunity to meet with C. Boyden Grey, the chief counsel to President Bush. In the ensuing discussion, Grey argued that not all gender distinctions should be criminalized because some gender differences are real. He tried to drive this point home with the flip observation that "boys will be boys, girls will be girls." The listeners had heard enough. Chanting "sexist pig," all but one of the women in the room stood up and left.[31] At Stanford, that was considered a successful conclusion to the discussion.
- In the spring of 1992, French professor Robert Cohn was forced into retirement after 32 years of work at Stanford. Cohn explained that his classes were emptied by student boycotts organized by faculty who disagreed with his conservative political views: "Stanford threw me away....The idea of going into class and finding no students was too painful. But it happened too often." In spite of Cohn's having received two Guggenheim awards, Stanford's Humanities Center refused to support his research projects. French professor Jean-Marie Apostolides blamed Cohn

for his own predicament: "A professor should be capable of renewing himself."[32]

- In an act of silent denunciation, one activist pointed a finger at Judge Richard Posner throughout his entire speech at Stanford Law School; when her arm got tired, she used the other one to prop it up. And, for good measure, she also cast a hex (a complicated series of hand movements, accompanied by hissing) on the libertarian judge and author.[33]
- In the fall of 1990, two row-house residents were given a choice: Either remove the Confederate flag from their room, or be thrown out of housing. In light of this, the first Otero incident, and numerous other threatened or actual removals, the response "You're outta housing" became a favorite reaction to speech critical of multiculturalism.[34]
- In the spring of 1989, former secretary of state George Shultz was pelted with a french fry (plus ketchup) at the Florence Moore dining hall. His crime consisted of having accepted the lunch invitation of several Stanford students.[35]
- In 1994, the naming of Yale law professor Stephen Carter as graduation speaker prompted an outcry. A liberal on most positions, Carter (who has questioned the "blackness" of black conservatives—see chapter 2) has nonetheless criticized some aspects of affirmative action. Apparently, Carter himself was not "black" enough for many campus activists. The leaders of the Black Student Union, among others, denounced the choice as evidence of a right-wing conspiracy of students and administrators seeking to rid the campus of minority students.[36]
- On numerous occasions, copies of the *Stanford Review*, a conservative and libertarian student newspaper critical of multiculturalism, were destroyed en masse. Mass removals from regular campus distribution sites occurred, for instance, after news articles on Stanford's controversial "domestic partners" policy and the MEChA hunger strike. The newspaper destroyers ironically compared the editors of the *Review* to "Nazis."[37] On every occasion, the University's Judicial Affairs Office refused to investigate the breech of freedom of the press.
- Stanford's Memorial Church has supported the expulsion of Bible studies from private dorm rooms. Byron Bland, a "minister" with the United Campus Christian Ministry (which runs Stanford's Memorial Church) called traditional Bible study groups "narrow" and urged them to study a broader "range of expression," including "the experiences and theologies of, for example, Latin Americans and feminists."[38]

- In the late 1980s, the Ronald Reagan Presidential Library Foundation wanted to site the Reagan Library at Stanford. A unique academic resource, the library would contain the papers of the Reagan presidency and further enhance the prestige of Stanford University. Nevertheless, students and faculty circulated petitions denouncing the proposal.[39] Others worried about its possible siting on an "ecologically sensitive" hill overlooking the campus. Within several months, the Foundation got the message and withdrew its proposal. English professor Ronald Rebholz was overjoyed: The decision to withdraw was "astonishing, surprising and wonderful. It's one of the few political victories I've had in my life."[40]
- Stanford's ROTC program was driven out by protests in the early 1970s and has never returned. The only thing that has changed in the intervening years is the preferred excuse: In the 1970s, opposition to the military was couched in terms of disagreement over the Vietnam War, whereas in the 1990s the attack is justified because of the military's "discrimination" against homosexuals and women. In practice, the only people who are directly hurt by this ideologically driven attack are the Stanford students on ROTC scholarships, who must make a one-hour commute to take the requisite classes at UC Berkeley's campus.
- Stanford Law School's Career Service Office (CSO) has taken the further measure of banning military recruiters from interviewing law students on campus. The "public interest," according to the CSO, does not include the U.S. military, but does encompass more "progressive" organizations like the Nicaraguan Marxist Women's Defense Fund.[41] Even the ban was not enough to satisfy law school dean Paul Brest. When a U.S. Marine Corps recruiter placed flyers in student mailboxes informing students of off-campus recruiting, Brest felt compelled to respond with a memo of his own, which he distributed to all students at the law school:

> Dear Friends,
> An unknown person has placed recruiting flyers for the U.S. Marine Corps Judge Advocate Program in many students' mailboxes. You should be aware that the Judge Advocate Program is not permitted to use the Law School's Career Services Office's facilities and services because it is not in compliance with the School's Non-Discrimination Policy with respect to sexual orientation.[42]

On its face, Brest's memo was simply gratuitous: Student mailboxes are not "facilities and services" of the CSO, and even an (ominous-sounding) "unknown person" may use them. Because the Marine Corps flyer could not be stopped in the first place, Brest tried to do the next best thing—denouncing and symbolically purging the military from Stanford Law School.

- Just before Education Secretary William Bennett's Stanford address in April 1988, Provost Jim Rosse encouraged radical student leaders to boo and hiss during Bennett's speech, so as to discredit Bennett's claims.[43] When Bennett instead received a standing ovation, President Kennedy shifted opprobrium onto Stanford's College Republicans, whom he accused of orchestrating a show of support.[44] For Stanford's multiculturalists, there is always someone to blame.

"Militant Action"

The targets of multiculturalism need not be outspokenly conservative, like the College Republicans or the *Stanford Review*, and they need not even have loosely conservative (or pro-American) connotations, like the Reagan Library or U.S. military. Although these targets are in some respects the easiest ones, it would be a major mistake to think that these ritual denunciations are in any way limited by ideology.

In the absence of obvious or compelling targets, others that are less obvious will be found. The multiculture's demand for oppressors will be met. Along these lines, it is worth stressing that the initial degree of differentiation from the prevailing orthodoxy can be very small indeed. So long as there is that initial difference, even if only in the minds of some of the observers, the violence that drives multicultural *ressentiment* can do the rest, transforming the mildest nonconformist into an enemy of the multicultural state.

The multicultural targets often have no idea what hit them: A bad joke, a slightly inappropriate comment, or the wrong turn of phrase can all generate a massive surge (and focusing) of multicultural anger. It is difficult to predict who the next targets will be. And although most individuals are careful not to give offense, not everybody will behave with perfect diligence all of the time. It only takes a spark to set off the multicultural explosions.

In the spring of 1992, shortly after the first verdicts were returned in the Rodney King trials, Stanford's multiculturalists were even more angry than usual. Everybody agreed that Rodney King had been a victim, and so it was time to look for a victimizer. The most obvious people responsible, the three police officers charged with the beating, were in Los

Angeles. That was too far away; a more proximate cause was needed and soon found.

On May 1, 1992, classes at Stanford Law School were cancelled so that students and faculty could participate in demonstrations. Speaker after speaker denounced the entire society that had ever allowed such a verdict. One speaker exhorted the crowd, "If it doesn't look bad to you, you aren't looking good."[45] About 1,000 protestors marched into downtown Palo Alto, a well-to-do suburban community near Stanford, protesting behind a banner that declared "Wake up, the revolution has begun again."[46] In several cities, notably Los Angeles and San Francisco, there had been violent riots, and nobody in Palo Alto quite knew what to expect. Several stores had closed for the day, and one, Copeland's (a sporting goods store), had taken the additional precaution of boarding its windows.[47]

This very precaution became the natural target of the demonstrators' anger. Multicultural Educator Greg Ricks declared that Copeland's boarding was "a huge insult" to "Stanford students on a peaceful march." Ricks added that Stanford students "are the most educated people in the country. We're not rioters, we're scholars."[48] He called for a boycott of Copeland's, paradoxically using rhetoric that evoked the images of a violent riot: "We're going to go down to University Avenue, the heart of this city....We're going to show some radical economic policy that's bigger than 20,000 fires. This is militant action. This is a serious thing."[49] Junior Terry Clay contradictorily declared, "We are taking things over in a peaceful and forceful manner."[50] All of the talk about a "forceful" takeover and "militant action" indicates that the line between a peaceful protest and violence was extremely thin. Even though there happened to be no riot in Palo Alto that day, the fears of anxious store owners were not unwarranted.

The boycott of an upscale sporting goods store in suburban Palo Alto would seem to be far removed from events in Los Angeles, from breaking the cycle of poverty in America's inner cities, or even from dealing with the problem of police violence. For the demonstrators, though, the day's events had been a tremendous success. The multicultural community had been galvanized and united, and the experience of collective anger had been wonderfully cathartic. At the end of the day, BSU leader Bacardi Jackson exulted, "We've all done a lot of work, and I'm really impressed by the way Stanford has mobilized. Take a look around. Let's say 'Thank God.' Thank somebody."[51] Ricks concluded that the response to the King verdict had been a "multicultural event," and for once he was right.[52]

Even Copeland's may not have been the most preposterous of the multiculturalists' targets. That prize may go to Jan Kerkhoven, a self-described "humanist" and third-year doctoral candidate in the School of Education. According to his advisor, feminist studies professor Nel

Noddings, Jan (pronounced "Yan") was "so interested in feminist studies that he [had] participated in a reading group."[53] Even such public displays of ideological commitment did not guarantee immunity from multicultural attacks, however.

In Spring 1991, Jan attempted to take "Feminist Methodology in the Social Sciences."[54] He was the sole male to enroll in the class. Jan told the class that he accepted the magnitude and pervasiveness of male dominance and oppression of women, but said he could not view the issue as pertaining only to women. Jan explained that he could not "see the oppression of women outside the larger context of the dehumanization of society." In a paper for the class, Jan elaborated:

> As a man I see no way to do women centered research, without implicitly conveying the message that serves to endorse the abominable system of gender in place. Women centered research by a man will further the partial truth that men have to give up their privilege and dominance as if these represent an absolute advantage of men over women.[55]

It is difficult to imagine greater devotion to the feminist cause. Yet Professor Susan Krieger responded to the paper by throwing Jan out of the class. According to Professor Krieger, Jan "didn't have the right commitment to a gendered outlook...[and might] divert the class discussion in an undesirable direction."[56] Some students found Jan's ideas "disturbing," and Professor Krieger concluded that Jan did not have the "right preparation." She suggested that he enroll in an introductory feminist class.[57]

The fact that Jan's comments were "disturbing" did not cause the seminar's participants to question their own assumptions. A much easier recourse was at hand: They could get rid of the "disturbing" person instead. For only minor deviations, Jan became a hapless target of multicultural *ressentiment.* Unaware of his crime or of what was really happening, Jan was simply flabbergasted: "It is shocking for me to be bumped off the one course that fully addresses the issues that I am struggling with."[58]

Jan's case is not unique or even unusual, but it does indicate that no objective parameters delineate the set of multicultural enemies. In a particular context, a former ally might become a new enemy, if for no other reason than that no other enemies are readily available. Jan may have had an illustrious career of following the party line and participating in his own multicultural denunciations, but he was unfortunately now stuck in a situation where others were hewing to the party line even more closely. It was therefore his turn to be denounced.

The fact that even Jan Kerkhoven became a target suggests that nobody is ever completely beyond reach. Joining the multicultural mob does not guarantee that one will be safe. And as we will see next, neither does membership in a preferred minority group.

Enemies Within

Even though some of Stanford's multiculturalists perceive all white males to be symbolic representatives of the West (and therefore a part of the enemy), it would be a mistake to think that these expulsions and witch-hunts are limited by race or gender.[59] If anything, the nonconforming members of preferred victim groups (for example, pro-life women, conservative blacks, or even Professor Stephen Carter) often receive even worse treatment than nonconforming white males. To many multiculturalists, it is a distinction between enemies and traitors.

Enemies, like white males and other superordinate peoples, just "do not understand" the oppression of the subordinated. Within the multicultural framework, it is expected that a white male will say something inappropriate every now and then; white males "just don't get it" (and are not really expected to, at least not on their own). On balance, their contretemps probably reassure multiculturalists, reminding them that there will always be ignorant people for them to reeducate and oppressors for them to despise. Traitors, on the other hand, like conservative blacks or pro-life women, cannot simply be dismissed as ignorant, since multiculturalists claim that these categories of people possess special knowledge. Because the very existence of such traitors threatens the foundations of the multicultural state, they must be dealt with in an especially harsh way. If they cannot be gotten rid of entirely, they must be muzzled at the very least.

Thus, for several years in the late 1980s, the Black Student Union kept a "blacklist" of black Stanford students who were insufficiently "Black"—that is, students who did not subscribe to the radical positions multiculturalism claims that all blacks must hold. One *Stanford Daily* columnist described how the "blacklist" worked:

> One thing that I won't forget is the "blacklist" that circulated around campus my freshman year, and that still exists today. It was a "list" of black students who were judged (by whom I don't know) to be oreos, pseudo, whitewashed. Apparently, those on the list didn't fit the mold of a typical black person, whatever that is. My friend was one of the students who was included on this list. Ironically, my friend is one of the "blackest" persons

> I know, in the sense that she is very proud of her African heritage, and she and her family reflect a strong African culture. More than that, my friend is also proud of her American culture. She's not down with baseball, apple pie and all that, but she has embraced her American culture, including its aesthetic, language and intellectual tradition. And for this, I suspect, she made the blacklist.[60]

Those on the "blacklist" were shunned by politically active black students and informally ostracized from Stanford's black community—an especially invidious punishment at a place like Stanford. Outside the multicultural state, such a list, though reprehensible, would not be psychologically devastating. Given a choice, after all, most of the students on such a list would not want to be friends with the people who put them there—and would instead choose their friends from among the rest of the student body. Under the multicultural regime, however, this is far more difficult to do. The multicultural axioms regarding intragroup unity and intergroup difference encourage friendships along racial lines. If one is black, it likely will be more difficult to form friendships with students of other races. The one place where such a list is necessary to maintain the prevailing regime is also the only place where something like the BSU's "blacklist" can really hurt people. Their mistreatment was not just a punishment, but a threat of what would happen to other "people of color" who stepped out of line—even just a little bit.[61]

The BSU's tactics for dealing with nonconformists were still quite gentle, at least compared to the methods devised by MEChA, Stanford's militant Chicano/Latino group. MEChA sought to promote "unity" under its leadership, with a stress on radical causes (like the grape boycott and hunger strike). Those in Stanford's Hispanic community who disagreed with these priorities were singled out as "disrupters," and subjected to personal attacks and harassment. One of the most frequent tactics, used against countless "disrupters," involved the physical "encirclement" of individual Hispanic students and staff who disagreed with MEChA. In such encirclements, five MEChA members would surround the lone "disrupter" and make pointed and abrasive statements until the student was intimidated into silence. The individual would be accused of lacking solidarity, betraying his people, and so on; a number of students were driven to tears in the process.[62]

In the spring of 1989, MEChA launched a takeover of El Centro Chicano, the university-funded Hispanic student center on campus. Director Juan Yniguez, who hoped to make the center open to the entire Hispanic community, was denounced because he "never envisioned unity in the community as a possibility in the first place."[63] Yniguez was subject to taunts, harassment, and abuse (no protection from fighting words here), and both he and his staff were constantly asked what their "employment plans are for the future."[64] MEChA's critics received degrading and menacing phone calls and had their places of work repeatedly vandalized.[65] For Yniguez, the last straw came when he and his four-year-old daughter encountered decapitated birds on their doorstep at home.[66] As a result of these tactics, Yniguez eventually resigned and someone more in line with the MEChistas replaced him.

Even more disturbing than these encirclements and systematic harassments, however, was the Stanford administration's response to MEChA's coup. When 40 Hispanic students sent a complaint to President Kennedy and Dean of Student Affairs James Lyons, the administration responded by informing MEChA of who the troublemakers were.[67] MEChA members proceeded to call the 40 students who had written the letter to pressure them into withdrawing it.[68] Predictably, MEChA accused the letter writers of undermining unity:

> The recent letter supposedly supported by 40 members of our community to Donald Kennedy is a destructive effort in that it only serves to keep our community from focusing on the true concerns of Chicanos and Latinos at Stanford....It has shocked many in our community....It is behavior such as this that creates a negative atmosphere in our community, not MEChA.[69]

The letter writers became subject to the very kinds of abuse they had complained about in the first place, as MEChA redoubled its harassment.

Unfortunately, these muzzling techniques worked. A number of students withdrew their names from the petition, and even those who did not withdraw their names did not push the matter any further: what would be the use, given the apparent complicity of the administration? As a result, MEChA achieved its main objective ("unity," or at least the appearance of unity, which was almost as good), and more than a year elapsed before this particular series of events came to light.[70] In the end, for many non-MEChA Hispanic students, the whole episode became an object lesson in the price of criticizing the new multicultural state. Much like Soviet dissidents writing letters to Premier Brezhnev complaining about the KGB's human rights violations, those who sought redress from the Kennedy administration for multicultural abuses—such as the 40 letter signers, or the seven Phi Delt protestors at Otero—often became the logical next targets of the very abuses they challenged.

Moral Luck

Taken separately, these episodes are easy to dismiss. Each incident involves a handful of targets or more often, only a single person. After the fact, with the benefit of 20/20 hindsight, it is always possible to identify ways in which the targets could have avoided opprobrium. It is then seductive to reinterpret their failure to do so as a kind of misbehavior. But taken together, these episodes cannot be dismissed. They bring a disturbing picture into focus. The multicultural hunt for nonexistent "oppressors" who can be held responsible for all of America's ills leads to the vilification of innocents. Individuals are held responsible for crimes they did not commit.

In the process, justice is not the only thing sacrificed. So is truth, the very mission of the university. Sustaining false accusations necessitates the replacement of facts with myths. A detailed case is rarely brought against individuals; rather, an accusation of wrongdoing simply requires identifying someone as a member of a mythical group of oppressors.

The problem with these myths is not exactly that they ignore cause and effect, but that they require an excess of cause and effect. Causal links are perceived even where none exist, or where only the most tenuous correlations can be drawn between an offense and the offending person. In Salem, old women identified as witches were blamed for all sorts of individual misfortunes and social problems. In that case, the mythical causal link between the women and the problems was that the witches had supposedly been casting evil spells on people. Similarly, primitive peoples assumed that gods or demons were responsible for illnesses and plagues. Multicultural superstition revolves around a similar primitivism.

Multiculturalists invent myths of causation when they blame Copeland's for contributing to the oppression of blacks or Jan Kerkhoven for contributing to the oppression of women. Certainly, a sporting goods store would appear to have no link to a police beating hundreds of miles away. But by creating an elaborate web of connections and arbitrarily focusing on a small subset of these connections, multiculturalists are able to isolate particular culprits as the parties responsible for societal ills. This mythical victimology is not falsifiable: If any links in the causal chain were shown to be fanciful, then new and circuitous routes of causation would spring up to replace them. For the most part, the multiculture's "oppressors" are never quite sure what hit them, because they never could have imagined their actions to have all of the ramifications perceived by the multicultural community.

The general direction in which this bizarre scapegoating ritual is leading is not difficult to discern. Institutions like Stanford University are indoctrinating the current generation of American graduates with a new mythology—a complete pantheon, filled with heroes and villains, deified victims and demonized oppressors. Like the shamans of primitive peoples, the high priests of multiculturalism provide their acolytes with a comprehensive doxology, offering explanations and connections to make sense of an otherwise mysterious and complex reality. This mythology allows them to point to deep structural problems for any mishaps and identify immediate culprits.

The multiculture is not only creating chronic malcontents; it is providing them with a lexicon of New Age crimes. These crimes have no objective indicators or causation. Much like the case of witchcraft, which could only be discerned by the "victims" of spells, their legitimacy is guaranteed by the mental states of the "victims" alone. Since every individual reacts and takes offense in unpredictable ways, nobody is safe from the multicultural witch-hunt. There are no principled rules—indeed, there are not even arbitrary guides—telling people how to conduct themselves in order not to give offense. The various episodes may fit a general pattern, but it is never clear when a particular event will meet the threshold to trigger a multicultural episode. Because multicultural causation is arbitrary, individuals are targeted almost at random; they are not in any meaningful sense morally culpable.

Multiculturalists often claim that they are merely holding individuals to account for the consequences of their actions. Little could be further from the truth. Multiculturalism is teaching a new generation to engage in wanton name-calling and senseless accusation. When a stray look could lead to a charge of sexual harassment or an ill-timed joke to a charge of a racial slur, careers and lives are needlessly destroyed. Hapless innocents get thrown out of housing, lose their jobs because of "insensitivity," or spend years fighting frivolous lawsuits. The accused are not morally flawed, just unlucky.

Busy Doing Nothing

While the specific details vary from episode to episode, the larger storyline always seems very much the same. Individuals or organizations embody or espouse views that are incompatible with the multiculture: a defense of traditional morality, of the free-enterprise system, or of Western civilization, or perhaps merely a minor dissent from the multicultural orthodoxy. The community finds this challenge (however miniscule and seemingly insignificant) intolerable, regardless of whether the challenge is presented seriously or humorously, is framed positively or negatively, or is advanced by a 70-year-old professor or a 19-year-old sophomore. The multicultural response seeks to achieve a unanimous (or near unanimous) condemnation of the critics, as the initial incident becomes the excuse for "educational" opportunities and a springboard for other "multicultural events."

These "multicultural events," more reminiscent of totalitarian show trials or medieval inquisitions than of the rational pursuit of truth, raise an important but troubling question: Do Stanford's faculty and administrators have nothing better to do with their time? Even if their causes were worthwhile, the extent of the effort still seems excessive. A Shakespeare teacher should have more interesting things to do than circulate petitions condemning a library, and a law school dean should have more pressing things to do than hand out fliers disavowing military recruiters. The silliness of these activities is matched only by the zeal of the respective advocates.

Nietzsche once noted that most people would rather believe in nothingness than in nothing. If the multiculturalists were true relativists, believing in nothing at all, then nothing would matter, and there would not even be a need or much of a point to any of these unsavory attacks and ritual denunciations. But, as already noted many times, the multiculturalists are not full-fledged nihilists. And because they would prefer an anti-Western nothingness to a relativistic nothing, they are left with the singular task of purging the community of those who might suggest alternatives. These systematic attacks, expulsions, and persecutions are at the very core of multiculturalism.

The multicultural explanations and rationalizations for these various "multicultural events" are likely to be incomplete, if not downright misleading. The major reason for the denunciation of Keith Rabois was not sensitivity towards homosexuals, just as the major reason for the opposition to the Reagan Library was not ecological and the major reason for the elimination of the Western Culture program was not curricular. Multicultural events are not primarily for the benefit of a handful of activists concerned about ecology or abstract ideals of nonpartisanship. One should not be distracted by what is taking place on the multicultural stage—by the morality plays of self-proclaimed "victims," who use their status to attack the politically incorrect representatives of the West. Of course, like the "witches" at Salem and the dissidents in the Soviet Union, the suffering inflicted on the "people's enemies" is very real. But for the multiculturalists, this suffering is just an incidental part of the price that must be paid to reconstitute the multicultural community in the only possible way—in perpetual opposition to the West.

The multicultural mob does best if it can find actual representatives of the West to persecute, just as the communist regimes of the 20th century could stage the most dramatic show trials on those rare occasions when they actually caught real subversives. For both of these regimes, however, the most important component is that the spectators believe the distortions and untruths that they are being told. Salem was not a community that was confronted with an epidemic of witchcraft, but merely a community that believed it was so confronted. In a similar way, the supposed Western representatives need not be particularly credible enemies of the multicultural state. As in the case of Copeland's, the Hispanic students attacked by MEChA, or the liberal male in the feminist studies class, the multicultural imagination can be counted on to do the rest. The theater of multiculturalism exists primarily for the benefit of the spectators, so that the entire community can release a kind of cathartic anger.

In light of these observations, it is worth considering the work of Romanian ethnologist Mircea Eliade. Eliade studied religious rituals and observed that in many archaic cultures, these sacred rites served a foundational purpose in describing the creation of the world. Because archaic societies subscribed to a cyclical rather than a linear (Western) conception of time, these rituals, from the point of view of the participants, actually reenacted the original creation of the world. Each new year involved a repetitious celebration of the cosmogony—of the passage from chaos to cosmos. Eliade summarizes the elements of the annual rituals accompanying the new year:

> Fasting, ablutions, and purifications; extinguishing the fire and ritually rekindling it in a second part of the ceremonial; expulsion of demons by noises, cries, blows (indoors), followed by their pursuit through the village with uproar and hullabaloo; this expulsion can be practiced under the form of the ritual sending away of an animal or of a man, regarded as the material vehicle through which the faults of the entire community are transported beyond the limits of the territory it inhabits.[71]

A successful completion of the sacred rituals guaranteed that the world (and the human community participating in these rituals) would go through the same eternal cycle anew.

The multiculture—with its hunger fasts, expulsions, and ritualized scapegoatings—bears some remarkable similarities to the archaic cultures studied by Eliade. Like archaic societies throughout the world, Stanford's multicultural tribe periodically reproduces the original event—the rejection of Western Culture—in which the multiculture had its genesis. All of the original components come back together for a mythical moment in time: the mob chanting slogans, the individual or institution that symbolizes the West (or some trace of the West), the elimination of the latter by the former, and the re-creation of the multicultural community in the process of this elimination. In this sense, the protest at Copeland's (or any of the other incidents described in this book) was not merely a "multicultural event," but became another incarnation of the original multicultural event itself.

Of course, Stanford's multiculturalists do not perceive themselves to be engaged in any sort of primitive scapegoating ritual. In this new (as in the very old) context, the true nature of the ritual must remain hidden if it is to be foundational. If the multiculturalists ever realized that they were themselves creating new victims, presumably their zeal for the process would cease. At the very least, they would lack the passionate conviction needed to transform each discrete event into another founding myth.

Nevertheless, no matter how evocative the parallels to the non-Western cultures studied by Eliade, there also are differences. Although the degree of uniformity is remarkable, the multiculture is unable to shut out all foreign ideas and thus cannot achieve the complete closure that it seeks. A unanimity of belief, regarding the proper allocation of guilt and innocence (and a consensus regarding who the victims and victimizers are), cannot be reached in the multiculture as it could in archaic cultures. At the end of the day, disagreements remain, so that no finite list of scapegoats satisfies everyone. Multiculturalism promises to found a new utopia, but only at an infinite price, as a never-ending list of the people's enemies must be denounced and expelled.

The multiculture will never reach "the new kind of community" sought by President Kennedy. Stanford under multiculturalism is not a New Jerusalem, the shining city on the hill envisioned by the Puritans of New England, providing a beacon of light to an unrepentant world. But more than any of Eliade's primitive tribes, perhaps, multicultural Stanford does resemble the day-to-day exigencies of 17th-century Salem, with its similarly explosive mixture of superstition and zeal. The denunciation "you witch, welcome to Salem" points to both the parallels and the differences. It evokes the imagery of Salem, of the lynching mob confronting the lone individual, while, on a deeper level, reminding us that Stanford is not Salem, for nobody in Salem would have ever used those words to signify what they today mean. In Salem, nobody seemed troubled by the notion that the so-called witches actually might be victims or scapegoats. Convinced of their righteousness, Salem's good citizens could be resolute in closing ranks against the offenders in their midst. Scapegoating depends on a misrecognition of the scapegoat, so that the efficacy of the scapegoating process is inversely proportional to a community's understanding of that process.

Unlike Salem's populace, today's multiculturalists are painfully aware of victimization and scapegoating—at least in the abstract. They speak of almost nothing else, and their words betray a level of knowledge that far surpasses the innocent ignorance of the archaic past. Multicultural discourse is filled with accounts of how societies and groups of people subordinate minorities and persecute outcasts. But these accounts are generally limited to other times and other places, and never applied to the one place where some immediate applications are necessary—the here and now, whether at Stanford University or in multicultural America. Rather, the extreme focus on victimization has become the method *par excellence* for a new round of victimization, with multiculturalists using their much-vaunted victim status as the proverbial stick with which to beat others over the head.

Ultimately, the liberation of Caliban—and, for once, it does not matter whether one prefers Shakespeare's original or Cesaire's revision, because the two authors are in agreement on this most fundamental point—means nothing more or less than the freedom to express his resentments without any restraint whatsoever. In a similar way, multicultural victimology has founded a new community that channels its collective anger in myriad directions.

In both the case of Caliban and multiculturalism, the underlying descriptive account of the world is not sufficient to justify the normative judgments that are drawn from this account. That is, even if Caliban were right about Prospero's oppressive "colonialism" and the multiculturalists were right about the West's uniquely baneful history of oppression, their normative formula—an eye for an eye, a tooth for a tooth—does not follow. The fact that Prospero oppressed Caliban does not imply that Caliban has a right to oppress Prospero. One must make other assumptions, and these are the ones that drive multicultural *ressentiment*: One must believe that there can be no limitation on grievances, that the ethics of revenge cannot be questioned, and, perhaps most fundamentally, that the primary religious directive of the West must be rejected—that there is no possibility for forgiveness, renewal, or salvation for certain classes of people.

In some respects, the rejection of the Biblical text, and of the Western religious tradition more generally, might seem like the wrong target for Stanford's multiculturalists. Among world religions, after all, only Judaism and Christianity consistently take the side of the victim. From the beginning, the Bible seeks to rehabilitate those who have been unjustly persecuted. Already in the Book of Genesis, the Bible sides with Abel over Cain, and with Joseph over the brothers who sold him into slavery. In Exodus, the focus shifts to the entire Jewish community—a community of people who collectively had been oppressed and mistreated in Egypt. And in the New Testament, Christ becomes the "victim," in juxtaposition to a murderous humanity. It would be no exaggeration to say that the Judeo-

Christian perspective, and the civilization (Western civilization) founded on this perspective, were absolutely necessary preconditions for a phenomenon like multiculturalism, with its appeal to rehabilitating the human subject. In Imperial China or Aztec Mesoamerica, "multiculturalists" who demanded that women's feet not be bound or that human sacrifices cease, on the basis that these people were "victims," would have encountered incomprehension, and then probably a nasty death. The very idea of victimage, and of its undesirability, was alien to non-Western cultures and religions.

Instead of representing an advance on the Western religious and cultural tradition, multiculturalism actually is its perversion. The Western religious tradition seeks to redeem all of humanity, not just select subgroups. Multiculturalists, by contrast, are interested in the rehabilitation only of those of a particular race, gender, class, or sexual preference who happen to share their ideological commitments. This difference is critical. For multiculturalists, the elimination of victimage has become a rhetorical means whereby one group of people can transform their historical mistreatment (both real and imagined) into a political program to oppress other groups of people in the present day. Multiculturalism provides a sort of counterfeit religion for those who do not want to stop hating particular groups of people (men, the bourgeoisie, whites, etc.) even if their hatreds are dressed in the guise of "compassion" and "sensitivity" towards others (women, the poor, racial minorities, etc.). Rather than breaking the cycle of human history, multiculturalism merely represents another link in the long chain of victimization and revenge.

Notes

1. David Stoffel, "Woman of the Year," *The Stanford Review*, January 10, 1994.

2. Felicity Barringer, "Campus Battle Pits Freedom of Speech Against Racial Slurs," *The New York Times*, April 25, 1989.

3. Thomas Grey, "Interpretation of Fundamental Standard deals with discriminatory verbal abuse," *Campus Report*, December 6, 1989.

4. An explanation of the thinking behind the new code was provided by Professor Charles Lawrence: "Words like 'nigger,' 'kike,' and 'faggot' produce physical symptoms that temporarily disable the victim, and the perpetrators often use these words with the intention of producing this effect. Many victims do not find words of response until well after the assault when the cowardly assaulter has departed....The subordinated victim of fighting words also is silenced by her relatively powerless position in society....The question of power, of the context of the power relationships within which speech takes place, must be considered as we decide how best to foster the freest and fullest dialogue within our communities. It is apparent that regulation of face-to-face verbal assault in the manner contemplated by the Stanford provision will make room for more speech than it chills. The provision is clearly within the spirit, if not the letter, of existing first amendment doctrine." *See* Charles Lawrence, "If He Hollers Let Him Go: Regulating Racist Speech On Campus," *Duke Law Journal*, vol. 1990, no. 431, June 1990.

5. Kim Bonnie and Lisa Koven, "Minority students cannot be prosecuted under speech code," *The Stanford Review*, January 19, 1993.

6. Lawrence, *supra* note 4.

7. *Ibid.*

8. Bonnie and Koven, *supra* note 5.

9. Molly Stephens, "Stanford speech code struck down by judge," *The Stanford Daily*, March 1, 1995. Ben Wildavsky, "Rethinking Campus Speech Codes," *The San Francisco Chronicle*, March 4, 1995. Thorvin Anderson, "Speech Code ruled unconstitutional," *The Stanford Review*, March 6, 1995.

10. Juthymas Harntha, "Two students can't be charged for hurling homophobic slurs," *The Stanford Daily*, February 3, 1992.

11. "If you plan on joining a housed fraternity, please reconsider," Resident Fellow Matthies wrote in a 1990 letter attacking fraternities. *See* Dennis Matthies, "Pluralistic ideals do not exist in housed fraternities," *The Stanford Daily*, April 3, 1990.

12. Harntha, *supra* note 10.

13. Keith Rabois, "Rabois: My intention was to make a provocative statement," *The Stanford Daily*, February 7, 1992.

14. Michael Jackson, "Community should condemn homophobic harassment," *The Stanford Daily*, February 4, 1992.

15. *See*, for example: Harntha, *supra* note 10; Steve McCarroll, "Officials to fight hate speech with public pressure," *The Stanford Daily*, February 4, 1992; June Cohen, "Rabois' comments on 'faggots' derided across University," *The Stanford Daily*, February 6, 1992; June Cohen, "Law School searches for the 'appropriate' response to Rabois," *The Stanford Daily*, February 11, 1992; and Anush Yegyazarian, "Matthies, Rabois called on views of hate speech," *The Stanford Daily*, February 20, 1992.

16. Donald Kennedy, "Kennedy: Sense of tolerance is weapon against provocation," *The Stanford Daily*, February 7, 1992.

17. Scott Kupor, "Fraternity founded on principles of tolerance," *The Stanford Daily*, February 6, 1992.

18. Robin Kennedy, "Lawyer claims Rabois will shame profession," *The Stanford Daily*, February 6, 1992.

19. Gina Durante, "Response necessary to inflammatory speech," *The Stanford Daily*, February 6, 1992.

20. Mario Huerta, "Gays and lesbians must take action to ensure rights," *The Stanford Daily*, February 7, 1992.

21. Cohen, "Law School," *supra* note 15.

22. "An Open Letter to the Stanford Community," *The Stanford Daily*, February 11, 1992.

23. Cohen, "Law School," *supra* note 15.

24. *Ibid.*

25. Jean-Michel Oughourlian, *The Puppet of Desire* (Stanford, CA: Stanford University Press, 1991).

26. Rabois, *supra* note 13.

27. W. R. McKelvy, "Name for party is offensive," *The Stanford Daily*, November 6, 1987.

28. Michelle Finkel and Vivian Vice, "Republicans aren't threatened like most minorities," *The Stanford Daily*, June 1, 1989.

29. Dan Levy, "Stanford Band Suspended for 'Insensitivity,'" *The San Francisco Chronicle*, October 31, 1990.

30. *Ibid.*

31. Interview with Kevin Warsh (class of 1992).

32. David Sacks, "Academic Harassment," *The Stanford Review*, May 11, 1992. *See also* Veronique Mistiaen, "Backlash of 'political incorrects,'" *Peninsula Times Tribune*, December 19, 1991.

33. Interview with Neil Morganbesser (Law School class of 1990).

34. Interview with John Abbott (class of 1992).

35. Interview with Norm Book (class of 1991).

36. Miranda Doyle, "Out of the loop, students fear 'conservative

agenda,'" *The Stanford Daily*, February 25, 1994.

37. Most of these attacks were anonymous, although one university employee warned *The Review* against responding. In a message on editor Daryl Joseffer's answering machine, he said: "Hi. My name is Robert Driscoll Norton. I'm with the staff of Stanford University.... I've just been informed by some people in the gay community that you're planning on printing a response to our response to your bigoted article in the last issue, and I would like to let you know that the Gay and Lesbian Association Against Defamation and several other gay and lesbian organizations have been notified of what you have printed....And when you do choose to print your response they'll be all over your butts, so I'd probably suggest not doing it because you're going to be in pretty deep crap as a publication." The university refused to take any action against Norton's threat. *See* Daryl Joseffer, "Homosexual Harassment," *The Stanford Review*, October 29, 1990.

38. Undergraduate Leslie Kaufman spearheaded the ban in *The Stanford Daily* at the beginning of the 1987 school year: "Because of its potential to divide a community, dorms should consider carefully the impact of a decision to host a Bible study group....It is my experience that no matter how private a Bible study—or for that matter how public—the results are always negative. Bible studies only serve to create strains of isolation and religious competitiveness or closedmindedness that will eventually undermine the solidarity of any dorm....Bible studies will best meet the needs of the students they serve and least offend everyone else if they are outside the dorms." Kaufman never explained why a prohibition of dorm-based Bible studies would impose less on Christians than the tolerance of such Bible studies imposes on non-Christians. Or, more generally, why a Bible study—held in the privacy of students' individual dorm rooms—is any more "irritating and even insulting" than those Res Ed programs that also cater only to certain groups. *See* Leslie Kaufman, "Bible groups alienate," *The Stanford Daily*, October 7, 1987. Byron Bland, "A profound, healthy religious questioning," *The Stanford Daily*, October 14, 1987.

39. Bob Beyers, "Faculty Senate Unanimously Criticizes Campbell, Moves To Review Reagan Library," *Stanford University News Services*, February 20, 1987.

40. George Marotta, "Partisanship, liberal bias blinded Stanford to library's value," *Peninsula Times Tribune*, June 17, 1987.

41. Neil Morganbesser, "Thank You, Dean Brest," *The Stanford Review*, February 12, 1990. Neil Morganbesser, "Recruiting Season Begins at Law School," *The Stanford Review*, November 5, 1989.

42. Morganbesser, "Thank You," *supra* note 41.

43. As one of the students organizing Bennett's campus speech (at 7:30 p.m., on April 18, 1988), Peter Thiel received a telephone call from Rosse's office that same afternoon, regarding a meeting to discuss "security arrangements" for the visit. At the meeting, Peter was surprised to discover that most of the other people invited were the leading student activists who had pushed for the elimination of the Western Culture program—precisely the people from whom one might expect "security" problems, if any. Peter was even more surprised, however, by what transpired next. Rosse denounced Bennett's use of a "bully pulpit" at Stanford, and informed the student activists that it would be "perfectly appropriate" to "boo and hiss, just a little bit." At the same time, with a Machiavellian twist, Rosse encouraged Stanford's radicals to carefully modulate the degree of booing and hissing. Several years earlier, United Nations Ambassador Jeanne Kirkpatrick had been unable to deliver a speech at UC Berkeley after the crowd had shouted her down—and Rosse wished to avoid a repeat of that fiasco at Stanford. Bennett had to be cast as the victimizer, and a riot in Cubberley Auditorium would only serve to credit some of Bennett's claims.

44. Kennedy blamed the College Republicans for orchestrating support in a televised debate with Bennett on the *MacNeil-Lehrer News Hour*, on April 19, 1988. *See* Neil Morganbesser, "Believe it or not, there are some right here at Stanford," *The Stanford Review*, April 1988. College Republicans President Jennifer Bryson explained why Kennedy's charge was preposterous: "The Stanford College Republicans is an organization of 300 members. Perhaps 100 of those members were present [at Bennett's speech], and even this is a generous estimate. This clearly did not constitute a majority or even a dominant voice in a crowd of over 800 that attended the program. Furthermore, President Kennedy, though invited, did not attend the program; he was in New York City. It seems doubtful that he was qualified to fairly judge the composition of the crowd." *See* Jennifer Bryson, "Kennedy misinformed about student response to Bennett," *The Stanford Review*, April 1988.

45. Andy Dworkin and Linda Friedlieb, "Ralliers call for justice," *The Stanford Daily*, May 4, 1992.

46. Andy Dworkin and Linda Friedlieb, "Students make peaceful march to Palo Alto, block intersections," *The Stanford Daily*, May 4, 1992.

47. *Ibid.*

48. *Ibid.*

49. *Ibid.*

50. *Ibid.*

51. *Ibid.*

52. *Ibid.*

53. David Sacks, "Student Excluded from Feminist Class for His

Ideology," *The Stanford Review*, May 20, 1991.

54. *Ibid.*

55. *Ibid.*

56. *Ibid.*

57. *Ibid.*

58. *Ibid.*

59. In practice, of course, not all white males are persecuted either. President Donald Kennedy is a white male, but he is also a leftist multiculturalist. "White male," in some ways, is more of a political epithet than a biological description. In an equal but opposite way, some blacks (i.e., conservative blacks) are considered not really "Black."

60. Corey Davis, "Accepting cultural roots," *The Stanford Daily*, April 11, 1990.

61. *Ibid.*

62. Daryl Joseffer, "Chicanos Allege Harassment," *The Stanford Review*, February 26, 1990.

63. *Ibid.*

64. *Ibid.*

65. Juan Yniguez, "League critics have endured harassment by peers," *The Stanford Daily*, June 7, 1990.

66. *Ibid.*

67. *Ibid.*

68. *Ibid.*

69. *Ibid.*

70. *The Stanford Review* was the first newspaper to break this story, in February 1990. Interestingly, MEChA's leadership proceeded to accuse *The Review* with charges very similar to the ones it had leveled against the "disrupters": "In a recent issue of *The Stanford Review*, a front-page article was run which serves to erode the gains the Chicano community made in the last year. By failing to acknowledge the tremendous progress made by the Chicano community, *The Review* has offered an uninformed and negatively-biased view which adversely affects the building of a multicultural university." Indirectly, the response actually verified *The Review*'s charges. *See* Jerry Porras et al., "Chicano community is forging positive future for all," *The Stanford Daily*, March 7, 1990.

71. Mircea Eliade, *Cosmos and History: The Myth of the Eternal Return* (New York: Garland, 1985).

7

The Egalitarian Elite

"The public just doesn't understand that the kind of government-funded research we do here at Stanford requires a certain ambience."
"I quite agree....More caviar, Donald?"

— A cartoon in the *San Jose Mercury News* depicting two voices emanating from a Stanford lofted high in the clouds[1]

On the morning of March 13, 1991, U.S. Representative John Dingell banged his gavel, and the House Subcommittee on Oversight and Investigations came to order. The committee's purpose that day was to determine whether Stanford University had misused federal funds.

"What we will hear today," Dingell announced in convening the hearing, "is a story of taxpayer dollars going to bloated overhead rather than to scientific research. It is a story of excess and arrogance, compounded by lax governmental oversight."[2] Federal investigators proceeded to make their case: During the 1980s, Stanford president Donald Kennedy's administration had diverted funds earmarked for research into other areas that it deemed more integral to the university's functioning.[3] While much of the misspent money had been used to fund a bloated campus bureaucracy, the auditors also chronicled an extensive list of personal abuses:

- Stanford billed the government $184,286 for depreciation on the *Victoria*, a 72-foot sailing yacht owned and operated by Stanford's sailing program. The boat's walnut and cherry paneling, marble counters, brass lamps, mirrors, and exquisite joinery made a pleasant setting for the multicultural elite.[4]
- Uncle Sam paid $6,200 for a football lunch and subsidized other

bashes for the faculty.[5]

- Taxpayers also laid out $185,872 for salaries and related administrative expenses for the Stanford Shopping Center.[6]
- Government money funded tuition costs for the children of Stanford faculty and staff.[7]
- Senior university administrators regularly traveled first class, at either government or alumni expense.[8]

While all these financial diversions were taking place, the congressmen proceeded to ask, where were the people entrusted with oversight responsibility? The evidence indicated they had been in on the racket.

Not even the university's Board of Trustees was clear. In one particularly egregious violation, the trustees had seen fit to take a $45,250 retreat at Lake Tahoe, once again at taxpayer expense. The expenses covered costs for water skiing and pontoon boats, as well as lodging for 126 people. (Stanford has only 32 trustees.)[9]

Perhaps even more embarrassing to the university were the revelations about its leading educator. Taxpayers had footed the bills for a number of lavish personal items in Kennedy's home. Here, too, the multicultural experiment had been pricey:

$12,084 for a pair of George II lead urns;
$7,000 in bedsheets and table linens;
$3,000 for a cedar-lined closet;
$2,500 to refurbish a grand piano;
$2,000 per month for flower arrangements;
The unspecified cost of enlarging Kennedy's bed;
$1,530 for personal laundry services for his family;
$1,500 apiece for two Voltaire chairs from Pierre Deux;
$1,200 for a fruitwood commode; and
$1,600 for a shower curtain and its installation.[10]

Taxpayers also had paid $400 for flowers for the dedication of the Stanford horse stables; $600,000 to make Hoover House, President Kennedy's official residence, earthquake-safe; $4,000 for a reception after the wedding of President Kennedy and his second wife, as well as for the cost of two meals before the wedding; and $10,000 in silverware for Hoover House.[11]

In at least one instance—that of the silverware—there appeared to have been deliberate manipulation. While the silverware had been appraised at $10,000 in total, the appraiser had broken it down into categories, such as knives, dinner forks, salad forks, and spoons, and appraised each category, apparently to escape the $500 capital expense limit that would have prevented Stanford from charging the whole set to the government in one year.[12] Federal investigators stopped short of actually claiming fraud, if only because they did not know the intent of the person who made the decision. But, criminal or not, the mind-boggling pattern of waste and abuse was now public record, and the fallout for Stanford and its multicultural leaders was just beginning.

Kennedy, for one, blamed American taxpayers for their failure to understand what it took to run a major university: "Some expenses associated with the operation of the President's residence" may be "sources of potential embarrassment," he allowed, but only because "the complexity of the cost accounting makes it difficult for us to gain public understanding of the legitimacy of these charges."[13] Taxpayers (and their elected representatives) simply misunderstood what constituted a research cost. Kennedy knew better: "They are in my judgment allowable. They just don't appear reasonable to most people."[14]

In Kennedy's case, it appeared that ideological extremism and bureaucratic arrogance went hand in hand. Both, in the end, were a function of the same loss of perspective engendered by the multicultural revolution. No matter how flagrant any of these violations might appear to outside observers, from inside the multiculture all such external standards had disappeared. Kennedy did not perceive himself as arrogant, because he did not (and could not) believe himself to have done anything wrong. "As a matter of fact," he concluded, "I wouldn't be embarrassed about saying that every damn flower in the house ought to be an indirect cost against research."[15]

Like Sandanista leader Daniel Ortega with his Gucci sunglasses (bought during a 1985 Manhattan shopping spree), Kennedy, who as president was paid more than $200,000 per year, did not perceive the irony of such an exorbitant lifestyle so transparently at odds with his egalitarian rhetoric. Bursting with revolutionary consciousness and run by a corrupt elite, Stanford truly had come to resemble something like the Third World.

One Man vs. The Multiculture

In contrast with the gilded luxury of President Kennedy's official residence, Paul Biddle's office was barely usable when he came to Stanford as the navy's resident representative in 1989. Having earned $142 an hour as a private consultant, Biddle gave up a lucrative accounting practice in 1985 to join the government. As an employee of the Defense Contract Audit Agency, the first government agency for which he worked, his starting salary was less than $18 an hour.[16] "I want to see if one person can make a difference," Biddle told his wife.[17]

Upon moving to Palo Alto, Biddle intended to do just that. His new position required him to manage the overhead on some 1,700 research contracts and grants the federal government had negotiated with Stanford. By 1990, the federal government funded most research conducted at Stanford, totaling nearly $400 million worth of contracts in fiscal year 1988–89.[18] Because much of this research has military-related applications, the monitoring was left to the Defense Department—in the case of Stanford, the Office of Naval Research (ONR). "Stanford is a major defense contractor in every sense of the word," Biddle explained.[19] The auditor hoped to determine whether taxpayers were getting their money's worth.

In the course of his review, Biddle opened a Pandora's box known as "indirect costs." Unlike direct costs, indirect costs are expenses that are not easily attributable to a specific project but are nevertheless necessary to conduct research—costs to maintain laboratories and other research buildings, even payments for roads, sewers, campus police protection, and the very accountants who prepare the bills. If a researcher uses a library for work on a federally sponsored research project, for instance, he incurs an indirect cost.[20] Direct costs, by contrast, include items fundamentally linked to a given research project, such as salaries, chemical solutions, and lab equipment.

When Stanford receives a government grant to complete research, Biddle knew, it also sends the government a bill for indirect costs, or overhead. Stanford, like many other private institutions, maintains that this bill is necessary to recover the full cost of performing government research, so as not to drain tuition or the endowment.[21] But while direct costs—for test tubes and salaries—are paid in full by the government, indirect costs—for heating, lighting, building depreciation, libraries, and administrative overheads—are paid for at a percentage rate negotiated with Washington.

Biddle soon discovered that Stanford had negotiated one of the highest indirect cost rates in the country—78 percent. Thus, a professor wanting to undertake $100,000 of research would require an additional $78,000 to pay university overhead. By 1990, indirect cost recovery constituted 30 percent of Stanford's operating budget, second only to tuition as a source of funds.[22] The university received nearly $122 million per year in overhead reimbursement.[23]

Stanford's indirect cost rate had risen continuously during the 1970s and 1980s. Less than two decades earlier, Stanford's rate had been a relatively modest 43 percent. Even in 1990, a number of other schools were able to make ends meet with rates in the 40 to 60 percent range; for example, Stanford's rival, UC Berkeley, charged an indirect cost rate of only 49 percent.[24] The rapid rise was a major source of discontent among research faculty at Stanford: Researchers feared that the university's relatively high rate would drive grants away from their projects to universities where research could be conducted more cheaply. "An increase in the rate doesn't mean more money comes from Washington (for the professor). It just means the university general fund gets a bigger slice," explained engineering professor William Spicer.[25] As the administration charged more money for overhead, researchers could expect to receive fewer grants. In effect, indirect costs represented a transfer payment from scientists to university bureaucrats.

In April 1990, *Science* magazine reported that Stanford faculty were preparing to stage a sit-in in President Kennedy's office after the news that Stanford's indirect costs would rise to 84 percent by 1993.[26] Faculty blamed the high rate on a bloated bureaucracy and Donald Kennedy's edifice complex—a campus-wide building fever with burdensome costs. Provost James Rosse acknowledged that the growth of Stanford's bureaucracy had caused much of the increase; in the 1980s, the University's staff had increased by 23 percent while faculty had grown by only 5 percent.[27]

Indeed, the multicultural "transformation" of the university had not come cheaply. Stanford employs nearly 7,000 staff and administrators—more than one bureaucrat for every undergraduate—and only 1,400 faculty.[28] Many of the new staff positions, such as Residential Education's $50,000-per-year Multicultural Educator, had been created to facilitate the multicultural revolution.[29] Nor did the large assortment of new departments (Feminist Studies, African American Studies, Chicano Studies), ethnic centers, Residential Education (which alone receives more than $3 million a year), or a multitude of new classes and trendy multicultural conferences come for free.[30]

At the same time costs were spiraling out of control, new sources of funding were limited. By the late 1980s, almost two-thirds of Stanford's undergraduates received financial aid.[31] Because these students and their families could not afford to pay any more, even Stanford's large tuition hikes—consistently above the rate of inflation and often around 10 percent a year—simply resulted in ever-increasing financial aid packages and yielded only incrementally greater revenues.[32] The one remaining source—which could be tapped with relative impunity—consisted of the American taxpayers at large. The latter could not see for themselves whether their money was misspent and would have to rely on others to provide the needed oversight. So long as this oversight was lacking, the progress of Stanford's "great experiment" would continue unchecked.

As an accounting matter, it is not possible to show that Stanford's rising indirect cost bill went directly to pay for its growing budget for multicultural programming and personnel, even though both increases occurred at the same time. Stanford makes public very little detailed information about how it funds line items in its operating budget, and any useful information, which could establish the link, is unlikely to be forthcoming. But that missing data is not necessary to reach an inescapable conclusion: Without the financial burden imposed by multiculturalism, the university could have operated with much lower overhead costs. OMD Director Sharon Parker admitted as much: Just as other departments would be fighting the budget cuts due to cuts in the indirect cost rate, she declared, she would be doing the same.[33] If Parker's statement meant that cuts in the indirect cost rate could be paid for with cuts in the OMD's budget, then the following corollary also must be true: A higher rate could have been avoided from the beginning if Stanford had never undertaken the "great experiment." With a bit more institutional modesty, Stanford could have avoided the unpleasant issue altogether.

Meanwhile, as Paul Biddle's own audit was turning up some of these, and other, irregularities, he—and not the irregularities—became the target of university denunciation. Janet Sweet, Stanford's assistant controller, reportedly warned him, "Paul, you're not here to do all these things. You are here to stamp, sign and pass the paper."[34] University officials were not used to operating under much oversight. Tom Dolan, head of the ONR, intervened on behalf of the university and reportedly threatened Biddle's job: "You've made waves here; you make more waves here, you're gone."[35] Biddle was told repeatedly not to waste time on his study and to get back to processing the agreements Stanford presented.

Biddle faced a crisis of conscience. As *Reader's Digest* reported, "Discouraged by repeated warnings and the lack of encouragement, Biddle considered taking a far better-paying job in private industry. But he knew he'd feel guilty if he left and allowed such a scandal to continue. One Sunday after church he approached his minister for advice. 'You've found coveting of taxpayers' money,' said his pastor. 'You have a duty to do something if you can.'"[36]

Biddle decided to stay and fight. On May 29, 1990, he picked up the phone and called Washington. The following week, three investigators from the House Energy and Commerce Committee came to campus and started combing through the university's files.[37] By December 1990, their audit would find the yacht, flowers, parties, and other abuses billed to the government as "indirect costs." The following March, the committee would show that the navy auditor's efforts had not been in vain, as misspent tax dollars began to be recouped.

In the aftermath of the indirect cost fiasco, the government instituted strict new spending controls and slashed Stanford's indirect cost rate to 55 percent. The university faced projected budget deficits of $110 million over three years ($44 million in 1992, $41 million in 1993, and $25 million in 1994).[38] By the end of 1992, the Stanford administration had shifted its focus from funding multicultural priorities to paring a budget deficit. Stanford's "great experiment" lost momentum and slowly ground to a halt.

Duping and Doling

In 1994, Stanford and the federal government reached a settlement on the indirect cost issue that cleared the university of any legal wrongdoing.[39] The university, of course, touted this as a victory and pointed out, justifiably, that a number of Biddle's more ambitious charges were unsubstantiated. But the settlement did not represent a complete or even partial vindication of Stanford's behavior, because the real scandal never had to do with the legalities of indirect cost accounting. As Mark Simon, a columnist for the *Peninsula Times Tribune*, observed: "The question never has been whether Stanford did wrong. The question was whether Stanford had done all it could to do right. In that sense, the university leadership was revealed as expedient rather than lofty. And in response to the scandal, the university leadership was revealed as arrogant, rather than earnest."[40] The real outrage concerned institutional conceit—the arrogance that led Stanford to believe it could dictate research costs to the government, the arrogance that led Stanford to believe it was a model for society, and, similarly, the personal arrogance that led Stanford's leaders to believe they were entitled to taxpayer-subsidized fruitwood commodes. This top-to-bottom immodesty, laid bare in the course of the debate over indirect costs, was always the real issue.

In particular, the Kennedy administration's reaction to the indirect cost scandal is more illuminating than any minutiae of misallocated money. President Kennedy's statements were rarely consistent from week to week, but they did seem designed to placate disgruntled alumni and others who were angry with him. When local newspapers first began reporting Biddle's charges of overbilling, the president laughed off the allegations. He joked glibly that the charges were "enough to send Trustees off to their cardiologists," but were "without foundation" and "entirely unrelated to impropriety or fraud."[41] Kennedy assured the faculty in September 1990 that his administration was "unusually well positioned" to defend itself and had "nothing to fear."[42] Provost James Rosse also reflected the calm before the storm: "There's nothing illegal about it. It's not as though anybody's building swimming pools or taking trips to Tahiti."[43]

As the investigation deepened, the administration's unseemly confidence became even more brazen; a good offense would be the best defense. In October 1990, Stanford released a "self-audit." It not only found no university wrongdoing in the school's assessment of indirect costs, but claimed that the government actually owed Stanford an additional $13 million—Stanford really deserved an even higher indirect cost rate of 84 percent![44] Taxpayers could rest easily, however; the university announced it would not try to claim the money.[45] Nor did Stanford faces turn red that November, when after initial denials Stanford officials reimbursed the government $184,286 for improper charges on the yacht *Victoria*.[46] Still, apologies were not forthcoming. "We have seen *no* evidence suggesting wrongdoing by Stanford personnel," Kennedy insisted.[47]

By the beginning of 1991, it had become clear that the inappropriate billings extended beyond Stanford's sailing program. House investigators found the flowers, piano, cedar-lined closet, antique commode, and other taxpayer-subsidized luxuries in Donald Kennedy's mansion.[48] The government had also paid for embarrassing entertainment expenses, such as a wedding reception for President Kennedy and his second wife.[49] These discoveries, unfortunately, were not only professionally compromising to the president; they dredged up personal rumors. His remarriage in 1987 to an attorney in the university's Legal Office had raised eyebrows, following just two months after Kennedy divorced his wife of 34 years.[50] Signs saying "He's No Kennedy" had even popped up in student dorms, a reference to Massachusetts Senator Ted Kennedy's reputation for infidelity. The wedding reception had been hosted by the Board of Trustees to smooth over Robin Kennedy's introduction to the university community "in her new role as the wife of Stanford's president and official hostess."[51] That old wound was now unkindly reopened.

Remarkably, every time Stanford's multicultural leaders tried to present their side, they lost further ground. During a special on ABC's *20/20* television show and during the House Oversight hearings, Kennedy lectured his audience on the priorities of higher education and the complexities of the university's accounting, which, he assured them, mere citizens could not possibly understand. But because Congress and the public understood all too well, Kennedy's performances further undermined the university's credibility. Kennedy became increasingly petulant:

> I don't care whether it's flowers, or dinners and receptions, or whether it's washing the table linen after it's been used, or buying an antique here or there, or refinishing a piano when its finish gets crappy, or repairing a closet and refinishing it—all these are investments in a University facility that serves a whole array of functions.[52]

In rushing to support Kennedy, the university's Board of Trustees echoed his indignant attitude. Chairman of the Board James Gaither likened Kennedy's residence to a "mini White House" deserving only the finest—paid for by taxpayers, of course. In a signed letter to Representative Dingell, Chairman Gaither, joined by several past chairmen of Stanford's

Board of Trustees (including future U.S. Secretary of State Warren Christopher), applauded President Kennedy for setting "the highest standards for the educational community." They also emphasized the importance of furnishing Kennedy's house "in a manner appropriate to its distinction," with "items such as silver, crystal, china, flower arrangements, table linen, antique tables, chairs, desks, and other furniture, expenses of refinishing the piano or other furnishings and the cost of upholstery, draperies, and carpets."[53]

Paul Biddle, who was perhaps not accustomed to living in such high style, interjected a little common sense: "How is the cost of putting cedar in a closet remotely relevant to organized research? They were gilding the lily."[54]

As publicity mounted, university officials announced that Stanford would withdraw about $500,000 of federal research billings that had been used to cover upkeep of the president's home and the residences of two other Stanford administrators.[55] Still, officials stipulated that they had not done anything wrong, but pulled the costs because of the possibility of public misperception.[56] The president, who earlier was "unusually well positioned to handle it," now blamed the scandal on public relations: "We've had no opportunity to tell our story first. It's always a disadvantage to be following up instead of leading. In that sense, I don't think it's possible for us to do a very good job."[57]

On March 13, 1991, the House oversight hearing publicly detailed the list of waste and abuse. Undaunted, the president reasserted his regime's innocence the next day, maintaining that "the hearing brought forth *no* evidence of wrongdoing at Stanford."[58] If "wrongdoing" were defined only in legal terms, Kennedy may have been correct. No intentional fraud could be proven. But for those operating under a more common sense definition of "wrongdoing," the hearing was hardly a vindication for Stanford. "Every single taxpayer knows the real issue here," proclaimed Representative Ron Wyden (D-Oregon), who earned a bachelor's degree in political science at Stanford in 1971 and whose mother works at Stanford's Green Library: "Billing the government for yachts and parties and baubles is wrong. Frittering away scarce government resources can't be justified under any circumstances and any interpretation of the rules."[59]

Kennedy's arrogant posture made him a particularly deserving target of recrimination. "The events today did not reflect well on the university or on you," Dingell lectured Kennedy, "or upon those who appear with you."[60] Kennedy's failure to admit the slightest wrongdoing only magnified the hearing's fallout. The *San Jose Mercury News* captured an angry public's sentiment: "The list of questionable expenses has grown too long to be attributed simply to bookkeeping errors. What has emerged is a picture of a greedy institution that saw the federal government as a vast reservoir to be tapped. The university negotiated the highest 'overhead' reimbursement rate it could and then threw in every possible expense into the pool to justify that rate."[61]

These financial improprieties had been no worse than many of the other abuses at Stanford—from the sacking of Western Culture to speech codes and the vilification of nonconformists. Each was a result of enforced orthodoxy, each a reflection of the same unyielding arrogance. But the financial abuses captured the public imagination like nothing else had. In curricular debates and even in rules of conduct, the public was generally willing to defer to the judgment of academic experts. But the financial abuses were different, because they involved tangible items that were obviously extravagant, if not totally inappropriate. No special expertise was needed for taxpayers to determine that their money had been misspent; they wanted it back.

Even many in the Stanford community began to suspect that things had gone badly off track. Observers on campus characterized Kennedy's appearance before the House as a disaster for the university.[62] Stanford faculty also were alarmed: Stanford's damaged reputation, as a university that wasted money, might make research grants more difficult to obtain in the future. Even some of the campus leftists joined the rising chorus of dissent. Professor John Manley, in a letter to President Kennedy, declared: "What is Stanford's image under your leadership? It is that of a venal institution caught, red-handed, robbing the American people. It is that of a university that cares more about getting every last dollar than moral issues."[63]

The president scrambled to revitalize his image. Speaking in Los Angeles on March 23, 1991, he told alumni what they wanted to hear: "I take full responsibility for the management of the institution, and I am sorry to have let you down."[64] But the damage control was too little, too late. By the beginning of April, the president felt compelled to respond to rumors of his imminent termination: "I hope you know that I would never prolong my own stay in the Presidency against Stanford's best interest. But I have good support from the Board, from most of the University's friends—and, I believe, from most of my faculty colleagues."[65]

Kennedy had miscalculated for the last time. Although many trustees had been friends of Kennedy's, they suspected that the barrage of bad press would not end until his departure. Stanford's Napoleon had suffered his Waterloo. Under pressure from the Board, Kennedy announced his resignation on July 29, 1991, effective August 1992. In the following months, almost all the university's top financial officials followed suit. It is "very difficult," Kennedy finally perceived, "for the person identified with a problem to be the spokesman for its solution."[66]

The Great Experimenters

Like a company selling an inferior product, Stanford's administration hoped to compensate with advertising efforts. And because the quality of the educational product is far more difficult to measure than the quality of something like an automobile, such a public relations effort did represent a fairly viable short-term strategy. In the long term, however, the public relations gloss could not hide the continuing abuses. On the contrary, Stanford's problems were allowed to grow unchecked and became all the more noticeable.

Indeed, as the multicultural revolution proceeded in the late 1980s and early 1990s and on-campus abuses mounted, Stanford's administration moved energetically to weaken the remaining checks on its authority. The most important such check consisted of the school's alumni. Up to that time, their primary source of information about the university had been the Stanford administration. Official university publications cultivated alumni with slick features about their *alma mater*, recalling fond memories of an institution that in truth no longer existed. But with the massive media focus on Stanford brought by the Western Culture debate and the indirect cost scandal, the administration's monopoly on information began to break down. This represented a tremendous problem for the administration: If alumni were to become aware of campus happenings, they might stop contributing money to the university. That would lead to accountability and force an immediate change.

To combat rival sources of information, the administration placed more and more resources into putting a positive "spin" on campus happenings. Campus instructors, including Professor Rosaldo (see chapter 1) and Professor Jackson (see chapter 3), began to spend time off-campus, to "educate" alumni about how everybody else was "misinformed." In the aftermath of the CIV debate, some of the new instructors were flown around the country to alumni gatherings, to rebut charges made in the *Wall Street Journal* and other major newspapers.

Symptomatic of the new stress on public relations was a nasty fight over the control and direction of Stanford's News Service, which publishes the *Stanford Observer*, a monthly alumni newsmagazine. Bob Beyers, a 28-year veteran who headed Stanford's News Service and was the recipient of many journalistic awards, was pushed to resign.[67] According to Robert Freelen, then vice president for public affairs, the university was not served by a news bureau that reported campus failures. Although the administration admitted that Beyers "is regarded by virtually everyone...as an individual of extraordinary dedication, loyalty, and commitment," it nevertheless condemned him for being "mired in a culture of independence" and for taking "a black-and-white, absolutist approach to questions about how the News Service should operate."[68] A "culture of independence" was not compatible with the culture of deference on which the great experiment hinged. Beyers resigned in January 1990 because the university was muzzling honest journalism in favor of "corporate"-style public relations.[69]

Despite these efforts of university leaders to collectively bury their heads in the sand, the indirect cost debacle brought many unpleasant truths to the forefront. One of these self-evident truths is that universities like Stanford are a part of the "real world." Stanford's utopian experiment was never a self-contained perpetual motion machine, but depended upon massive transfer payments from the rest of American society. Once these transfer payments ceased, the engine driving the multicultural machine began to run out of fuel. Stanford's experiment was a hothouse product dependent upon others to maintain its artificial environment. This lack of self-containment represented a significant flaw in President Kennedy's experiment. Because nobody outside America would be able to foot the bill for an American multicultural transformation (in the same manner outside funding maintained Stanford's momentum), Stanford University did not represent an accurate microcosm or experimental laboratory. A similar experiment—if it should be called that—could never be pulled off with nearly as much success in America as a whole. It would collapse for lack of funding at a far earlier stage. But this was not the only, or even most important, problem Biddle's revelations raised.

The fundamental mistake had involved the strange notion that such a "great experiment" could be conducted in the first place. Experimenters require freedom to exercise control over the experimental objects. In the natural sciences, such a distinction between the freedom of the "researcher" and the constraints placed on the "object of research" is possible, but in the human realm it collapses. The Great Experimenters are, by definition, a part of the multicultural community—that is, part of the very experiment they are conducting. Such an experiment, then, would seem to require a degree of control over the Great Experimenters similar to the control they exercise over everyone else. Since the Great Experimenters had to place themselves beyond such control, the resulting "experiment" was a fraud from the start.

Plato's version of this conundrum took the form of a question, never asked by Aime Cesaire of CIV fame: "And who will guard the guardians?" If we need multicultural administrators to guard against bad people, how can we ensure that the multiculturalists will be good? The partial answer of the founding of our country involved a system of "checks and balances," in which the various guardians check one another. If there are many guardians and none is too powerful, one or a few bad ones will not be able to do too much damage. The multicultural experiment, with its vanguard of Great Experimenters, who stood above the law and beyond review, constructed a political ordering radically antithetical to the American one.

Unable to maintain the impartiality their experiment required, Stanford's multicultural leaders simply set themselves above the law or any other standards of decency—not to mention any of the rules they would have others follow. There would be no need to guard against the guardians if the guardians were infallible. A government of men began to replace a government of laws.

But, of course, Stanford's high priests were very much fallible, and their veneer of infallibility eventually cracked. The consequent scandals were really quite inevitable, as the multicultural state came to resemble a despotic Third World regime not only in its fervent ideology, but also in the endemic corruption throughout its ranks:

- If the president of Stanford thought that the world was obliged to furnish him with a lavish lifestyle, then it is hardly surprising that his subordinates tried to make their own little fiefdoms yield such personal bounty as they could. A case in point involved the Stanford Bookstore, which holds a virtual monopoly on textbook sales to Stanford students. As a nonprofit organization, the bookstore operates a complex refund system, under which some of its profits are returned to customers in the form of rebates. But many of the bookstore's revenues never made it into the "profits" column in the first place, as the store's management obtained a number of benefits for itself, unheard of elsewhere in the college bookstore industry: a vacation home, a motor home, sailboat, Cadillacs, and sports cars.[70] Bookstore profits also paid for $69,000 worth of improvements to the vacation home, including a hot tub and satellite dish. In another unusual arrangement, the bookstore leased the vacation home from two of its top employees, whose mortgage payments effectively were paid by the bookstore.

Members of the bookstore's board of directors either did not know about these matters or did not care. Law professor Robert Weisberg "personally was unaware of the matters that were disclosed," whereas history professor Peter Stansky, also a board member, considered the vacation home a "quite splendid" perquisite.[71] For many in the Stanford community, these financial abuses hardly raised an eyebrow. "We've gotten a good chuckle out of it," explained junior Heather Weaver, a member of the bookstore association (a group of 30 faculty, staff, and students responsible for selecting the board members). "There's a little resentment and some disgust, but it's the same old thing—another one of Stanford's little scandals."[72]

California's Deputy Attorney General James Schwartz did not consider these abuses quite as amusing. During the 1992–93 school year, he began investigating whether the bookstore's unorthodox spending violated its nonprofit status.[73] Over the next year, the board sold the vacation home, terminated the car leases, and appointed directors with business expertise.[74] In the meantime, however, the costs of the DA's investigation added another $900,000 to the bookstore's bills.[75] Because of the store's virtual monopoly status, these costs were passed on to Stanford students, in the form of more expensive textbooks. The "joke" was on them.

- The prize for hypocrisy may go to Diana Conklin, the head of Stanford's Res Ed system. Conklin had acquired a reputation as a particularly vigilant promoter of the new morality—she had helped organize the grape boycott, punished fraternities for alcohol use, and drafted Stanford's restrictive "Controlled Substances and Alcohol Policy." But on June 24, 1990, Conklin herself was caught red-handed: After using a vial of cocaine in her home, she called paramedics, who rushed her to the hospital, where she received treatment and a police citation.[76] A municipal judge later placed Stanford's Res Ed leader into a drug counseling program.

Conklin's story was bizarre: She claimed that she had found a vial of cocaine left in her closet years before and, feeling depressed, had used it on a momentary impulse.[77] Stanford's senior administrators, however, could not bring themselves to say that Conklin had done anything wrong, or even ask whether her drug use might affect (or have affected) her professional duties in enforcing Stanford's drug and alcohol policy. Acting Dean of Student Affairs Norm Robinson declared that "what people do with their private lives is their own business."[78] Of course, a similar standard had not been applied to the many policies Conklin had promoted. If people could use cocaine in their private lives, then why could they not cut loose and drink grape juice or study the Bible? The university did not try to explain. Conklin retained her position; her sole punishment consisted of a token letter of reprimand.[79]

- Perhaps the most bizarre double standard involved Stanford's militant dean Keith Archuleta, the director of the Black Community Center. Archuleta had played a leading role in the Copeland's protest. But only several weeks later, it was revealed that Archuleta had for years invited young women, many of whom were black, to his residence for amateur photography sessions. The women were encouraged to change into various costumes in an adjacent room. While they were changing, Archuleta secretly filmed the women in various stages of undress—"kind of like a Peeping Tom," according to District Attorney Margo Smith.[80] In some tapes, he spliced together scenes of women undressing, often repeating a given scene several times in a row. Although some of the women suspected that the video camera was on (because of a red light), most trusted Archuleta when he assured them it was not so. A student who did not trust Archuleta's explanation reported the event to the police in May of 1992, and the dean's arrest quickly followed.[81]

Even with all the evidence before them, Stanford's leaders refused to admit that Archuleta had abused his position of confidence. Dean of Student Affairs Michael Jackson expressed his sympathies for Archuleta, rather than the exploited women: "We are deeply distressed by this situation and regret that an employee who has made significant contributions to the university finds himself in such a position."[82] Not until several days later, when complaints by the filmed women did not stop and local publicity mounted, did Jackson deem Archuleta's conduct "totally unacceptable." The only basis for self-criticism among the egalitarian elite, it seemed, was the same thing that made Kennedy's enrichment unacceptable—public outcry.

By the early 1990s, there were no internal checks left. No Stanford University accountant complained about Kennedy's overhead billings, the bookstore's board acted only after the investigation by California's attorney general, and the administration calibrated its responses to the Conklin and Archuleta episodes in proportion to the level of public outcry. It is unclear whether anybody in authority at Stanford believed that the Great Experimenters actually could make great mistakes, and it did not matter. Out of fear or ignorance, no Stanford administrators stood against the multiculture.

By placing themselves above their own rules, the Great Experimenters made self-examination almost impossible and self-criticism unthinkable. Indeed, as problems mounted, the scapegoat of choice became the outside world—the federal government, the American taxpayers, and, more generally, the entire society that had held Stanford's guardians to a higher standard than they had set for themselves. There was no better example than President Kennedy himself. Kennedy's commencement address to Stanford's class of 1992 marked his last major speech as Stanford's leader, and he used the opportunity to make clear that he had learned nothing from the indirect cost ordeal. After the hubris and fall, there was no hamartia or tragic insight, only the bathos of a daytime soap opera. Kennedy used the opportunity to lecture his audience on the need for personal responsibility:

> And that brings me to the section of this farewell that is headed "Parting Advice"; because there is an aspect of what you have done that will, if you can conserve it and use it, do more for our society than you can possibly

> imagine. It has to do with the capacity for taking responsibility, the disappearance of which is creating a tragic national vacuum.[83]

Kennedy, apparently, viewed the flight from responsibility as a national problem:

> Public scapegoating in high places is now exhibit A of our national failure to take personal responsibility....No mistake is irreversible, and nearly all stains wash out in time. But the hasty grab for the nearest excuse only makes the marks more permanent. Raise your hand, acknowledge the foul, and take the penalty.[84]

Kennedy's account of "the hasty grab for the nearest excuse" offered a fairly accurate description of why he had lost his job as Stanford's president several months earlier. But one should not be misled by Kennedy's use of the inclusive "our." He considered himself the totally innocent victim, who had been misunderstood and scapegoated by the dullards of American society:

> Above all, I hope you will not shrink from that special form of responsibility that will require you to stand up, state the program, accept the risks and bear the consequences. Even at their worst, and you are hearing this from an expert, they're not intolerable—not if you acted from conviction and know you did the right thing.[85]

By the end of the speech, the fact that Kennedy had been attacked became transformed into evidence of victimhood and, *ipso facto,* confirmation that he had done "the right thing." The self-righteous tone of Kennedy's lecture was nothing new to most students, but many parents and guests were simply stunned. Most of the audience recognized that Kennedy was not exactly the best person to preach about responsibility.

The hypocrisy was compounded in Fall 1993, when Kennedy returned to Stanford as a full-time professor. The first subject he would teach: ethics. According to the *Stanford Daily,* Kennedy would offer "the first comprehensive examination of ethics of university life offered anywhere," a course entitled "Professional Responsibility and Academic Duty." "I think it will be terribly informative to me," Kennedy pronounced, "and I hope it will be to [the students]."[86] The irony did not end there. From his tenured perch in semiretirement, Kennedy reflected upon the university's budget woes, pontificating about the greed of the 1980s: "I think we're starting to pay off for the 12 binge years from 1980–1992."[87] Although Kennedy was referring to Republican administrations, the dates 1980 to 1992 ironically refer to his term in office as well—"12 binge years" if there ever were. Still busy looking for scapegoats, Kennedy would rather blame Stanford's problems on the president of the United States than on the president of Stanford.

Metamorphosis

Caliban's rebellion succeeded at Stanford. By the early 1990s, the multicultural leaders had taken control. They had expelled the West and many of its defenders. But their success—if it should be called that—was replete with contradictions. Though in no way bullish about capitalism, the multicultural vanguard behaved just like their caricature of the hated "robber barons"—looters who squeezed every penny out of others. In seeking to impose egalitarianism, they made themselves an elite. In seeking to eliminate what they perceived as oppression, they acted far more tyrannically. In enacting new codes of conduct and creating new-age crimes, they exempted themselves from common standards of decency.

The comparison between Donald Kennedy and Stanford's founder, Leland Stanford, is particularly telling. The original Stanford had been one of the West's premier railroad builders, one of the legendary captains of industry, or, less positively, "robber barons." But the original Stanford had been more charitable than the latter caricature might suggest: He contributed his vast fortune to the establishment of a university in memory of his son, who died at age 15. He hoped hoping to provide others with the education his only child never had the opportunity to receive. Such nuances have been lost upon Stanford's current generation of leaders, who piously rail against the capitalist sins of those who came before them. Under Kennedy's leadership, any reminders of Stanford's capitalist founding family were gradually expunged, to the point that even the group statue of the first family (father, mother, and son) was relegated to a forsaken lot (see chapter 4).

Donald Kennedy certainly is no Stanford. Any comparison is flattering to the former, not the latter: Kennedy operated by spending the public's money rather than his own, and in the process almost destroyed the institution Stanford had built. Whether the university's hard-working founder was really a "robber baron" or deservedly earned the money is open to debate. But Kennedy actually fit the bill rather nicely. A refined acquisitiveness ensured the best lifestyle capitalist loot could buy, but without the hindrance of capitalist or even democratic restraints, such as a respect for taxpayers' property or the kind of accountability the American polity requires. In a final bizarre twist, Donald Kennedy's life had come to bear a striking resemblance to the vilified image of Leland Stanford.

If Caliban's liberation implied that he would be free to do whatever he pleased, then Stanford's Calibans—the Great Experimenters—had chosen to exercise their freedom in a most peculiar way: They had become like Prospero—or, more precisely, like their distorted image of Shakespeare's Prospero, the vile character depicted in Cesaire's angry book. Like Cesaire's Prospero, who did not realize that he was a "colonial addict" or "anti-nature," Stanford's Great Experimenters suffered a similar blind spot regarding their own transgressions.

Yet oddly enough, such a transformation seemed to follow ineluctably from the logic of the multiculture itself. The only roles that could be conceived of in the multicultural production were those of victim and victimizer, Caliban and Prospero. On the multicultural stage, if one no longer played the role of Caliban, then one must have become Prospero. The sort of "liberation" achieved by Stanford's egalitarian elite simply amounted to an inversion of who was doing the controlling.

For the multicultural vanguard, there was no escape from the historical dialectic between the class of the oppressed and the class of the oppressors. There could be, at best, a substitution of roles, with new groups of victims—the American taxpayers—to take the place of the old. A third possibility, of the true individual, whose ontological status depends neither on being a gnostic victim nor on being an ignorant oppressor, could not even be imagined. At the end of their remarkable metamorphosis, Stanford's multicultural leaders had become their own worst enemies.

Notes

1. Scott Willis, *The San Jose Mercury News*, January 25, 1991.

2. Joel Shurkin, "Congressional Committee Criticizes Stanford's Accounting Procedures, Suggests Some Employees May Be Guilty of Fraud in Indirect Cost Issue," *Stanford University News Service*, March 14, 1991.

3. This was the finding of Fred Newton, deputy director of the DCAA (Defense Contracting Auditing Agency), whose auditors conducted an on-site investigation. Milton Socolar, special assistant to the comptroller general of the General Accounting Office (GAO), the investigative branch of Congress, testified that "serious deficiencies in Stanford's cost allocation and charging practices, combined with inadequate oversight by ONR [Office of Naval Research], had led to significant overcharges to the government. We identified over $3.6 million in unallowable and inappropriate charges, of which almost $1 million was erroneously charged to the government." *Ibid.*

4. John Wagner, "In troubled waters; Stanford billed yacht costs to U.S.; revelation raises ire of congressman," *The Stanford Daily*, December 5, 1990.

5. Eugene Methvin, "He Caught the Campus Chiselers," *Reader's Digest*, January 1992. Marcia Barinaga, "John Dingell Takes on Stanford," *Science*, February 15, 1991.

6. According to the GAO, the university eliminated the shopping center charges in 1988, but the charges for 1986 and 1987 were never corrected. As a result, the government paid more than $185,000 of the shopping center's bills. Shurkin, *supra* note 2.

7. Paul Biddle, Letter to James Gaither, *Stanford University News Service*, January 26, 1992.

8. *Ibid.*

9. John Dingell, "Deserving projects are underfunded as Stanford overcharges taxpayers," *The Peninsula Times Tribune*, March 31, 1991. Shurkin, *supra* note 2.

10. John Wagner, "University may retreat on costs," *The Stanford Daily*, January 14, 1991. Maria Shao, "The Cracks In Stanford's Ivory Tower," *Business Week*, March 11, 1991. John Wagner, "House subcommittee lambastes Stanford; Hearing reveals more embarrassing charges, hints of 'criminal liability,'" *The Stanford Daily*, March 14, 1991. Methvin, *supra* note 5.

11. Dingell, *supra* note 9. Jeff Gottlieb, "U.S. probe of Stanford may cost other schools," *The San Jose Mercury News*, January 22, 1991. Philip Hager, "Grants Helped Pay for Reception," *The Los Angeles Times*, February 16, 1991. The wedding reception charges were withdrawn from Stanford's

bill to the government in January 1991. Donald Kennedy, "Statement by Donald Kennedy, President, Stanford University," Subcommittee on Oversight and Investigations, House Committee on Energy and Commerce, March 13, 1991. Shurkin, *supra* note 2.

12. Shurkin, *supra* note 2.

13. Donald Kennedy, "Statement on Indirect Costs," *Campus Report*, January 8, 1991.

14. Shao, *supra* note 10.

15. Wagner, "University may retreat," *supra* note 10.

16. Lisa Koven, "Man of the Year Paul Biddle," *The Stanford Review*, January 27, 1992.

17. Methvin, *supra* note 5.

18. Jeff Gottlieb, "Stanford investigated for research billing," *The San Jose Mercury News*, September 13, 1990.

19. Koven, *supra* note 16.

20. John Wagner, "Stanford vulnerable on indirect cost issues," *The Stanford Daily*, October 16, 1990.

21. Tracie Reynolds, "Probes of grant funding," *The Peninsula Times Tribune*, September 13, 1990.

22. Faculty Task Force on Indirect Costs, "Task Force reports on indirect costs," *Campus Report*, April 6, 1988.

23. Jeff Gottlieb, "U.S. probe of Stanford may cost other schools," *The San Jose Mercury News*, January 22, 1991.

24. Lynn Ludlow, "Stanford probed on costs of U.S. research," *The San Francisco Examiner*, September 13, 1990.

25. Gottlieb, *supra* note 23.

26. Marcia Barinaga, "Stanford Erupts Over Indirect Costs," *Science*, April 1990.

27. *Ibid.*

28. Norm Book, "Is Stanford's spending out of control?" *The Stanford Review*, January 1988.

29. Heather Heal, "No budget cuts here: Stanford seeks new multicultural educator," *The Stanford Review*, January 19, 1993.

30. Andy Dworkin, "No cuts for student centers," *The Stanford Daily*, April 8, 1994. Christopher Yeh, "Res Ed Trims the Fat: Director promises to preserve essential services and staff," *The Stanford Review*, February 3, 1992.

31. Jeff Gottlieb, "Stanford raises its tuition by 5.5 percent: Year on The Farm to cost the same as a BMW 325i," *The San Jose Mercury News*, February 9, 1995.

32. Mary Madison, "Stanford to raise tuition 5.5%: Undergrad costs will be $26,749 with room, board," *The San Francisco Chronicle*, February 9, 1995.

33. David Sacks, "Departments Paid Bonuses for Minority Hiring," *The Stanford Review*, November 4, 1991.

34. Biddle, *supra* note 7.

35. *Ibid.*

36. Methvin, *supra* note 5.

37. *Ibid.*

38. Peter Robison, "Casper finds improving Stanford image a slow, difficult process," *The Stanford Daily*, February 26, 1993.

39. Gerhard Casper, "Statement on the Resolution of Outstanding Disputes Between Stanford and the Government on Indirect Costs Issues," Stanford University, October 18, 1994.

40. Mark Simon, "Out of scandal, Stanford has a chance to redefine itself and seek greatness," *The Peninsula Times Tribune*, July 28, 1991.

41. Donald Kennedy, "Statement to the Stanford Faculty Senate on Various Reviews of Indirect Cost Recovery," September 27, 1990.

42. Kennedy explained: "While the degree of attention being paid to indirect costs will be intense, we are unusually well positioned to handle it. In our Controller and his senior financial staff, we have highly respected professionals with years of experience with indirect costs. I have great confidence in the competence and integrity of these colleagues, and I believe we have nothing to fear from a fair and thorough examination." *Ibid.*

43. Wagner, *supra* note 20.

44. John Wagner, "Stanford self-study finds no wrongdoing on indirect costs," *The Stanford Daily*, October 17, 1990. Jeff Gottlieb, "Stanford report denied overcharging U.S.," *The San Jose Mercury News*, October 18, 1990.

45. John Wagner, "Rosse: Stanford won't collect money it says government owes," *The Stanford Daily*, October 19, 1990.

46. Wagner, *supra* note 4.

47. Donald Kennedy, "Statement on Indirect Costs," *Campus Report*, January 8, 1991.

48. Wagner, "University may retreat," *supra* note 10.

49. Jeff Gottlieb, "Stanford withdraws bill; Taxpayers won't have to pay for wedding reception," *The San Jose Mercury News*, February 14, 1991. Hager, *supra* note 11.

50. Shao, *supra* note 10.

51. Gottlieb, *supra* note 49.

52. Wagner, "University may retreat," *supra* note 10.

53. The chairmen explained: "Our view has been and continues to be that the Hoover House expenditures are important, reasonable and appropriate ones for Stanford University....[The] services provided to the president and his family, such as the salaries of staff and household help and

their reimbursement for mileage in connection with errands which may be wholly or partly personal to the president or his family, payment for phone service, other utilities and the like...are also appropriate Stanford expenses." *See* James Gaither, Warren Christopher, William Kimball, Peter Bing, Chairmen of the Board 1976–1991, Letter to Representative John Dingell, *Stanford University News Service*, March 1, 1991.

54. Shao, *supra* note 10.

55. Gottlieb, *supra* note 49. *See also* John Cox, "Probes, fines tarnish Stanford's golden image," *The Sacramento Bee Final*, January 31, 1991.

56. Jeff Gottlieb, "Stanford appoints two to oversight committee," *The San Jose Mercury News*, February 16, 1991.

57. John Wagner, "Elite image a liability in controversy," *The Stanford Daily*, January 29, 1991.

58. Donald Kennedy, "Statement by Donald Kennedy, President of Stanford University," *Stanford University News Service*, March 14, 1991.

59. Shurkin, *supra* note 2.

60. *Ibid.*

61. "Stanford's image," *The San Jose Mercury News*, March 17, 1991.

62. Howard Libit, "Controversy's glare scorched Kennedy: The politics of indirect costs proved too hot for Stanford's eighth president," *The Stanford Daily*, May 22, 1992.

63. John Manley, Letter to President Kennedy, *Stanford University News Service*, April 18, 1991.

64. Donald Kennedy, "What have we learned? Our obligation is to do what is right, Kennedy asserts," *Campus Report*, April 3, 1991. Jeff Gottlieb, "Kennedy apologizes to alumni," *The San Jose Mercury News*, March 24, 1991.

65. Donald Kennedy, "Message to the Faculty," *Stanford University News Service*, April 4, 1991.

66. "Chronological guide to indirect costs at Stanford," *The Stanford Daily*, May 28, 1992.

67. John F. Burness, "Report of Public Affairs/News Services Site Visit: Stanford University 31 May – 2 June 1989," *Stanford University News Service*, July 14, 1989.

68. *Ibid.*

69. *Ibid.* More specifically, Beyers wrote in an addendum to the report, the administration had "Mandated publication of bowdlerized reports; Forbidden our staffers from contacting public agencies; Ordered photographers not to take their pictures at a public demonstration; and Suggested that editors stonewall legitimate news inquiries." *See also* Skip Schwartz, "'A fact sheet?' Faculty Senate expresses control over Casper's control of Campus Report," *The Stanford Daily*, March 5, 1993.

70. John Wagner, "Bookstore brass enjoys perks unheard of else-

where," *The Stanford Daily*, February 5, 1992.

71. *Ibid.* Juthymas Harntha, "Store directors not fully aware of perks," *The Stanford Daily*, February 7, 1992.

72. *Ibid.*

73. Steve McCarroll, "Attorney general intensifies Bookstore investigation," *The Stanford Daily*, October 1, 1992. *See also* John Wagner, "Bookstore perks were 'inappropriate,' review finds," *The Stanford Daily*, May 18, 1992; and Steve McCarroll, "Bookstore's lease on campus called sweetheart deal," *The Stanford Daily*, May 28, 1992.

74. "Bookstore getting rid of perquisites," *The Stanford Weekly*, August 20, 1992. Miranda Doyle, "Bookstore to sell vacation home: Pricey perk on the market for 'ambitious' $425,000," *The Stanford Daily*, February 11, 1993.

75. Miranda Doyle, "Bookstore costs from state probe near $900K," *The Stanford Daily*, February 12, 1993.

76. Cecilia Tom, "Conklin arrested for using cocaine," *The Stanford Weekly*, July 4, 1990. *See also* John Cox, "Probes, fines tarnish Stanford's golden image," *The Sacramento Bee Final*, January 31, 1991.

77. Anne Stroock, "Drug Program for Stanford Dean," *The San Francisco Chronicle*, July 26, 1990.

78. Tom, *supra* note 76.

79. Stroock, *supra* note 77.

80. Rajiv Chandrasekaran, "Archuleta sentenced to probation, service," *The Stanford Weekly*, July 2, 1992.

81. Martha Brockenbrough, "Archuleta resigns, admits a 'problem': Long-time administrator arrested for secretly videotaping women," *The Stanford Daily*, June 3, 1992.

82. Terry Shepard, "Assistant Dean Archuleta arrested, placed on leave," *Stanford University News Service*, May 30, 1992.

83. Donald Kennedy, "Fond farewell: 'You have made me proud to be president," *The Stanford Observer*, May–June 1992.

84. *Ibid.*

85. *Ibid.*

86. Julie Makinen, "Kennedy teaches hard lessons," *The Stanford Daily*, September 30, 1993.

87. Interview with Donald Kennedy, *The Stanford Weekly*, July 1, 1993.

8

Caliban's Kingdom

Western civilization has suffered a setback at Stanford. Civilization will recover. Whether Stanford will is another question.[1]

— Charles Krauthammer

It was time for a change. On March 18, 1992, Gerhard Casper, the dean of the University of Chicago Law School, was named Stanford's ninth president.[2] The silver-haired legal scholar's most important credential was perhaps his status as an outsider, in no way tarnished by the indirect cost scandal. Hailed as "the right white knight to lead the university into the 21st century," the first president from outside the university in 25 years acknowledged Stanford's position as a chastened institution and sought to convey an austere, academic tone.[3] The trustees, Casper told local newspapers, wanted him to refocus Stanford's attention "on the central purposes of the University, that is, teaching and research, not being diverted by all these political controversies."[4]

Casper's back-to-basics message resonated in the wake of an administrative regime that had lost perspective on reality. "One of the advantages I have as an outsider is I have a sense of balance about Stanford," Casper noted.[5] Donald Kennedy's replacement lifted a cloud hanging over Stanford's image. Casper admitted that errors had taken place ("Stanford is a human institution," he allowed)[6] and indicated that he did not take the indirect cost scandal lightly. He also began making frequent trips to Washington, D.C., and Sacramento, where he impressed elected officials as straight-forward and low-key.[7] "By all accounts an even-keeled person," the *New York Times* reported, "Mr. Casper is seen as an ideal antidote for Stanford's ills. His style is deliberate and considered, even meticulous, while Stanford has been accused of laxity."[8]

Upon taking office, Casper's first major initiative was to clean house—reducing the number of vice presidents from ten (under Donald Kennedy) to four and cutting about $1 million of bureaucracy.[9] Much of the savings were diverted to Stanford's withering libraries.[10] "I wanted to make it simpler, and I also wanted to make sure that symbolically the administrative organization shows that we are primarily here to support teaching and research of both faculty and students," Casper announced.[11] The Office of Public Affairs, so integral to the Kennedy administration's attempts at spin control, was reduced in scope, and Bob Freelen, then Kennedy's vice president for public affairs, was asked to leave.[12] The following year, Casper dissolved the Office of Public Affairs altogether.[13]

Turning his attention to the undergraduate curriculum and to what he called "multidisciplinary illiteracy," President Casper toughened the grading system by bringing back the "F."[14] And in April 1993, he established a "Commission on Undergraduate Education" to "focus more intently on the basic objectives of the institution."[15] Its far-reaching mission was "to clarify the goals of a Stanford undergraduate education."[16] Casper suggested that "the humanities need some more care and some strengthening," and said campuses should be more efficient in what they teach.[17] He railed against exotic programs he called "orchid subjects, because like orchids, they are rare and nice, but they serve no purpose."[18] Of course, there is no need for an institution to be born again if it gets it right the first time, and Casper's sweeping reassessment of purposes and priorities implied that he believed that Stanford's priorities had gone badly off track.

Casper's most principled reforms appeared to come in the political realm. He established warmer relations with the Hoover Institution, naming its director, John Raisian, to the President's Cabinet of Advisers. (Raisian, in return, provided a small getaway office for Casper in Hoover Tower.)[19] The president also stood up for freedom of speech: "When it comes to defending the freedom of speech at the University, I will defend everybody's freedom of speech. That's part of my function—not to limit it."[20] He returned Stanford's motto ("The Winds of Freedom Blow") to the university seal, and spoke out in his timely inauguration speech against intellectual "fashions" and "orthodoxy."[21]

Signalling a new, lower-profile political role for the university and the president's office, Casper vowed to keep his political views private. "Nobody here who is in an administrative position has been chosen to represent anybody politically," Casper told 100 students at a dorm visit. "If I take a political position and do it in my role as president of Stanford University, I am abusing my role."[22] Recalling the takeover of German universities during the 1930s by the Nazis, who "in no time destroyed the universities by turning them into political vehicles for the regime," Casper warned, "The minute I would take a position—and indeed, your professors would take a position—...they are ending the discussion by silencing those who disagree."[23]

Nevertheless, as positive as some of Casper's statements have been, his first years in office have not quite lived up to the media's "white knight" image. While Casper has been willing to resist multicultural initiatives where his predecessor probably would have led the charge, he has moved slowly, or even backtracked, in areas where he has encountered heated opposition. His lack of ideological fervor has been accompanied by, and perhaps subordinated to, a resolute pragmatism. Whereas Kennedy seemed to relish political confrontations, Casper's instinct is to head for cover. Before moving ahead with a policy, the new president likes to float trial balloons; if the waters test cold, as they often do, he backs off. Consequently, Casper has not been able to follow through on any of his boldest initiatives:

- In December 1992, Casper refused to condemn Professor Kennell Jackson's "Black Hair" class as frivolous. However laudable his rule about academic "orchids," it is doubtful that Casper would ever be willing to anger any member of a major university constituency in order to enforce the principle.[24]
- In 1994, President Casper placed Stanford's ethnic centers on the university's fundraising priority list.[25] In addition, after unrelenting protests by MEChA and other minority groups, the ethnic centers, as well as the Lesbian, Gay, and Bisexual Community Center, were among the few organizations on campus spared any budget cuts.[26] The ethnic centers' budget apparently was the price of peace.
- In December 1992, Casper signed Stanford's "domestic partners" policy into law. According to Kate O'Hanlan, who authored the proposal, "the trustees only needed to hear from Casper." O'Hanlan promised that she and her partner would be the first in line to collect the new benefits; the policy would cost the University on the order of $100,000 a year or more.[27] Casper rationalized his failure to oppose the politically driven proposal: "If I took a position I would have possibly forced the trustees to choose between backing up their new president or rejecting their new president. I didn't want the trustees to be in that position."[28]
- Although Casper has pointed out that the campus is "a University, not a political commune," he has reaffirmed the university's commitment to multiculturalism numerous times.[29] He has defended ethnic theme dorms and separate commencement ceremonies as "congregation" rather than "segregation."[30] In September 1993, he directed Provost Rice to appoint a new vice provost for the special purpose of recruiting minority professors.[31]

Perhaps the most disappointing development of Casper's presidency has been the Commission on Undergraduate Education (CUE), which had raised the possibility of sweeping reform. In June 1994, the CUE issued its preliminary findings: Its report proposed "no single dramatic revolutionary change," announced history professor James Sheehan, the chair of the commission. Rather, it contained a large number of recommendations designed to "reform, reinvigorate and improve a number of things we do."[32] Law professor Robert Weisberg explained that the CUE was reluctant to change the graduation requirements too drastically, considering the debate that ensued when the university switched from Western Culture to CIV: "The real issue is what should be the common denominator. We didn't have the stomach to take on that whole issue again."[33]

Indeed, the new administration does not have the "stomach" to truly end Stanford's multicultural experiment once and for all and begin anew. While it has identified problem areas—such as Residential Education and CIV—it has done nothing to address these problems. In the case of Res Ed, the CUE simply encouraged "those involved in residential education to review and clarify their various missions."[34] Specific recommendations were altogether lacking. "I'm not sure we have taken the look at Res Ed that we should have," admitted Professor Weisberg. "I don't think anyone wants to look at it, and I think that's a problem."[35] The combination of apathy and angst often produced as a result of multiculturalism had now gripped the faculty and administration and immobilized them. Although most suspected that multiculturalism (at least in the form of Res Ed) was flawed, they had no idea what might replace it.

The CUE's recommendations for CIV were similarly confused. The commission suggested replacing CIV with a three-quarter "culture core" that would fold in both the race studies and non-Western-culture DRs. The overwhelming majority of students, Professor Sheehan explained, were dissatisfied with CIV. (A *Stanford Daily* poll indicated that 72 percent of undergraduates felt CIV should be changed—about the same percentage who had thought in 1988 that Western Culture should be left alone.)[36] Once again, however, the general sentiment that things had broken down was not accompanied by a sense of why, or even where to go from there. Professor Sheehan, for one, offered precisely the wrong diagnosis: The problem with CIV, he said, is that it "never really lost the residue of its beginning in Western Culture."[37] Certainly, no one conceived that the problems with CIV and Res Ed were connected—or, more accurately, were one and the same. It was almost as if an earthquake had struck campus during summer vacation and destroyed two buildings on different sides of campus. When the vacationers returned, they observed the sites independently without deducing a root cause of the wreckage.

While any reduction in the number of DRs would be a positive step, the proposed "culture core" may not be much better than CIV. The reading list offered by sophomore Jodie Dyl suggested that the new track might be more politicized than anything before it—without even a "residue" of the great books: "You could read 'A Room of One's Own' as an example of what Western women need, along with a Third World feminist. I'd rather see it integrated."[38] Senior Todd Gilcrest agreed: "CIV is an examination of cultures, not great books. You're using books as tools to look at a culture and see how they relate to themselves and to outsiders. CIV is not intended to give you your ideas—that was the whole debate of the '80s. You will learn ideas indirectly, but the real goal is culture."[39] On a fundamental level, nothing could change because nothing had been learned.

In the final analysis, Casper's greatest success may simply consist of his failure to lead the multiculture. In May 1994, Casper warned that political pressure (such as the MEChA hunger strike) hampered Stanford's ability to pursue the best academic programs:

> We cannot work for Stanford's future in an environment dominated by the politics of ultimatum. If we shortcut argument and reason, we abandon the essence of the University. If universities make their substantive decisions for political rather than academic reasons, they have no claims for untrammeled existence.[40]

Professor Ross Schachter, a multicultural activist, explained his frustration: "We don't have any momentum right now on the multicultural agenda. It takes presidential leadership to move ahead."[41] In a further blow to multicultural momentum, the OMD declared that it would limit its focus to affirmative action issues.[42]

Unlike Kennedy, who seemed to focus and distill campus passions, Casper has had a calming influence.[43] With a reputation for charm and humility, Casper's personal style could not have been more different from that of his predecessor.[44] His sense of humor has helped boost morale, rather than undercut it: The German-born Casper joked that he had been selected because the board wanted a president who could finally pronounce the university motto, "Die Luft der Freiheit weht" ("The Winds of Freedom Blow").[45] "What the university needed after the period of malaise was a sense of calm leadership," observed history professor Barton Bernstein.[46] The nonideological Casper performs a delicate balancing act—attempting to halt Stanford's slide, without rocking the boat.

Beyond the Wasteland

If one were optimistic about the intentions of the new Stanford administration (and we are), then one would still have to be quite concerned about the prospects for the University as a whole. For, in spite of the widespread recognition that something has gone badly wrong with multiculturalism, Stanford's new leaders are unwilling or unable to effect many of the needed changes. Although the momentum towards multiculturalism has slowed, no genuine reversal has taken place. Even relatively modest proposals of a procedural nature—raising academic standards or checking the growth of multicultural programs—meet with fierce opposition and do not get far. A more fundamental shift, such as the restoration of a Western civilization requirement, remains utterly unthinkable. On the levels of the faculty and the lower reaches of the administration, the multicultural structures appear firmly entrenched.

Without aggressive leadership from the top, however, the various resentments from below largely remain diffuse, occasionally exploding into a protest or two, but rarely gathering enough force to provide a rallying point for the entire community. A telling example occurred in May 1994, when Asian Americans, usually considered a success story among America's immigrant minorities, declared themselves the latest victim group on campus. One week after MEChA's hunger strike, a group of protestors demanding the creation of an Asian American studies major sneaked into a Faculty Senate meeting and forced its adjournment. (Among the concessions won by the hunger strikers was the formation of a Chicano studies major.)

"We demonstrated to the senate that this is a very real, intellectually viable issue that they are going to have to deal with at some point," pronounced coalition member Davina Chen.[47] The difference between a protest and an "intellectual issue" still was not understood. Junior Ken Tan allowed that he felt "marginalized" by the lack of an Asian American studies major and said the group "will not be asking the administration for this program; we will be demanding it."[48] As had been the case with the Western Culture "revival meetings," several protestors seemed visibly shaken, fighting back tears and comforting one another.[49]

However striking the emotional and ritualistic similarities to the Western Culture protests, there was one significant difference: Most students hardly took notice. The protestors did not enjoy wide support or even interest among their peers; the activists appeared hackneyed rather than revolutionary. Increasingly, multiculturalism fails to fire the imaginations of many students. Student President Ying-Ying Goh described the new atmosphere: "There are gripes that you hear on campus like 'Multiculturalism is being shoved down our throat.' It wasn't just a small minority of students. It was almost becoming an 'in' thing to say."[50] In a show of discontent, students rejected the annual fee requests of the BSU, MEChA, and the Rape Education Project in the April 1994 student government elections.[51]

While the rest of the student body is increasingly indifferent, the advocates of multiculturalism seem to share a cult-like passion and, according to the *Stanford Daily*, "a growing feeling of paranoia."[52] Many think President Casper (a Democrat, certainly no right-winger) secretly harbors a "conservative agenda." BSU Chairman Anietie Ekanem and junior Emily Haine, for instance, had picked up on small things—"little, slight, underhand things."[53] These signs included the choice of Stephen Carter as graduation speaker in 1994 and Casper's suggestion that faculty members should not take political stands.[54] Casper, who had recently thrown his weight behind Stanford's speech code and placed the ethnic centers on his fundraising priority list, seemed genuinely puzzled by the conspiratorial charges, unaware that he was simply the latest person to blame.

Nevertheless, despite the overwhelming multicultural edifice, these activists correctly perceive their victory to be on shaky ground. For the edifice is hollow; after more than seven years of great experimentation, a positive vision of the multicultural future remains altogether absent. Because the multiculture is derivative from the West, and depends on an ongoing, ritualistic expulsion of the latter, any total triumph would completely deprive the multiculturalists of their enemies. In the hour of its final victory over the West, the multiculture itself would be doomed to perish. Like parasites that have finished consuming the carcasses of their hosts, multiculturalists may turn on one another for a brief while, but in the end they will starve for lack of sustenance.

Something like that already may have happened on the Stanford campus. Western civilization and classical liberal arts education truly are dead, killed off in the same multicultural epidemic that expunged "dead white males" from the reading list. But the multicultural cult of the dead—a defiant nothingness, involving the destruction and deconstruction of all possible meaning—has gradually dissolved into nothing at all. To be certain, the buildings are well maintained, the lawns are well watered, the football team plays for cheering throngs of fans, the faculty and staff are well paid, and the students attend classes and receive diplomas. The institution can keep going for a while on autopilot. But the heart of the university's humanities program—involving the quest for universal truth—has decayed into dust. The university has become a whitewashed sepulchre, a hidden reminder, not just of the Western tradition upon which it was founded, but also of the anti-Western multiculture that sought to replace it.

There are unlikely to be any easy or direct reversals. Even the most explicit and dramatic repudiation of multiculturalism would not necessarily entail a return to the West. For many of the faculty hired in the last 20 years, such a return would be literally impossible—they have become as ignorant of the despised Western civilization as the students they purport to instruct. (The CUE admitted as much in its final report: "Even if such a core list could be collectively compiled, it would substantially restrict the number of faculty members willing and able to teach the course.")[55] On an intellectual level, the multiculture's cycle of destruction may have eliminated too much of the past foundation on which any future recovery would have to be based.

In many cases, of course, the professors, appointed out of political motives and less talented academically than their own students, would not want to go back to teaching. They would rather stick to that which they can do reasonably well, explicating the scholastic nuances of multicultural liturgy, never subject to critical review. And so, even as the multicultural community of belief starts to disintegrate—as multiculturalism shifts from a sweeping cultural and religious force to a pale image of its former self, little more than a particularist cult—the same rituals will be continued, out of habit if not from belief. The multicultural congregations may be dwindling and the church bells all broken, but no other alternative can be conceived. There is no Tiresias to herald a renewal of life in the wasteland, to bring an end to the springless winter.

Of course, none of this implies that institutions like Stanford will serve no function whatsoever. In the hard sciences and the engineering fields, our top colleges and universities will graduate people who have amassed an impressive array of scientific knowledge and technical skills. At the same time, the business, law, and medical schools will continue to churn out trained professionals. From the outside perspective of companies seeking to hire new computer engineers, biochemists, or investment bankers, everything will continue as before.

But in the process, Stanford will have become a technical and vocational school, along the lines of MIT or Cal Tech—highly esteemed in narrow areas of expertise but not much more. Behind the facade of normalcy, much will have been lost. The university will have become transformed into a multiversity, no longer capable of providing a universal framework that enables students to integrate a wide assortment of knowledge into a coherent whole. That kind of framework, so essential for thinking about the larger problems facing individuals and societies, simply cannot be provided by science; it must be gleaned from the humanities, and can be reached only after rigorous study—in philosophy, literature, history. Though the loss of this framework cannot readily be translated into dollars and cents, it will be felt keenly nonetheless, by a generation of students increasingly alienated from an incoherent and senseless world, unable even to diagnose the source of their troubles.

The nature and scope of the loss was hinted at, indirectly, by one of President Casper's most sweeping proposals, in which he suggested eliminating the college major and replacing the four-year undergraduate degree with a three-year degree.[56] His proposed three-year degree was particularly heretical, because it suggested that students were not getting much added value out of a fourth year at Stanford and that the university's burdensome distribution requirements might need to be scrapped: "If resources were available, I'd say four years are wonderful, the more the better. On a cost-benefit analysis, there will be more questions as to whether these four years are sustainable in the long run."[57] In a narrow sense, Casper was clearly right: If there was no real humanities program left, then a technically focused education over a three-year time frame would represent a sensible change. At the same time, however, the call for such a drastic remedy indicated how much had been lost and how little else could be done about this loss.

In the early 20th century, the Argentinean writer Jorge Luis Borges envisioned a vast and fantastic library—infinite in size—that would contain every possible book, consisting of every possible combination of letters. Some of these books would contain great knowledge—the Grand Unified Theory of physics, the complete works of Shakespeare, the first million digits of the decimal expansion to pi, the true theory of religion, a dictionary from English to Maya, the code for the human genome, the perfect game of chess. Far more of the books would involve mistakes of one sort or another—there would be a hundred false refutations of Einstein's theory of relativity, a thousand false histories of the world, a million false reference books for the library itself. The overwhelming majority would be wholly meaningless—a book consisting of a string of the letters "AAA," perhaps, or of some random string of letters resembling the work of a monkey on a typewriter. The Borgesian library simultaneously contains all the information in the world and none at all. And it provides a useful image for what the multicultural university has become: a vast repository of information, taken from all the corners of the planet, but with no framework to distill the information, to determine what is true and what is false, or even what is important and what is trivial. If one tries to find one's way around this intellectual Byzantium, one will only become ever more lost.

If intellectual life in America is not altogether finished, then it may be in the process of a massive and unprecedented displacement. An intellectual renaissance in our traditional centers of higher learning may be a long time coming (*see* for instance, the excellent Independent Institute book *The Academy in Crisis: The Political Economy of Higher Education*[58]), but this does not necessarily imply that people simply will stop thinking in the intervening years. To the extent that it continues, intellectual life will shift from elite universities to historically less significant colleges that have survived the multicultural transformation, or move altogether outside the academic context.

There is some precedent for such a displacement in other areas, such as the communications media, where in recent years cable television and radio talk shows have grown dramatically, in response to the failure by the major television networks to provide the desired programming. In a similar way, new educational venues may arise and meet demands that are no longer being satisfied by the existing institutions. One particularly promising area involves a number of new computer networks, in which people can connect with one another from disparate parts of the country, to discuss or learn about matters of common interest. Not surprisingly, a number of these networks are focusing on areas that no longer have much of a place in the multicultural academy, such as free-market economics or Thomistic theology. Because learning need not take place in the classroom, this sort of technological breakthrough may in time undermine the near-monopoly on higher education currently enjoyed by America's elite universities.

But this sort of intellectual displacement will not occur as smoothly as the shift from network to cable television, in large measure because the idea of a university may have no ready substitute. There are reasons why its structure, centered on faculty committed to teaching and students committed to learning, served its function so well for so long. The benefits from an interactive education, from the total immersion in the learning process, and even from the economies of scale that exist at large Western universities may not have any real replacements. In addition, there seems to be a considerable danger that the learning process, even outside the multiversity, will acquire a distinctly Borgesian flavor. For every person who manages to find an Ariadne's thread of sorts, there may be many others striving to untie Gordian knots that were bypassed long ago. Without external standards to guide them, people will take the immediate as a good approximation for the important, and focus on developing particular skills; larger and more fundamental issues may recede into the background.

Nevertheless, even if Stanford University does not survive the destruction of Western civilization on campus, chances are that Western civilization will survive the decline of universities like Stanford. In spite of the hurdles and difficulties, some people will continue to ask the same questions about life and the universe that vexed Plato—even if there no longer is any academic or cultural elite to guide them in their quest for answers or even to encourage them to ask the right questions. Those who wish to learn the truth will still have that opportunity, but henceforth may have to do so on their own, with no direction from anyone.

The Culture of Blame

Even if multiculturalism were only intellectual in nature, it should be of great concern to all Americans that our leading universities are turning into academic wastelands. But multiculturalism goes much deeper, and much more is at stake in these debates than the direction of our leading academies. The multicultural movement, taken as a whole, is concerned with a radical reordering of the entire culture—that is, not just with an assortment of new ideas, but also with the application of these new ideas throughout the country. Multiculturalism matters because it promises to transform America in a large number of fundamental ways, including race and gender relations, art and religion, the rules of law, and the ways in which different communities exist and relate.

Many commentators have noted that America is quickly becoming a nation of victims. To extend the metaphor already used throughout this book, multiculturalism is turning America, like Stanford, into a kingdom of victims—a "Caliban's kingdom"—the likes of which were foreshadowed, but never explicitly described, in the plays of both Shakespeare and Cesaire. This alternative world represents a future in which Caliban's multicultural revolt over Prospero had been successful, a new kingdom in which self-proclaimed victims had become the kings.

Shakespeare probably had an inkling of what Caliban's revolt might lead to, but decided to spare his audience all the sordid details. Cesaire's characterization of Caliban—as a sort of noble savage who would achieve genuine "liberation" by getting rid of Prospero once and for all—seemed little more than wishful thinking. But in important respects, Cesaire's dream has become today's reality, for increasingly we live in a culture of victimization, a hypertherapeutic world where "dysfunction" has become the standard and victims get to dominate.

Rehabilitating victims is an American virtue as significant in our day as the Protestant work ethic was in an earlier era. In almost any situation, the way to win arguments and popular sympathy—as well as large settlements in court—is to portray oneself as the victim. In a celebrated case recently, an 81-year-old woman won a $2.9 million judgment from McDonald's for burns suffered when its coffee spilled out of a cup she held between her legs in a moving car.[59] Victims can do no wrong, it seems. Lyle and Erik Menendez admitted to killing their parents, but were not convicted after a jury heard that the brothers were abused.[60] Every day, guests on *Oprah*, *Donahue*, or even the evening news describe in unabashed detail matters once called family secrets, as well as an assortment of more mundane personal misfortunes, including but not limited to their blind dates, skin problems, and sexual deficiencies (circumstances that might otherwise warrant some sympathy, were commiseration not so obviously the desired goal). A sense of modesty or shame can only be an impediment in convincing others that one is a victim. The highest-rated talk show host, Oprah Winfrey, herself claims that she was abused, an unfortunate experience no doubt, but one indispensable to her role as an ambassador of sorts for the culture of victimization.[61]

The more tragic extremes to which people will go to cast themselves as victims was revealed by the *New York Times*, which recently reported that many homosexual men in San Francisco have again begun practicing unprotected anal intercourse in a *deliberate* attempt to contract AIDS and achieve the victim status the disease confers.[62] "I thought if I was H.I.V.-positive I'd be so much gayer," explained a recently infected 32-year-old airline mechanic. "People are looking for that red badge of courage and you get that when you convert" from being H.I.V. negative to carrying the virus, he added.[63] Experts say this attitude is so prevalent that the once-stable infection rate in San Francisco has doubled and for men under 25, has quadrupled.[64]

The deliberate contraction of H.I.V. is only the most extraordinary case of people trading almost anything (their privacy, their health, even their lives) for the regal social station victimhood confers, even if this status may be as short-lived as 15 minutes of fame on daytime television or the 5- to 10-year incubation period of a deadly disease. As the name implies, Caliban's kingdom (a kingdom run by the oppressed) leads to such bizarrerie because it is profoundly self-contradictory. If the only people suited to be the "kings" are "victims" and if these "victims" have indeed become the "kings," then in what sense can the new rulers still be thought of as genuine victims? Will the existence of this new culture not undermine the very reasons that gave birth to it in the first place?*

This tension is reflected by the transmogrification of the Afrocentric movement, which, having succeeded in its initial goals to see racism wane and the legal playing field leveled, has shifted its purpose from ending racism (liberating Caliban) to promoting racial superiority (taking over the kingdom). Among its fantastical teachings are the beliefs that the ancient Egyptians were all black, that blacks really built the pyramids (and have been robbed of the credit for doing so), and even that melanin is some kind of chemical that makes people of color stronger, smarter, and more humane than light-skinned people.[65] "Melanin allows us to receive the vibrations

---

* This problem is somewhat analogous to the status of the Communist Party in the aftermath of the Leninist revolution. If that revolution truly emancipated the proletariat, then why would there still be a need for a proletarian vanguard? The solution of the Marxist-Leninist regime was to distinguish between a Communist end-state and an intermediate Socialist state, and to use the latter to justify the indefinite deferral of the former.

of the universe," declares Professor Leonard Jeffries from his tenured perch at City College of New York.[66] These incredulities are the subject of *African-American Baseline Essays*, a textbook published in 1987 by the Portland school district, which is currently being used in public school and college classes in Atlanta, Detroit, Fort Lauderdale, and other cities.[67]

The spread of Afrocentrism is intimately related to events at Stanford. The phenomenon is dependent upon the same multicultural principles that at Stanford render the *gnosis* of "victims" beyond reproach. For once one has agreed to suspend one's rational faculties and learn whatever a particular group claims is its special knowledge, it is difficult to explain why anything that group tells you is wrong. There is no logical limiting principle. Nobody can point out that the Afrocentrists are incorrect without also saying there are universal standards that transcend particular groups. Consequently, the Afrocentric position, unsubstantiated by facts and unsupported by reason, has been legitimized in schools and colleges, if not by open endorsements then by a failure to oppose its inclusion. By virtue of their putative victim status and accompanying *gnosis*, the Afrocentrists have achieved a privileged, kinglike position—even if, upon taking the throne, the one-time victims of racism have become the new racists.

The multiculture is too busy manufacturing new victims and new grievances to notice these contradictions. The question asked by Oprah, Donahue, and Geraldo no longer is whether one has been victimized, but to what extent. By imagining that they are still "victims," today's Calibans can pretend that their revolution is not successfully completed and can defer confronting their problematic vanguard status indefinitely.

The disappearing distinction between real victims and self-proclaimed ones is evidenced by demands among a growing number of American blacks that they should receive restitution for slavery. Congress sparked the reparations movement in 1988, when it awarded payments of $20,000 to all Japanese-Americans interned during World War II, making some blacks wonder why they should not be entitled to similar treatment.[68] Subsequently, U.S. Representative John Conyers introduced a bill in the House calling for a commission to study the question of reparations for blacks.[69]

Unlike some Japanese Americans, however, there are no black Americans alive today who have suffered internment. Nor are there any former slave owners to pay reparations. Presumably, the descendents of slave owners would have to pay, but some reparations advocates intimate that all whites in this country might have to pay. In either case, the bill would be substantial (the National Coalition of Blacks for Reparations in America, the leading proponent of African American reparations, suggests $60,000 payments to individuals, depending on their needs, and awards of

$100,000 to families).[70] Just as the reparations movement makes no distinction between real victims (slaves) and false ones (the descendants of slaves), it makes no distinction between imaginary oppressors (whites today) and real ones (the slave owners of yesteryear).

It is never made clear why those who did not inflict the harms of slavery should have to pay any more than it is explained why those who did not suffer these harms deserve to be paid. But the reparations movement is not concerned with a factual account of who did what to whom. Rather, it is more interested in depicting a larger story in which blacks are the universal victims and whites are the universal oppressors. This myth, which substitutes for a historical account, visits the sins of the great-great-great-grandfather upon the son. It is a multicultural version of the Fall from Grace, in which the descendents of particular groups are still tarnished with the guilt of original sin, passed down from generation to generation. They can do nothing to redeem themselves, and neither, one suspects, will their great-great-great grandchildren a hundred years hence.

None of this melodrama would be quite so problematic if the culture of victimization did not lead to a culture of blame. But to maintain his identity, each multicultural actor requires a second, interdependent, yet antagonistic half. To reassure themselves that they are "victims," multiculturalists must constantly seek out "victimizers." As soon as multiculturalists vanquish their most recent enemy, a new one appears on the scene. This feature is not contingent—that is, a result of our not having tried hard enough or waited long enough for all the nonmulticulturalists to disappear—but a necessary consequence of the way multiculturalism works. What is true for each particular multicultural actor is true of the multiculture as a whole: In order to exist, Caliban's kingdom must be divided against itself.

A culture of blame might not be unjust if the accused were actually guilty of real crimes. Nothing would have been wrong with Salem's witch trials either if the accused women really had cast harmful spells on the rest of the populace. As in the case of Salem, however, the multiculture's victims are imaginary, and so, too, are the victimizers, who become targets of mythical accusations. In the case of reparations, the descendents of slave-owners, if not all whites, are held accountable. For Oprah as for the Menendez brothers, their parents are to blame for their current problems. For gays contracting AIDS in San Francisco, it is "homophobic" society. At Stanford, the Western tradition itself (or whoever was perceived as its incarnation) was singled out and attacked; the new Salem had no shortage of enemies and ritual expulsions, which served to refound the new culture periodically.

Nevertheless, the Stanford community never fully paid the price of the multicultural experiment. Financially, U.S. taxpayers footed much of the bill. But the larger American society also provided for the multicultural experiment in a more intangible way: It constituted the imaginary oppressor, the missing half needed to complete Stanford's multiculture. Whatever measure of peace Stanford's multiculturalists achieved on campus resulted from the direction of the community's anger and resentments outward, against American society or the West at large. So long as Stanford could hate America, it would not have to hate itself. As multiculturalism moves from Stanford to America and from there to the rest of the world, this escape valve is gradually disappearing. With no outside left and no others to attack or to deconstruct, the citizens of Caliban's kingdom may be increasingly forced to turn against one another.

The consequences of this division have been particularly serious and troubling in the realm of gender relations, which have rarely seemed more strained. Recent events at the Department of Transportation are just one indicator of how some of the multicultural victimology is being implemented in America. In a bizarre (but by no means unusual) episode in June 1992, the Federal Aviation Administration held a sensitivity training workshop on gender relations where male employees allegedly were forced to walk through a gauntlet of women who fondled the men's genitals and ridiculed their sexual prowess.[71] "Women were also asked to look at photographs of penises in various states of arousal and were told to use them to rate their male colleagues' sexual attributes," reported the *Washington Times.* The purpose of this session was to "educate" the men about "how it feels to be a woman."[72]

Once again, there are eerie similarities to the Stanford experiment. On campus, the *raison d'etre* of sensitivity training is that men "just don't get it." That is, men do not understand the special perspective of women and thus behave inappropriately around them. The belief that men and women fail to communicate is part and parcel of the more radical feminist view that the natural way men (the patriarchy) and women interact is antagonistically. Men victimize women, and it is high time for women to get them back. It is hardly surprising that to the extent "sensitivity" trainers are receptive to radical feminism, they become insensitive or hostile to men. The results are the same on the federal level, once the government has bought into the radical feminist position about "how it feels to be a woman" in its efforts to "educate" men.

Gender strife hits home in a way that the reparations movement or plight of gays in San Francisco does not. How men and women interact determines the nature and composition of families, the building blocks of communities and society. Over the last few centuries, for instance, the replacement of the extended family with the nuclear family has precipitated a seismic shift in the social order. As bonds of family have dissipated, the federal government has come to play an increasing role in providing a safety net (though cause and effect here are the subject of much debate). The multicultural reshaping of the family will likely have ramifications of similar magnitude, in directions we may only guess.

Gender relations affect everybody's life in a central way, and so it is not surprising that a sensational case like that of Lorena and John Wayne Bobbitt grabs people's attention. While men generally squirm, wince, and cross their legs when they think about Mr. Bobbitt's fate, many women react to Lorena Bobbitt's cutting off of the penis of her allegedly abusive husband with a different state of mind. *Time Magazine* essayist Barbara Ehrenreich has described this "grass-roots female backing for Ms. Bobbitt":

> The woman in the streets is making *V* signs by raising two fingers and bringing them together with a snipping motion....And, without any prompting from NOW, thousands of women are sporting bumper stickers identifying themselves as BEYOND BITCH and buying T shirts that say TOUGH ENOUGH or make unflattering comparisons between cucumbers and men.[73]

The emergence of the new family, comprised of "beyond bitch" mothers (should they choose to bear children at all) and men who are tough enough to stand them, certainly represents a sea change from Ozzie and Harriet. Interestingly, Ms. Ehrenreich herself makes the multicultural connection, identifying Lorena Bobbitt as a "multicultural manicurist."[74]

This description is curious, though, because most manicurists are not well versed in the intricacies of black hairstyles, group communications, pizza consumption, and other multicultural dogma. While Ms. Bobbitt likely would not think of herself as a "multiculturalist," the notable aspect of the reaction to her is that she is perceived as such, a subtle recognition of her role as a catalyst of the "Beyond Bitch" culture. The primary reason for her embrace by multicultural America is that, in the new atmosphere of gender antagonism, her story functions on an allegorical level. It is not the story of one disturbed woman injuring one man who may have abused her. It is the story of All Women being liberated from All Men. As Ehrenreich explains, "The retail clerks who send her letters of support, the homemakers who cackle wildly every time they sharpen the butcher knife are...tired of *being* victims. And they're eager to see women fight back by whatever means necessary."[75] Lorena Bobbitt is portrayed as striking a blow (literally) for women all over the world. And similarly, John Bobbitt, who stars in this multicultural production as the Man, is perceived as the victimizer, rather than the unsuspecting victim of the cruel punishment inflicted upon him.

Reduced to allegorical form for popular consumption, the episode is reminiscent of a Greek myth, which is not meant to convey a factual account of events but rather a moral virtue or message about society. "I'm not willing to wait another decade or two for gender peace to prevail," Ehrenreich finally concludes. "And if a fellow insists on using his penis as a weapon, I say that, one way or another, he ought to be swiftly disarmed."[76] So what Lorena Bobbitt did to John Wayne Bobbitt, or what John did to Lorena, becomes symbolic of what women do to men or men do to women. It is part of a larger story line in the saga of the gender war, the unstated implication of Ehrenreich's suggestion that "gender peace" is absent. To the extent that Lorena plays the role of victim in this myth, she is indeed "multicultural." As for her unfortunate husband, he is relegated to guest spots on the *Howard Stern Show*.

The Bobbitts are just one case where history has been mythologized into a broader story of heroes and villains. The reparations movement invokes a similar pattern, where whole classes of people (the descendents of slaves and the descendents of slave owners) become the victims and oppressors. Many reparations advocates expand the myth to include all the world's people, maintaining that Western nations should redress African nations and other Third World countries. Closer to home, we have such allegorical tales as the Tawana Brawley hoax, about which *The Nation* editorialized, "In cultural perspective, if not in fact, it doesn't matter whether the crime occurred or not."[77] "The facts were irrelevant, it seems," columnist John Leo observed, "because Brawley's story line reflected the broader reality that whites have abused blacks for centuries. In other words, forget about the facts. Just tell stories that convey emotional truth."[78] One is reminded of the anthem of Group Comm—"I don't care about facts, I care about how you feel." Nevertheless, every time such a hoax is revealed, one also has to wonder about the accuracy of the underlying story line, whose credibility would seem to depend on the empirical accuracy of some of the specific stories. How could one possibly know that any of these cases are truthful, if educated people are in the habit of fictionalizing reality and Stanford graduates can turn a candlelight vigil into a KKK rally?

Myth is integral to the new culture because a historically grounded view of the world would completely undermine Caliban's kingdom; a factual account of events would reveal that many self-proclaimed victims have never been wronged and that many supposed victimizers have been falsely accused. Indeed, while a culture of victimization and blame makes every misfortune the fault of someone else, a civilization based on history recognizes two other possibilities—that an individual can bring a problem upon himself, or that nobody at all is at fault. Even though the very possibility of tragedy is anathema to the culture of blame, the unfortunate reality is that not all bad things that happen to good people are caused by other human beings.

Just as multicultural attitudes towards sex are turning America's genders against one another, multicultural attitudes towards economic matters focus people's unhappiness with their current income levels outwards. The target of these resentments are rich people, and capitalism more generally. In the multicultural allegory, the wealthy are *per se* oppressive, because their success creates misfortune for others. The other two possible causes of poverty—bad fortune or bad choices—are rejected *a priori*. Quite naturally, multiculturalists conveniently overlook the fact that without productive people paying taxes, there could be no welfare for the poor.

The Clinton administration has effectively tapped into such sentiments of class warfare in pushing its policies. In his book *The Agenda*, *Washington Post* reporter Bob Woodward (no conservative) describes the president's glee at punishing the rich with higher tax rates:

> At 10:15 p.m...the [budget vote count went over the top, to 218]....Clinton grabbed his head with his fingers and thumbs, digging in like a madman. He whooped and threw his arms around each of his aides....Clinton said that Carville was the only one of them making top-tax-bracket money, and he would be the one paying the tax increase....He would gladly pay it all, someone joked. Clinton bent Carville over his big Oval Office desk to pick his pocket....About 20 of them posed around the desk with Clinton's hand in Carville's pocket, the populist president fleecing the rich....Clinton finally released the wallet from Carville's back pocket. Some $80 in cash was inside. The president took it out and started throwing the $20 bills around the Oval Office, symbolically redistributing the wealth.[79]

It is difficult to imagine a similar spectacle occurring in Franklin Roosevelt's Oval Office or that of Lyndon Johnson. To former presidents, taxes on the rich were simply the means for the liberal welfare state. Within the multicultural administration, by contrast, taxing the rich seems to have become an end in itself. In Woodward's account, Clinton does not take particular care to distribute the money in an equitable way. He seems to care very little where the money goes; as long as the rich (represented by Carville) no longer possess it, he seems happy.

But politics are usually a lagging, not a leading, indicator. Woodward is correct that, appearances notwithstanding, Clinton is acting like a "populist president." The administration's class warfare rhetoric represents a salient political strategy because it taps into a culture of blame.

Hillary Clinton, at least, understands this. Woodward reveals that part of her political strategy for gaining public support of her health care program was to generate myths blaming one class of people for the deprivations of another:

> [Hillary] told her staff, they had to find a story to tell, with heroes and villains....Research showed the enormous profits of drug companies, and Hillary was poised to denounce them. Hillary wanted to find more villains. She ruled out family doctors, since most people liked their physicians; but she had no problem going after specialists, such as plastic surgeons who performed face-lifts and other expensive cosmetic operations. AMA, one of the best financed and most powerful lobbying groups in the country, was an obvious, lush target, but for the very reason of its power would have to get a pass. She decided on the insurance companies.[80]

Tellingly, those with the most power, such as the AMA, "have to get a pass." Only the relatively powerless can suffer the vilification of being labelled a "victimizer."

The most remarkable feature of the culture of blame is that it has nothing to do with questions of actual guilt or innocence. One suspects that no monetary payoff, whatever the amount, would make reparations advocates happy, because their carping has nothing whatsoever to do with real grievances. Nor is it likely that any amount of academic recognition would satisfy the Afrocentrists, or that public recognition would appease the homosexuals who deliberately contracted H.I.V. Similarly, no particular change in the behavior of pharmaceutical companies would end their vilification, because no specific action they took led to their scapegoating. They are just the morally unlucky, unwilling participants in the self-indulgence of others. These myths are not the means to some larger end (the rare exception, perhaps, being their cynical invocation by a politician). In the culture of blame, they have become an end in themselves.

The Problem and the Solution

Because the multiculture represents a cultural phenomenon, we have examined it as such, applying the techniques any good anthropologist might use. We have focused on the way this new culture is organized, how personal identity is conceived, what domains are sacred and which ones are taboo, and, more generally, how all of these different pieces fit together. We have found that the multiculture can perhaps best be thought of as a neoprimitive culture in which individuals are not recognized as such and, in some sense, do not even exist. Instead, people conceive of their identity relationally, in a way that is profoundly dysfunctional: racial minorities in relation to racism, women in relation to sexism, homosexuals in relation to homophobia. These interdividual identities drive multicultural *ressentiment* and require multiculturalists to expel and denounce their (largely imaginary) enemies; instead of the rule of law, one sees an archaic scapegoating ritual gone berserk. The multiculture is profoundly antirational and seems singularly incapable of perceiving itself as it really is—perhaps one of the main reasons the whole edifice has continued for so long. As a result, the multicultural academy appears shallow and hypocritical, but these are merely symptoms of the underlying illness: The core problem with the multiculture is interdividuality itself, and any satisfactory solution to that problem will require people to transcend their interdividual identities.

As a historical matter, we have seen that the multiculture largely can be traced back to the protest movements of the 1960s. This should hardly be surprising, since many leading multiculturalists (whether faculty at Stanford or the president of the United States) were student activists back then, and today see themselves as pushing the struggles of that era to a logical conclusion. But at the same time, there has been a broadening of the focus, from immediate political goals (for example, civil rights or the removal of the U.S. from Vietnam) towards sweeping cultural transformation. Or, to frame the matter in another way, the political field of activity has been widened, to the point where just about everything has become political—from cartoons in bathroom stalls to church sermons to the relationships between men and women. No refuge from the new political order—no space for the individual—appears to be left.

One of the especially telling slogans of 1960s activists had declared, "If you're not part of the solution, you're part of the problem." The slogan denoted a neat division of people, between those who stood on the side of Progress (or History) and those who were opposed to it. The multiculture has developed a similar distinction with respect to "victims" and "victimizers"; the former are privileged in the multiculture, whereas the latter ("part of the problem") must be excluded. More complex possibilities—that the roles of victim and victimizer are less clearly defined (so that the same person can be both in different contexts, or even in the same context), that all people are simultaneously part of the problem and part of the solution, and that real solutions start on an individual (rather than a collective) level—are implicitly precluded. Once again, it is this very interdividual mind-set that has become the real problem: There are too many people who think that everything is political, that "top-level curriculum decisions all the way down to what you'll be eating for dinner tonight" affect the ordering of society, that, in short, "if you're not part of the solution, you're part of the problem."

A priori, there are several possible approaches one might envision towards counteracting the multiculture. One sort of response is political in nature: If we could systematically undo the damage wrought by multiculturalists, then perhaps we would undo the multiculture itself. A second sort of response goes somewhat deeper and is cultural in nature: If the multiculture represents the ascension of a new culture over the West, then perhaps we could move beyond multiculturalism through a further round of cultural innovation—for example, through some sort of a counter-counterculture to attack and displace the multicultural counterculture. We will consider and reject both of these approaches as inadequate and conclude by outlining a third, very different framework. We believe that only a civilization centered on individual rights offers the possibility for a genuine escape from the problems that underlie the multiculture.

The Political Response. The most natural inclination, perhaps, is to address each of the symptoms of the multiculture, one at a time—from unjust hiring preferences to speech restrictions, from mistaken curricular priorities to the funding of obscene art, from domestic-partner programs for homosexuals to racially gerrymandered election districts. According to this approach, the multicultural disease will be cured by treating all of its symptoms. If Americans would only elect the right president (along with representatives and senators committed to fighting the multiculture), if universities would only appoint better leaders and hire more responsible faculty, then, so goes the reasoning, we could solve each of these problems once and for all.

If multiculturalism were no more than a set of poorly conceived policies and entitlements, such a political approach might suffice. But it is much more than that: At a very minimum, the multiculture also includes the attitudes, habits, and beliefs—the character—of the people who are implementing these diverse policies. As a result, any specific repeal effort would not stop the future enactment of similar programs, so long as the underlying worldviews and psychological makeup of the multicultural actors remained essentially unaffected. A political response is necessary but not sufficient: Unless much else changes at the same time, such a response is akin to cutting off the tip of an iceberg, only to see another piece emerge from the angry sea.

Indeed, even a perfectly crafted political response would not address most of the existing and ongoing multicultural phenomena. As described in this book, most of these phenomena took place on the microlevel—in the classroom, in the dormitory, in the church—and one generally cannot microlegislate, prospectively preventing the decisions of tenured professors to offer debased curricula or of government officials to promulgate multicultural directives. In this respect, at least, the multiculture represents an extraordinarily intractable problem, an obstacle that is present everywhere and therefore cannot be pinned down anywhere. Unlike the great political successes of the 20th century—such as the American triumph in World War II or the Apollo space program—the means and the ends are far less clear this time around. We must face the very real possibility that there may not be a silver bullet to finish off the multicultural hydra.

Political leadership often lags cultural trends, and there is little reason to believe that the case of the multiculture is any different. Or to put the matter another way: Multicultural politics became possible only after the multiculture itself had captured the hearts and minds of millions of American voters. This is not to deny the ability of leaders to exacerbate certain trends and to tinker at the margins of the cultural debates sweeping America, but it is to suggest that to focus on conventional politics is to misperceive the scope and nature of the problem. Along these lines, it is worth stressing that we do not place most of the blame for the multicultural mess on President Clinton or Hillary Clinton or Donald Kennedy or some other culprit. Instead, it would be more accurate to say that the multiculture, along with the ethos of resentment it promoted, paved the way for Clinton's election and Kennedy's great experiment. A rejection of this culture may lead to Clinton's defeat, but neither Clinton's defeat nor any other electoral success will suffice to stop the multiculture.

The fundamental difficulty with any purely political response is that such a response perceives the people who are enacting multicultural policies to be the problem—and views the solution simply as getting rid of these people. In important respects, this response is just the mirror image of the 1960s attitude—it involves a substitution of "the problem" for "the solution" and vice versa. But it is unlikely to be any more successful: Just as there are millions of Americans who disagree with the multiculture, there also are millions who agree with it, at least in part. We should stop multicultural policies whenever we can, but we cannot and should not stop the multiculture by disenfranchising all of its advocates. Just as the former Soviet Union could not have broken with the spirit of communism by sending all 25 million card-carrying members of the Communist Party away to the Gulag, we cannot break with the ethos of the multiculture by turning its self-proclaimed victims into real ones. Because excessive politicization is a major symptom of the disease, any purely political solution does not promise much of a cure.

The Cultural Response. If multiculturalism represents a triumph of the 1960s counterculture, then perhaps one might address the problem by going back to the Western culture which this counterculture replaced. This sort of a tack, favored by a number of traditional conservatives, has the advantage over the purely political response in that it at least acknowledges the cultural dimension of the problem.

One fairly popular version of the cultural response envisions returning America to a more homogeneous, functioning whole. America is sometimes described as a "melting pot," in which the cultures of the world came together to forge a new hybrid culture. Might this hybrid culture not present a viable alternative to the multiculture? This approach does not really work, however, because its account of the American past is only half true: Although the old cultures were dissipated and weakened, no new American culture ever really replaced them. Bosnians and Serbs do not kill each other in America, not because they have discovered some new cultural identity, but merely because they have given up their old identities as Bosnians and Serbs (that is, their old interdividual identities as one another's enemies). The exact same could be said of Eritreans and Ethiopians, Koreans and Japanese, and Irish Protestants and Irish Catholics, to the extent that each has been assimilated in the United States. The melting pot did not melt cultural identities together; it melted them away.

From the time of its founding, America represented an opportunity for individuals to break with the cultures of their pasts—first the cultures of Western Europe, and later those of the rest of the world—and to forge their own destinies in the New World. For better and for worse, the rejection of culture has been carried further than anywhere else in history. As a result, America's common ground is no longer defined in terms of cultural particulars (such as dress, food, or customs, or even art, music, or literature), but in terms of abstract principles (freedom of speech and religion, property rights, freedom of the individual *vis à vis* the state, etc.), and it is an allegiance to these abstract principles that informs the constitutional framework of the United States. The multiculture, with its focus on culture creation, represents not a culmination of American civilization, but an aberrant regression towards something very different. As a historical matter, America has always been anticultural, at least in the classical sense of the word, with a vengeance.

Even if some sort of cultural return were possible in the American context, the cultural response presents other difficulties. An immediate issue centers on the following conundrum: If one does not like the multiculture, then one would presumably not want to go back to the culture that gave rise to it. Multiculturalism may have its historical roots in the protest movements of the 1960s, but these movements in turn reflected that not all was well with America more generally. A society that was in perfect shape would never have been torn asunder from within, as was the United States in the last years of that tumultuous decade.

This theoretical problem becomes even more acute when one reflects about details. "Western culture," it must be remembered, was not a single well-defined entity; instead, it consisted of many distinct cultures, in different countries at different times. It is not clear how one would decide which Western culture we should return to—for example, should we go back to the America of the 1950s or the America of the 18th century, or Victorian England, or Salem in the 17th century, or pre-revolutionary France, or the Italy of the Renaissance, or the Athens of Pericles? This question aside, a return to the cultural systems of Periclean Athens, Bourbon France, Puritan Massachusetts, or even Victorian England would not, on balance, represent a tremendous improvement on modern America, which can do without slaves, serfs, or witch-hunts. Salem was not a better place than Stanford.

In any event, a restoration of or return to any specific cultural system—involving the implementation of particular rules and, even more important, the distribution of precise interrelated positions to its citizens—would today meet with fierce opposition. People no longer are willing to accept assigned stations in a Great Chain of Being. In the Western world of the late 20th century, the sort of unspoken and unanimous (or near-unanimous) agreement that enabled earlier cultures (be they "Western" or "non-Western") to function has disintegrated. Even if there are many who would like to return to some culture of the past (or, like the multiculturalists, forge some altogether new cultural entity), no faction holds a decisive majority. Too many people refuse to sacrifice whatever measure of individuality they now possess—but such a sacrifice would be the necessary price for any such return. As a result of this lack of consensus, any attempt to implement a new (or old) culture results in failure or tends towards authoritarianism or both. The experience of the multiculture was not the exception, but the rule.

The Individualist Alternative. The multiculture exists to destroy Western culture, and this destruction has been ferocious and indiscriminate; the multicultural bulldozer has not drawn any distinctions between the good and the bad in Western culture. Both the historic cultures of the West, which admittedly were deeply flawed, and the transcultural civilization of the West, which has much to offer, were expelled in one and the same movement. The mother was thrown out with the bathwater.

If there is something positive to be gleaned from the multicultural cataclysm, then it is this: The bathwater has indeed been thrown out, once and for all, and many of the bad aspects of the historic cultures of the West are truly dead now, at least in America. It is utterly inconceivable that we would return to a society in which blacks are slaves, women are disenfranchised, or people's stations are determined at birth. Nor does it seem even remotely plausible that people would once again be burned at the stake as witches or put to death on account of their religion. There has been that much progress, at least.

The real dispute, we suggest, is not about the *desirability* of that progress (everybody agrees on that), but about the *cause* of that progress. Multiculturalists postulate that progress is the result of an increasing distance from the West, led by people with a special *gnosis* enabling them to understand and perceive the West as unjust. Here the picture becomes very murky, however, since it is never clear where exactly this *gnosis* is supposed to come from.

One common suggestion is that the *gnosis* has been learned from archaic, non-Western, or "Third World" cultures, but this claim cannot really be taken seriously. None of these other cultures had much to say about the evils of slavery, the emancipation of women, or anything else of that sort. In addition, these cultures suffered from unique injustices, in many respects worse than those of the West (footbinding in China, clitorectomies in the Islamic world and Africa, suttee in India, to name a few), and therefore would not appear to provide particularly promising vehicles for achieving personal liberation.

The other common multicultural argument is that the *gnosis* has arisen at the margins of the West. Much of the multiculture's obsession with victims and victimizers relates to this point: Those who are subordinated in our society are the only ones able to describe it as it truly is, and so everybody else should listen to them. Even at its best, however, the argument remains unconvincing and incomplete. It does not explain why such an insight was possible in the West and not elsewhere, when all other cultures on the planet have had their own sets of outcasts and misfits. If subordination was all that it took to achieve *gnosis*, then every culture on the planet should have produced its own multicultural movement. But these other multicultures are strangely absent.

Only a very different interpretation can explain the progress achieved by the West. There is no need to invoke esoteric modes of knowledge, but there is a need to acknowledge a fundamental breakthrough that occurred in the history of the Western world. The breakthrough involved a single revolutionary idea: that individuals exist and have rights, and that these rights are independent of the cultures these individuals happen to inhabit. This idea provided the Archimedean lever with which to move the world. The Declaration of Independence, at the time of the American Founding, was one of the first documents to make all of this perfectly clear: "We hold these Truths to be self-evident, that all Men are created equal, that they are endowed by their Creator with certain unalienable Rights, that among these are Life, Liberty, and the Pursuit of Happiness." These rights are grounded in nature, and do not depend on whether one is British, French, Zulu, or Aztec. The concept of the individual, with rights that transcend any particular cultural system, is the cornerstone of civilization.

These natural rights (or, in 20th-century parlance, human rights) are not recognized in every society, to be sure, but this nonrecognition does not negate their reality. Instead, the natural rights framework requires us to consider those societies (or cultures) that do not respect human rights to be fundamentally unjust. For the first time in history, the rights of the individual were greater than the needs of the collective.

Of course, there are disputes over where these rights came from and how exactly this breakthrough in understanding occurred. The two prime candidates, perhaps, are philosophy and religion—more specifically, the classical natural rights tradition of Socrates and the Judeo-Christian revelation—but we will not attempt to resolve the debate between Athens and Jerusalem here. For present purposes, all that matters is that the breakthrough occurred. And though it may have been quite sudden for particular individuals, it took many centuries to percolate through the historic cultures of Western Europe. For a long time, indeed, these cultures remained essentially hostile to the idea of the individual, which invariably challenged their most foundational institutions.

Eventually, however, the notion of individual human rights came to be applied in many contexts, and a political transformation leading to the abandonment of Western cultures and the simultaneous rise of a more or less unified Western civilization became inevitable. The recognition of the individual freedom of conscience brought the religious wars of the 16th and 17th centuries to a close. The individual right to property and contract undermined the feudal and mercantile systems, and made possible the capitalist revolution of the 19th century. The individual right to self-expression gave rise to a free press and a marketplace of ideas. Blacks and women were recognized as individuals, resulting in the abolition of slavery and the emancipation of women.

Although this distinction is not acknowledged by the multicultural bulldozer, "Western culture" is thus a confusing term because it denotes two very different things. On the one hand, it refers to the historic cultures of the West—to their languages, customs, and injustices. It is also often used synonymously with Western civilization—the transcultural framework within which the notion of individual rights first became articulated. The two meanings arose because the transcultural framework originated in the same societies that contained the historic cultures. But the two meanings were rarely harmonious, because little of Western culture (understood historically) would prove to be compatible with the transcultural framework.

This transcultural framework was applied first to Western cultures, because these cultures were the ones closest at hand. In large measure, the historic cultures of the West have not survived the test. Like the culture of the Confederate South, they have gone the way of the dinosaur. These cultures have been indicted by their own history books, and have disintegrated in direct proportion to their past violations of individual rights. Cultural institutions that were not compatible with the rights of individuals, such as slavery or the medieval Inquisition, have gradually disappeared. In a sense, the multicultural movement simply represents yet another, though largely unnecessary, phase of this cultural disintegration, denouncing oppressive institutions that have been virtually nonexistent for some time.

Of course, it was inevitable that the transcultural framework which disintegrated the West's historic cultures would encounter and be applied to cultures outside the West, with similar results. This stage, which multiculturalists refuse to understand or acknowledge, has already been going on for some time, and has driven archaic and non-Western cultures to the brink of extinction as well. The multicultural rhetoric about studying other cultures, if it were ever truly implemented, would only accelerate this process tremendously. The history books of non-Western cultures are as replete with savagery and violations of individual rights as the history books of the West; once these books are read as closely as those of the West have been, and subjected to the same level of scrutiny, the non-Western cultural alternatives will lose much of their allure.

If this process is carried to a successful conclusion, there will be liberation, but it will be of a sort quite different from anything ever envisioned by the likes of Aime Cesaire or Sonia Johnson. The liberation of the individual requires the triumph of civilization over all cultures, not just Western ones. The multicultural movement simultaneously goes too far and not far enough. It goes too far because it seeks to liberate people from Western civilization as well as Western culture. It does not go far enough because, in replacing the West with a neoprimitive multiculture, it does not seek to liberate people from the one cultural system right at hand. In short, the antidote to the multiculture is civilization—the same transcultural framework that has made individual rights possible and dissolved other primitive cultures.

Liberation from the multiculture must occur one individual at a time, outside the politico-cultural realm. The true human subject (or person or individual) will not emerge as the object of some collective, utopian experiment, but only in the rejection of all such pretensions. Individuals must strike out and set their own destinies, free from both the historical cultures of the past and the newer multiculture.

Instead of a "great experiment," a better metaphor for the history of our age might be a "great adventure," consisting of the unique stories of the lives of countless individuals. This adventure cannot be reduced to a mere formula or verbal description. It is far richer, more exciting, interesting, and wonderful than anything dreamt in the philosophy of social scientists or totalitarian bureaucrats. If a comprehensive account exists anywhere, then it does so only in the mind of God. By rejecting all utopian delusions, we will embrace this truth, and it will set us free.

Notes

1. Charles Krauthammer, "The Tribalization of America," *The Washington Post*, August 6, 1990.

2. Sue Hutchison, "Nobody found any dirt about Gerhard Casper," *The San Jose Mercury News*, March 19, 1992.

3. Peter Robison, "Tone returns Stanford's sight to academics," *The Stanford Daily*, October 5, 1992.

4. *Ibid.*

5. Barbara Koh, "A new agenda at Stanford; Stressing the good, Casper confronts the difficult," *The San Jose Mercury News*, March 22, 1992.

6. Gerhard Casper, "'Stanford is a human institution,'" *The San Jose Mercury News*, March 22, 1992.

7. Mark Simon, "Stanford Image Repairman," *The San Francisco Chronicle*, April 28, 1993.

8. Anthony DePalma, "Stanford Names Chicago Provost As Its President; Scholar to Take Over a University in Turmoil," *The New York Times*, March 19, 1992.

9. Peter Robison, "Casper shrinks Stanford administration; Total number of top University bureaucrats reduced as first move," *The Stanford Daily*, September 28, 1992. Confronted with drastic budget shortfalls, the incoming president suggested that a comprehensive response to the cost crisis might require some deep cuts in the size of the administration. Calling today's universities "mini–welfare states," because of the size of their administrations and the many services they offer, Casper explained that there must be a point at which a university says "this is a service we are no longer willing to supply." The president even suggested that the elimination of tenure is "something we may have to consider in the long run." Peter Robison, "Casper finds improving Stanford image a slow, difficult process," *The Stanford Daily*, February 26, 1993. John Ford and Martha Brockenbrough, "Casper takes a hard look at tuition, financial aid," *The Stanford Daily*, April 21, 1992. Peter Robison, "Casper makes first dorm visit; After-dinner chat on money, PC," *The Stanford Daily*, April 22, 1992. Barbara Koh, "Stanford tuition will go up 5%; Total costs expected to exceed $25,000," *The San Jose Mercury News*, February 9, 1994.

10. George de Lama, "Diversity of Stanford tests former UC provost," *The Chicago Tribune*, December 6, 1992.

11. Robison, "Casper shrinks," *supra* note 9.

12. Rajiv Chandrasekaran, "Casper to eliminate the Office of Public Affairs," *The Stanford Daily*, February 23, 1994.

13. *Ibid.* In March 1994, Casper also eliminated the position of secretary to the Board of Trustees and a handful of gratuitous administrative positions in the president's office. *See* Rajiv Chandrasekaran, "Budget

cuts to trim staff in Building 10; Casper eliminated secretary to the trustees," *The Stanford Daily*, March 9, 1994.

14. David Margolick, "Stanford Brings Back the F and Toughens Rules on Course Selection," *The New York Times*, June 4, 1994.

15. Karen Bartholomew, "Casper announces creation of Commission on Undergraduate Education," *Stanford University News Service*, May 5, 1993. Skip Schwartz, "Casper plans review of undergrad studies; Speech questions DR system, four-year-degree," *The Stanford Daily*, April 30, 1993.

16. Gerhard Casper, "Charge to the Commission on Undergraduate Education," *Stanford University News Service*, November 19, 1993.

17. Koh, *supra* note 5.

18. Barbara Kantrowitz, "The Calm After the Storm; For president, Stanford picks a hot commodity," *Newsweek*, March 30, 1992.

19. "Changes For Hoover, Stanford," *The San Francisco Chronicle*, May 28, 1993.

20. Peter Robison, "Casper defends free speech; No 'Casper doctrine' outlining political endorsements," *The Stanford Daily*, October 29, 1992.

21. George Ely, "Casper gives Stanford seal a facelift," *The Stanford Review*, November 23, 1992. In his speech, Casper announced: "A university's freedom must be the freedom to challenge new orthodoxy. Just as traditions should not be embraced merely because they are traditions, the newest intellectual fashions should not rule just because they are new....A university's freedom must be the freedom of its members, faculty and students to think and speak for themselves. A university must not have dominant ways of thinking. No university can thrive unless each member is accepted as an autonomous individual and can speak and will be listened to without regard to labels and stereotypes." *See* Gerhard Casper, "A university's freedom should be the freedom to seek and to know," *The Chicago Tribune*, November 20, 1992.

22. Peter Robison, "Casper vows to keep personality public, politics private," *The Stanford Daily*, October 7, 1992.

23. *Ibid.* A registered Democrat who is pro-choice on the abortion issue, Casper nonetheless explained that if he were approached by a group buying an advertisement in the *New York Times* to support Bill Clinton, he would not sign his name to it: "I would not possibly do such a thing, nor would I do it for Clinton's opponent." He added, "This has nothing to do with whatever the views of the trustees might be, but reflects long-standing views of my own." Casper's comments were particularly poignant. The previous May, 700 faculty and staff members had signed a full-page advertisement in *The New York Times* in response to the Rodney King verdict and subsequent civil disorder. The strongly worded ad condemned "pervasive racism, the abandonment of our cities, the heartless misallocation of federal and state funds, and the politics of deprivation." It urged "all

citizens to vote for candidates committed to using our nation's abundant resources in the service of justice and equality." English professor Albert Gelpi explained that the signatories wanted to "take a position that was public and collective rather than private and personal." In response to Casper's admonitions, Professor Gelpi warned: "I think that if there were a real attempt to keep faculty from expressing their political views there would be strong resistance." *See also* Robison, *supra* note 20.

24. Lisa Koven, "Stanford University's Ninth President: Gerhard Casper," *The Stanford Review*, January 4, 1993.

25. Miranda Doyle, "Out of the loop, students fear 'conservative agenda,'" *The Stanford Daily*, February 25, 1994.

26 Andy Dworkin, "No cuts for student centers: Student Affairs will trim $1 million next year; budget knife spares ethnic centers, other groups," *The Stanford Daily*, April 8, 1994.

27. Mike McDevitt, "Same-sex partners of Stanford staff and faculty also will get benefits," *The Peninsula Times Tribune*, December 9, 1992. Bill Workman, "Stanford Faculty Backs Domestic Partners Plan," *The San Francisco Chronicle*, October 30, 1992. Barbara Koh, "Stanford OKs gay partner benefits," *The San Jose Mercury News*, December 9, 1992.

28. William Honan, "At the Top of the Ivory Tower the Watchword Is Silence," *The New York Times*, July 24, 1994.

29. Michael Slemmer, "Casper defends University policies at ASSU meeting," *The Stanford Daily*, April 28, 1993.

30. Bill Workman, "Chief Says Stanford Isn't for Separatism; Congregating doesn't mean 'segregating,'" *The San Francisco Chronicle*, September 24, 1993.

31. Bill Workman, "Stanford Renews Commitment to Diversity; President wants campus of 'interactive pluralism,'" *The San Francisco Chronicle*, September 23, 1993.

32. Karen Bartholomew, "Commission preview: new introductory courses; no formal 3-year degree," *Stanford University News Service*, June 14, 1994.

33. Sarah Katz, "Its info gathered, CUE poised to hash out final report," *The Stanford Daily*, June 1, 1994.

34. Bartholomew, *supra* note 32.

35. Katz, *supra* note 33.

36. Romesh Ratnesar and Skip Schwartz, "Under the looking glass: Faculty, students critique CIV program," *The Stanford Daily*, December 8, 1993.

37. Bartholomew, *supra* note 32.

38. Sarah Katz, "Students rap about CIV, DRs," *The Stanford Daily*, February 25, 1994.

39. *Ibid.*

40. Andy Dworkin, "Casper: politics and academia don't mix," *The Stanford Daily*, May 13, 1994.

41. Barbara Koh, "Stanford's president defends his record on multiculturalism," *The San Jose Mercury News*, May 28, 1993.

42. Romesh Ratnesar, "Multicultural office narrows focus," *The Stanford Daily*, September 23, 1993.

43. Louis Freedberg, "Stanford Weathers Storm of Scandal," *The San Francisco Chronicle*, February 2, 1993.

44. Lisa Lapin, "Incoming Stanford chief sees a chance to rebuild," *The Sacramento Bee*, March 30, 1992.

45. Kantrowitz, *supra* note 18.

46. Robison, "Casper finds," *supra* note 9.

47. Colleen Krueger, "Asian-American Studies protest disrupts Fac Sen; Students want major created," *The Stanford Daily*, May 13, 1994.

48. Nick Kuritzky, "'Asian-American studies now'; 70 protest lack of autonomous major, march to Casper's office," *The Stanford Daily*, April 20, 1993.

49. Krueger, *supra* note 47.

50. Doyle, *supra* note 25.

51. Jim Luh, "When voters say no," *The Stanford Daily*, April 18, 1994.

52. Doyle, *supra* note 25.

53. *Ibid.*

54. In addition, BSU Chairman Ekanem criticized the fact that the ethnic centers were primarily dealing with three black administrators—Provost Condoleezza Rice, Vice Provost Mary Edmonds, and Dean of Students Michael Jackson. "If it wasn't planned, it's a darned good way of going about business," said Ekanem. Apparently, some black administrators were less equal than others. Casper was nonplussed: "I have in the past and I continue to break glass ceilings—when that happens, for that to be turned around as an argument against me I find just incredibly offensive." Casper also noted that Edmonds and Jackson had been appointed by Donald Kennedy, whose record can by no means be called unsympathetic to multiculturalism (see chapter 2). *Ibid.*

55. James J. Sheehan, et al., "Report of the Commission on Undergraduate Education," Stanford University, 1994.

56. Louis Freedberg and Bill Workman, "Stanford Chief Questions Value of School Major," *The San Francisco Chronicle*, September 23, 1993. Louis Freedberg, "Stanford President Challenges Sanctity of 4-Year Degree," *The San Francisco Chronicle*, January 26, 1993.

57. Freedberg, *supra* note 56.

58. Sommer, John W., ed. *The Academy in Crisis: The Political Economy of Higher Education* (New Brunswick, NJ: Transaction Publishers, 1995). *See* also page viii.

59. "A Case for Iced Coffee," *The Wall Street Journal*, August 26, 1994.

60. Linda Deutsch, "Another Menendez Mistrial; Elder Brother's Jury Also Can't Reach Verdict," *The Record*, January 29, 1994.

61. Brian Lowry, "Changing Channels; Television promotes culture of victimization," *Daily Variety*, February 2, 1994.

62. Jane Gross, "Second Wave of AIDS Feared By Officials in San Francisco," *The New York Times*, December 11, 1993.

63. *Ibid.*

64. *Ibid.*

65. Leon Jaroff, "Teaching Reverse Racism," *Time*, April 4, 1994.

66. *Ibid.*

67. *Ibid.*

68. Eloise Salholz, "Paying for Sins of the Past; Blacks debate the issue of reparations for slavery," *Newsweek*, May 22, 1989.

69. *Ibid.*

70. Ruth Bond, "Hundreds of Years in Arrears," *Washington City Paper*, May 24, 1991.

71. Ruth Larsen, "FAA men charge 'Tailhook II,'" *The Washington Times*, September 8, 1994. *See also* Megan Garvey, "Male FAA Worker Sues, Alleging Female 'Gantlet' Demeaned Him," *The Washington Post*, September 9, 1994.

72. *Ibid.*

73. Barbara Ehrenreich, "Feminism Confronts Bobbittry," *Time*, January 24, 1994.

74. *Ibid.*

75. *Ibid.*

76. *Ibid.*

77. John Leo, "The junking of history," *U.S. News and World Report*, February 28, 1994.

78. *Ibid.*

79. Bob Woodward, *The Agenda* (New York: Simon & Schuster, 1994).

80. *Ibid.*

About the Authors

DAVID O. SACKS is a research fellow at The Independent Institute and a consultant at McKinsey & Company. He has worked as a legislative aide for U.S. Representative Christopher Cox and as a research assistant for judges Richard A. Posner and Robert H. Bork. During his time in Washington, *National Journal* identified Mr. Sacks as one of Capitol Hill's "rising stars." He received his A.B. in economics from Stanford University, where he served as editor-in-chief of the weekly, *The Stanford Review*, and *Campus*, a national magazine. Subsequently, he earned his J.D. from the University of Chicago, where he was an Olin Fellow in Law and Economics and a member of the Law Review. He has appeared on PBS's Firing Line, regularly comments on the news for C-SPAN, and writes articles for The Wall Street Journal, as well as numerous other newspapers and public policy magazines.

PETER A. THIEL is a research fellow at the Independent Institute and heads up Thiel Capital International, LLC, a hedge fund based in Palo Alto, California. He received his A.B. in philosophy (1989) and J.D. (1992) from Stanford University, where he also was the founding editor of *The Stanford Review*. Mr. Thiel has written for *The Wall Street Journal*, and is a regular commentator on the PBS program "Debates Debates" and the C-SPAN show "Washington Journal."

Index